*To Emanuela, the young European
who walks beside me.*

Alternative Religions among European Youth

Edited by
LUIGI TOMASI
University of Trento, Italy

LONDON AND NEW YORK

First published 1999 by Ashgate Publishing

Reissued 2018 by Routledge
2 Park Square, Milton Park, Abingdon, Oxon, OX14 4RN
711 Third Avenue, New York, NY 10017

Routledge is an imprint of the Taylor & Francis Group, an informa business

Copyright © Luigi Tomasi 1999

All rights reserved. No part of this book may be reprinted or reproduced or utilised in any form or by any electronic, mechanical, or other means, now known or hereafter invented, including photocopying and recording, or in any information storage or retrieval system, without permission in writing from the publishers.

Notice:
Product or corporate names may be trademarks or registered trademarks, and are used only for identification and explanation without intent to infringe.

Publisher's Note
The publisher has gone to great lengths to ensure the quality of this reprint but points out that some imperfections in the original copies may be apparent.

Disclaimer
The publisher has made every effort to trace copyright holders and welcomes correspondence from those they have been unable to contact.

A Library of Congress record exists under LC control number: 99072980

ISBN 13: 978-1-138-62470-2 (hbk)
ISBN 13: 978-1-138-62472-6 (pbk)
ISBN 13: 978-0-429-46054-8 (ebk)

Contents

Introduction
Luigi Tomasi 1
1. Sociological theory and NRMs 1
2. Spiritual responses to normative breakdown 6
3. The differentiation and plurality of faiths without membership ... 7
4. Alternative religions and young people 10

1 The new religious paradigms and European youth
   Yves Lambert 15
   Introduction 15
   1. Modernity as a new axial period 16
   2. Searching for the distinctive religious features of modernity ... 18
   3. The new religious paradigms against the background of a general
      model of the relationships between religion and modernity ... 22
   4. Why have parallel beliefs and NRMs burgeoned in the past thirty years? ... 27
   Conclusion 29

2 The new perspective of youth: religion in Europe towards
   the end of the millennium
   Luigi Tomasi 31
   Introduction 31
   1. The youth of Western Europe and religion 33
   2. The theory of materialism/postmaterialism 39
   Conclusion 41

3 New Age: re-enchantment of the world?
   Franz Höllinger 45
   Introduction 45
   1. Enchantment and magic 47
   2. The goals and results of esoteric practices 49
   3. Intended and non-intended consequences of new esotericism ... 53

4 The abstract image of God: the case of Dutch youth
Jacques Janssen   57
Introduction   57
1. The diversity of the religiosity of Dutch youth   61
2. What young people do and think: prayer and the image of God   73
Conclusion   79

5 New religious movements and youth culture in Great Britain
Michael York   83

6 Ecstasy as 'this-worldly path to salvation': the techno youth scene as a proto-religious collective
Michael Corsten   91
Introduction   91
1. Theoretical considerations: scenes as 'cool places' for young people   92
   1.1 Scenes: a sociological definition   92
   1.2 Experience of scene events   93
      1.2.1 Locality: time-spatio arrangements and social atmosphere of scene events 94
      1.2.2 Audience: the social characteristics of persons at scene events 94
2. The collective assignment of scene specificities and the proto-religious dimension of its validation: salvation ways of scene practices 95
   2.1 The symbolic structural differentiation of validating scene practices   97
   2.2 Youth scenes: local audiences of adolescents   98
   2.3 Social specificities of music and dance activities   101
3. Interpretive analysis of symbolic practices   103
   3.1 Design: text analysis of described practices and their experience   103
      3.1.1 Methodological standpoint   103
      3.1.2 Implications for the research design   104
   3.2 Data collection   105
   3.3 Data analysis   105
4. Results   107
   4.1 Symbolic structuring of scene events   107
   4.2 The spatial arrangement   110
   4.3 Non-verbal rules of validating symbolized identity   116
      4.3.1 Non-verbal constitution of interpersonal encounter   116
      4.3.2 Erotic playfulness of dancing bodies   118
Conclusion   120

7 New religious phenomena in Eastern Europe
Tadeusz Doktór   125
Introduction   125
1. Church religiosity   127
2. Alternative religiosity   130
3. Characteristics of members   138
4. Reactions to NRMs   140

8 Alternative creeds among Russian youth
   Mikhail F. Chernysh   147
   Introduction   147
   1. The evolution of the young   149
   2. Qualitative analysis   151
      2.1 Family problems   151
      2.2 Blind alley situation   153
      2.3 Conflict of values   154
      2.4 The generation gap   155
   Conclusion   155

9 *Pagus et urbanus* in Iceland: conjunctions and disjunctions in neo-pagan religion
   William H. Swatos, Jr. and Loftur Reimar Gissurarson   157
   Introduction   157
   1. The Icelandic case   157
   2. Iceland and the modern project   162
   3. Nýall   166
   4. Ásatrú   168
   Conclusion   173

Index   175
Contributors   181

Introduction

LUIGI TOMASI

For some time now, sociological theory has concerned itself with the phenomenon generally referred to as alternative religions and which comprises 'new religious movements' (NRMs) as the expression of a return to religion that grows increasingly evident in contemporary society.

This revival of the religious is manifest in a society which is a victim of its own contradictions, and in which religion is presented as a remedy for the shortcomings of the modern world – that same modern world which has undergone, and still undergoes, the process of secularization. The resurgence of orthodoxy takes such disparate forms as, for instance, the re-Islamization of Muslim society, the recovery of the *Thora* in Judaism, charismatic movements, esotericism and occultism. Often, moreover, one witnesses a revaluation of the sources, a return to original truths, and an authentic spiritual quest.

It is therefore within the setting of a global and differentiated reality that religion has reappeared. The processes that frame these religious phenomena – migrations, movements for cultural integration, the growth of values-systems, socialization – concern less the recomposition of the religious field than the evolution of society in diverse aspects of modernity. It frequently seems that the onset of NRMs is a reaction to a modern society characterized by the dissolution of shared values and by pronounced existential impoverishment.

1. Sociological theory and NRMs

Over the last twenty years a number of interesting theories have been developed in explanation of the rise of NRMs and of their significance. A first and important contribution to the debate was Bryan Wilson's contention that *the NRMs provide confirmation of secularization*: they should be viewed as indicative of the extent to which religion has become *inconsequential* for society.[1]

---

[1] Bryan Wilson, *Religion in Sociological Perspective* (Oxford: Oxford University Press, 1982).

2   *Alternative religions among European youth*

Arguing that society is dominated by impersonal bureaucratic roles, Wilson claims that charismatic leaders survive only in the cramped social space still available for collective behaviour and spontaneous faith.[2] On this view, religion has been reduced to an *exotic consumption good* and an *ornament of the person*. Consequently, its *purchasers* choose among a diversified array of spiritual products.

Wilson goes on to argue that since religion offers personal and individual redemption and is not susceptible to rational procedures or cost-efficiency criteria, it can only be supplied in a community.[3] Consequently, when the community ceases to be the principal foundation of the social organization, and society develops in a *societal* manner based on rational organization,[4] control becomes impersonal and amoral, and moreover with the passage of time grows increasingly computerized.

Wilson explains secularization as both the cause and effect of the decline of the community. The functional rationality that unifies the economic and political system pushes religion into an increasingly marginal role in society. As a consequence, the symbols and values of traditional faiths are superseded, and the new religions, consumerist and ornamental, are able to survive precisely because society is secularized.

Wilson's thesis – which is antithetical to Andrew Greeley's contention that the NRMs show that religion has not lost its essential significance in society[5] – coincides with Richard Fenn's discussion[6] of contemporary religious variables and with the secularization/privatization analysis conducted by Peter Berger and Thomas Luckmann.[7] Moreover, it receives support from Harvey Cox,[8] who criticises the way that oriental mysticism has become a consumption good of mass capitalist culture.

Like Luckmann, Wilson and Bell, Richard Fenn maintains that the process of institutional differentiation has been crucial for advanced industrial society. He categorically rejects Talcott Parsons' claim that the relations among social structure, culture and personality are congruent and essentially guided by shared values. According to Fenn, the secularization

---

2   Bryan Wilson, *The Noble Savages: The Primitive Origins of Charisma and its Contemporary Survival* (Berkeley: University of California Press, 1975), p. 125.
3   Bryan Wilson, 'Aspects of Secularization in the West', *Japanese Journal of Religious Studies*, 3, 1976, p. 273.
4   Wilson, *Religion in Sociological Perspective*, p. 63.
5   Andrew Greeley, *Unsecular Man* (New York: Schocken, 1972).
6   Richard Fenn, 'Toward a New Sociology of Religion', *Journal for the Scientific Study of Religion*, 11, 1972, pp. 16-32.
7   Peter Berger, *The Sacred Canopy* (New York: Doubleday, 1967); Thomas Luckmann, *The Invisible Religion* (New York: Macmillan, 1967).
8   Harvey Cox, *Turning East* (New York: Simon and Schuster, 1977).

process is by now so advanced that the social order can no longer be based on normative aspects. Religious values have apparently very little relevance to the world of politics and work. Hence it follows that the social order is instead the outcome of ties among individuals with different values, roles and personalities, and as a consequence societies are *integrated* but not *cohesive*.

A second theoretical interpretation which aids understanding of the proliferation of NRMs centres on the *search for community* in a mass urbanized society dominated by impersonal bureaucratic structures. The extreme isolation of the nuclear family has intensified discussion of expressive familial roles and on the impersonal roles that pervade the instrumental environment. A distinctive response to this disjunction takes the form of the *youth movements* that arise in contexts where affectivity can be combined with universalist mystical values.[9] A frequent feature of contemporary NRMs, and of orientalist groups in particular, is the growth of gratifying interpersonal relationships among converts – as happens, for example, among Pentecostalists, who believe themselves to be in possession of the Holy Spirit.[10]

The problem of community in modern societies is exacerbated by the *weakening of the traditional structures of mediation between the individual and an abstract political system*. Groups of this kind, often replaced by new social 'inventions' like *communes* and *encounter groups*,[11] have in the past served as surrogates for the family or as *part-time communities* which seek to *re-socialize* the individual in isolation from family norms and values, thereby reconstituting the collectivities that mediate between primary groups and society at large. By furnishing compensatory expressive gratification which mitigates the oppressive aspects of involvement in impersonal formal structures, the new communities help their members to orient their aspirations within an impersonal instrumental milieu.

The NRMs perform integrative functions for the social system and therapeutic ones for their adherents. Roland Robertson has written that 'intra-individual mysticism stands in a functional, mutually reinforcing relationship with a form of bureaucratic asceticism'.[12] This is not to gainsay, however, that this integrative function may be obscured by the long-term sociocultural

---

9   Samuel Eistenstadt, *From Generation to Generation* (New York: Free Press, 1956).
10 Thomas Robbins and Anthony Dick, 'Getting Straight with Meher Baba: A Study of Drug-Rehabilitation, Mysticism and Post-Adolescent Role-Conflict', *Journal for the Scientific Study of Religion*, 11, 2, 1972, pp. 122-40.
11 James Coleman, 'Social Inventions', *Social Forces*, 1970, pp. 163-73.
12 Roland Robertson, 'On the Analysis of Mysticism: Pre-Weberian Perspective', *Sociological Analysis*, 36, 1975, p. 264.

disintegrative and *transformative* consequences described by Edward Tiryakian.[13]

A third interpretative strand links the current spiritual ferment with *normative breakdown* and *moral dissent*. According to Charles Glock, the growth of scientific-social determinism has eroded the traditional assumptions of personal autonomy and free will, and it has devalued the ethic based on personal responsibility. The widespread socio-cultural protest and experimentation of the 1960s, in fact, reflected the crisis of meaning and its legitimation; and this generated a constant search for new forms and structures of meaning.[14]

Perhaps the most provocative version of the crisis-of-values perspective has been formulated by Robert N. Bellah, who views the alternative religions and therapeutic mysticisms of today as *succession movements* springing from the counter-culture of the 1960s, which demonstrated the incapacity of individualism to provide a meaningful basis for personal and social existence.[15]

The political-moral ferment of recent years has bred acute disenchantment with the hegemony of reason and instrumental values, and it has generated a new conceptualization of the issue of ends. The movements that arose from the crisis of values seek to reconcile the *humanism of the 1960s* with *utilitarian individualism*. This feature has been analysed by Steve Tipton in studies on the moral ideologies of the members of various American *Zen movements* and converts to the *Jesus* movement, focusing on the counter-cultural moral ethos of spontaneity.[16]

A further interpretation of NRMs has been proposed by Rodney Stark and William S. Bainbridge. These two authors view secularization as a process which affects not only society but also individual religious organizations, and which in its turn stimulates a religious and innovatory revival. This theory is obviously contrary to that put forward by Wilson and

---

13 Edward Tiryakian, *On the Margin of the Visible: Sociology, the Esoteric, and the Occult* (New York: Wiley, 1974).
14 Charles Glock, 'Consciousness Among Contemporary Youth: An Interpretation' in Charles Glock and Robert Bellah (eds.), *The New Religious Consciousness* (Berkeley: California University Press, 1976).
15 Bellah, 'The New Religious Consciousness and the Crisis of Modernity', in Charles Glock and Bellah (eds.), *New Religious Consciousness*, pp. 133-52.
16 Steve M. Tipton, 'The Ethical Outlook of American Zen Students', paper presented at the Annual Meeting of the Society for the Scientific Study of Religion, 1978.

Luckmann, who argue that the diffusion of NRMs is an integral part of the secularization process.[17]

Other scholars claim that the factors responsible for the fragmentation of the life-space into diverse and specific social roles has weakened personal identities and increased the attraction of groups offering the bases for holistic conceptions of the self. There is a constant need to *re-design* a global vision of society either by reverting to a theocratic society now consigned to the European past, or by adapting a complex of mystical and esoteric beliefs asserting the ends of salvation *hic et nunc*, techniques to gear the psyche to the rituals and lifestyles of rational action, and an array of faiths without membership.

The traditional types of social movement are now being supplanted by ideological groups oriented principally towards cultural change. These associations use dynamic techniques to transform the identities of their members and to fashion a 'look' by reinterpreting personal experience and biographical past as a whole. Many yoga, meditation and therapy movements can be viewed as expressions of the *cult of man*, which Émile Durkheim foresaw as the *quasi-religious mysticism* that would constitute the integrative consensual substrate of higher and more complex society. In a society of this kind, individuals belong to a limited extent to numerous collectivities without their lives being dominated by any group in particular, conceiving themselves as autonomous individuals possessed of immanent sacred power.[18]

Although these interpretations are useful and provocative, and not necessarily in conflict with each other, the moral dissent approach seems to have particular theoretical value because it can be used to draw up a typology in which the various NRMs embody different responses to normative breakdown.

---

17   William S. Bainbridge, 'Secularization, Revival and Cult Formation', *The Annual Review of the Social Science of Religion*, 4, 1980, pp. 85-119; Rodney Stark and William S. Bainbridge, *Concepts for a Theory of New Religious Mouvement*, in Joseph H. Fichter (ed.), *Alternatives to American Mainline Religion* (New York: Rose of Sharon Press, 1981); Rodney Stark and William S. Bainbridge, *The Future of Religion* (Berkeley: University of California Press, 1985).
18   Frances Westley, 'The Cult of Man: Durkheim's Predictions and New Religious Movements', *Sociological Analysis*, 39, 2, 1978, pp. 135-45.

2. Spiritual responses to normative breakdown

Various macrosociological approaches have sought to explain the fragmentation of religiosity. According to Jurgen Habermas, capitalism has failed to produce adequate legitimation, and the synthesis of Christianity with utilitarianism that Max Weber called the spirit of capitalism does not provide the social order with sufficient validity.[19]

Daniel Bell has linked conflicts among cultural, religious and economic factors with the birth of non-conventional religiosity, arguing that when religion dies, cults arise.[20] Other authors have claimed that the majority of converts to NRMs are seeking moral alternatives to the disintegration of the Protestant and Catholic ethics. They argue that this disintegration is due to the development of urbanized mass society and of an economy dominated by bureaucracies. Both these approaches emphasise the structural plausibility of the assumptions of personal autonomy and control that were crucial to the absolutist moral perspective in the spirit of capitalism. Consumerism, encouraged by managerial capitalism, has eroded the intrinsic asceticism of traditional religiosity.[21]

Colin Campbell argues that the drift towards secularism is interrelated with the growth of spiritual and mystical religion, which for Ernst Troeltsch is the third form of the Christian religion,[22] typically and radically individualistic, syncretic and tolerant. According to Campbell, mystical religiosity is growing increasingly compatible with the other forms within a more differentiated society and a relativized culture.[23]

---

19 Jurgen Habermas, *Legitimation Crisis* (New York: Beacon, 1973).
20 Daniel Bell, *The Cultural Contradictions of Capitalism* (New York: Basic, 1976).
21 In 1980, Daniel Bell claimed that the concept of secularization is confused and that religion has indeed a future, for it necessarily performs an integrative function in post-industrial society. Bell distinguished between the 'secularization of the social system' and the 'profanation of culture'. Consequently, there is a need for new forms of religion which return to the past in search of tradition, recovering those elements that give a person a set of ties which posit the continuity of death and life. Bell also envisaged the birth of three types of religion (of modernization, redemption and mysticism). These new forms are reactions against the hegemony of purely utilitarian norms and values. Bell's theory departs radically from the Parsonian functionalist model of the normative integration of industrial societies, and also from Bryan Wilson's notion of societalization. Existential questions require new responses, and this explains the rationale of the new religious movements.
22 Ernst Troeltsch, *Die Soziallehren der Christlichen Kirchen und Gruppen* (Tübingen: Mohr, 1923).
23 Colin Campbell, 'Clarifying Cults', *British Journal of Sociology*, 28, 3, 1977, pp. 375-88. Anthony and Robbins have argued that many converts to NRMs are in search of moral alternatives to the disintegration of the Protestant ethic. According to these authors, this phenomenon is due to the growth of organized mass society and to an economy subject to corporatist and state bureaucracies. Also interesting is Lorne L. Dawson, *Cults in Context. Readings in the Study of Religious Movements* (Toronto: Canadian Scholars' Press, 1996).

The birth of NRMs and of *alternative* cults therefore emerged as a *counter-cultural dimension* at the beginning of the 1960s.[24] In this regard, whereas during the 1950s and a large part of the 1960s, study of religious behaviour was dominated by the *church sect*, towards the end of the 1960s and in the early 1970s sociologists of religion were obliged to address what has been called the 'new religious ferment'. The theory arose that the youth counter-culture had served as a *communitarian laboratory* in an endeavour to furnish alternatives to disintegrating social philosophy and religion. Today, these NRMs reaffirm elements of traditional moral absolutism in exaggerated and strident terms which sometimes conflict with other groups sustaining systems of relativistic and subjective meaning.

There is a *fundamentalist syndrome* whereby a person from a Christian or Catholic background passes through a period of counter-cultural rebellion against the values of his or her parents, who are in their turn partly involved. There are, moreover, various types of movement with different implications for the socio-political and cultural orientations of their members. While some offer legitimation for the *status quo*, others encourage their adherents to work for social justice in an evolutionary rather than revolutionary manner.

Movements like Scientology, Hare Krishna or New Age appear generally pragmatic and empirical, as well as being 'scientific' to their converts and able to satisfy the need for monistic commitment. These are movements comprising individuals pervaded to a large extent by a distinctive scientific rationalism. Charismatic movements, by contrast, affirm value orientations and seek further legitimacy through the veneration and emulation of leaders held up as examples of advanced consciousness.

Frequently, devotion to the master is considered spiritually more vital than the standardized practice of techniques.

3. The differentiation and plurality of faiths without membership

I continue my discussion by turning to another aspect of the question, one which may be usefully addressed in terms of Niklas Luhmann's theory that

---

24 On the religious beliefs of young Europeans see Luigi Tomasi 'La condizione post-totalitaria e la "nuova" Europa: gli orientamenti valoriali dei giovani', in Luigi Tomasi (ed.), *The young People of Eastern and Western Europe: Values, Ideologies and Prospects* (Trento: Reverdito, 1991), pp. 7-22, and Luigi Tomasi 'The New Europe and the Values Orientations of Young People: East-West Comparisons', in William Swatos Jr. (ed.), *Politics and Religion in Central and Eastern Europe. Traditions and Transitions* (Westport: Praeger Publisher, 1994), pp. 47-64.

secularization is the consequence of the high degree of *functional differentiation* distinctive of modern society.[25] This differentiation began in the Middle Ages and persisted through the eighteenth century in science and education and then later invested the family.

Secularization is *the repercussion of functional changes on the religious system and on societal development*. According to Luhmann, in other cultures the functional subsystems that used to be geared to internal communicative social processes have gained in importance, and especially the political and legal system. There has thus arisen a set of contingent problems resulting from uncontrollable and complex physical-chemical/organic-psychic development which religion has incorporated and developed as a *religion of faith*.

In the modern age, the subsystems have acquired greater significance by increasing their control over society and depriving the traditional religious subsystem of its functions. In Luhmann's view, the latter subsystem has been stripped of those which, at a higher level than the religious one, control physical-chemical/organic-psychic problems. The result has been the birth of *a new type of religion suited to a functionally differentiated society*.

According to this theory, all the subsystems reciprocally develop within society, and they should prevent the operations that produce insoluble problems in other subsystems.

Integration is therefore based on predictions of the consequences of the *inter-subsystem of systemic actions*. All subsystems should know and respect the functional specialization of every other subsystem. Consequently, when a society depends, and continues to depend, on the religious function, there will always be social repression and the restriction of religious practice. Moreover, in asserting that integration is based on knowledge rather than mechanisms, those subsystems of society primarily based on cognitive processes, like science and economics, will be able to develop to the greatest extent. Hence it follows *that religion is only one subsystem of society, and that its negation will not cause any loss of credit in other sectors*.

---

25 To understand the role that Niklas Luhmann assigns to religion, one must bear in mind that he conceives *differentiation* not only as a process but also as a change in the differentiation principle from segmentation, through stratification, to specialization based on functional competence. This evolution produces a series of more specific meanings. Luhmann takes interpretation of the meaning of an increasingly complex and differentiated world to be a constant of human society. However, he has frequently been criticised for failing to give an adequate explanation as why the principle of differentiation has changed into *segmentation* and *stratification*, and finally into *functional specificity*.

Besides Luhmann's authoritative interpretation, mention should be made of two hypotheses advanced by F. Xaver Kaufmann and of a certain importance in interpreting secularization.[26] The first is that *an entirely unprecedented form of Catholicism* developed in the nineteenth century. The centralization of the Church, the sacralization of the organizational structure and the subcultural religious *'vis-à-vis'* have pushed religion into the innermost life of believers. The present differentiation between the Catholic religion and economic and political activities contrasts with the past. Xaver Kaufmann's second hypothesis is that *since the Council of Trent, Christianity has assumed progressively greater organization, and this has also been the case of Protestantism.*

These studies show that society is currently passing through a period of transition in which the prime concern is to find a *new historical form for the religious message* (Christian in particular) suited to modern social differentiation.

It has also been pointed out that the crisis of the Church and the consequent alienation of Christians from ecclesiastical organizations is not a unique phenomenon, for people have abandoned institutional forms in other subsystems as well. Kaufmann's study therefore seems more oriented to *playing down* the crisis of Christianity in the West, rather than further emphasising secularization.

Karel Dobbelaere has argued that changes in the social structure have both achieved control over the substructures (economy, science, education, family, leisure activities), thereby destroying the beliefs of many individuals, and also given rise to a personal God for those who still believe.[27] Hence the social differentiation brought about by the stratification of society into classes has been replaced by a *differentiation which has eroded the traditional concept of God and the beliefs connected with it, imposing a reformulation of the concept of God and of religion in general in terms more acceptable to people who live in a functionally differentiated society*. This religious change not only entails organizational and doctrinal and sometimes political modifications but also stimulates adherence to new organizations like sects and NRMs.

Within this process of differentiation, uncertainty has provoked a crisis of meaning, and it is in the space of the sacred that the need for meaning is

---

26 Xaver F. Kaufmann and Johann B. Metz, *Zukunftsfähigkeit. Suchbewegungen im Christentum* (Freiburg: Herder, 1987).
27 Karel Dobbelaere, 'Secularization Theories and Sociological Paradigms: Convergences and Divergences', *Social Compass*, 32, 2-3, 1984, pp. 199-219.

naturally expressed. According to Thomas Luckmann,[28] it is the atomization of meaning systems that characterizes the sacred in modern industrial societies, and this stems directly from the breakdown in the bond between belief and practice – a split that Michel de Certeau places at the centre of his analysis of contemporary Christianity.[29] Thus produced is a kaleidoscope of meanings which Luckmann denotes with the term 'analogue': the paradox being that the crisis of Churches is accompanied by a resurgence of *new religiosities*.

The decline of religious practice and the flourishing of NRMs live side by side in contemporary Europe. Lay communities arise endowed with a strong capacity for social integration and exacting requirements for membership. The marked diversification of the religious panorama, on the one hand, and its flexibility and ability to become a specific institutional component of systems of social protection and promotion, on the other, mean that religion is a source of both instability and strength in the Europe of the twenty-first century.

4. Alternative religions and young people

The foregoing discussion has shown that the members of NRMs tend to be influenced by counter-cultural values, and that they rely on these values because they help them adjust to the normative context and to the bureaucratized and rationalized milieu in which they live.

The concept of *normative breakdown* aids interpretation of the *privatized transcendent* in a European reality where disparate events have fragmented the life-space into specific social roles, weakening personal identities and heightening the attractiveness of groups able to provide holistic conceptions of the self.

Many of these movements have originated in the cultural change that has occurred in Europe over the last twenty years. In this context religion may rightly be considered a factor that invades everyday discourse together with

---

28 Thomas Luckmann, following Durkheim, believes that a non-institutional and non-specific form of religion is emerging in response to the declining significance of Church-based religion in modern societies. He also believes that Church religion will persist, and that in the future new forms of religion will arise. Flexible arrangements based on personal priorities and not mediated by special institutions, these new religious forms will be confined to the personal sphere and personal sentiments. This suggests that the image of the autonomous individual is constituted by ideas concerning the sacred nature of 'self-expression' and 'self-fulfilment'. Luckmann, *The Invisible Religion*.

29 Michel de Certeau and Jean M. Domenach, *Le christianisme éclaté* (Paris: Seuil, 1974); for another useful discussion of these topics see James A. Beckford, *Religion and Advanced Industrial Society* (London: Unwin Hyman, 1989).

others, furnishing para-religious forms and encouraging churches to adapt to the logic of the world.

The first point to address concerns the crisis of modernity and the falseness of the view that religion has been ineluctably expelled from society. The notion of modernity, with its twofold meaning of autonomous consciousness and changed mentality, so that man finds fulfilment in subjectivity, has now been superseded by a post-modernity defined as the dissolution of the values of modernity: a process that has produced a spiritual and ethical malaise which traverses contemporary European youth.

A second point concerns the distinctive capacity of our age to produce wealth in proportions that elevate it to a universal value or the ultimate goal of life. This ethical hegemony of production disfigures the individual and generates a *vacuum of meaning*. The consequence is an identity destructured and fragmented by the lack of a life-project and symbolized by the pronounced spiritual malaise lying at the core of the contemporary age.

Hence derives that crisis of identity – in religion as well – which can only be understood in the light of the general devaluation of the multiple identities distinctive of modern society – a society dominated by multiple faiths and flexible, personalized beliefs shaped by an anti-conformism which soon becomes conformism. An insistence on the immediate, the emotional charge of the present, the search for novelty, the unyielding desire to exercise will for personal growth: these are its principal manifestations.

Europe's traditional past, with its Christian imagery and values tied to the history of the West, is increasingly cast in doubt, while the emphasis is placed on imported values and symbols that have no counterpart in Western culture. It is this that has provoked the general crisis of post-modernity and its incessant production of novelty which alienates individuals from whatever they create, until they are no longer able to nominate and make sense of the social and cultural environment that surrounds them.

Mankind finds itself in an age in which nothing can be taken for granted, neither knowledge and expertise nor social and affective support. The decline of meaning breeds individual attempts to reappropriate it, and alternative religious groups constitute a distinctive form of this endeavour. A characteristic shared by these alternative groups is their deliberate choice of extraneity, their decision to be extraneous by election, to stand as a distinct and voluntary option external to the mainstream symbolic universe. Not coincidentally, common to all these aggregates is the concept of New Age, as a historical epoch and symbolic reality antithetical to a modernity viewed as embodying scientism, technocracy, and Aristotelian-Galilean rationality, and the other ills of the West.

The essays in this book give a clear description of the attitudes of young Europeans towards the alternative religions. The birth of new religious paradigms among young people through redefinitions of Christianity, new religious movements and parallel beliefs, is discussed by Yves Lambert, who proposes a general model for the analysis of the relations between religion and modernity in terms of 'axial changes'. In Lambert's view, modernity has had four effects on religion: decline, adaptation and reinterpretation, conservative reaction, and innovation. The new paradigms acquire importance, especially among young people, with personal spirituality, para-scientificism, and rapprochement with the divine. Lambert sets these and other processes in relation to the characteristics of the current phase of modernity.

These new paradigms can be discerned, although they are not explicitly described, in Luigi Tomasi's essay, which discusses the spread of religiosity based on the spontaneity of the individual and which increasingly supplants strict observance of ecclesiastical doctrine. In this case too, the evolution of the sacred is interpreted in close relation to the modernization that has produced changes in values, beliefs and attitudes so great that religion has now become an individual choice in modern society.

This general rejection of traditional culture is paralleled by a covert search for *re-enchantment of the world*, to use Max Weber's expression, an endeavour to develop an alternative mythology, strong axiological systems, communitarian mental spaces, a totalizing vision of the world. There is no alternative religion, in fact, which does not take the form of a *consecrated community* able to furnish a new definition of the world, a new cosmology, a new anthropology, a new faith in eschatological realities like the destiny of the soul, life after death, and the meaning to give to existence. All these aspects are defined in explicit contrast to the universe of values characteristic of tradition. New Age – perhaps the most significant of the alternative religious movements – is extensively discussed by Franz Höllinger. Treating this movement as part of the process of re-enchantment of the world, Höllinger highlights the existence of a system of consciousness that was abandoned with the advent of modernity. New Age, in fact, with its heterogeneous range of beliefs, represents a new way of thinking which looks to the traditions of all mythologies and to oriental wisdom, re-synthesising spiritual, philosophical and even scientific values to give rise to a new civilization, a new planetary consciousness.

The new paradigms of the sacred are well evidenced by Jacques Janssen's essay. It seems that religion in the traditional sense of the term does not play a structural or central role in the lives of young Dutch people. Janssen pays particularly close attention to culture, given that in contemporary society it is increasingly difficult to transmit from one generation to the next. It seems that youth culture is not objectively identical with young people, but rather with *being young* in a particular social system and context.

Like culture, also the religion of contemporary youth is constantly reinvented, and in some manner young people themselves create their religion. This individualized religion, Janssen acutely points out, is not a symptom of *de-Christianization*; instead, it perhaps provides the basis for the *recomposition* of religion.

Michael York describes youth culture in Great Britain and deals in particular with the *youth Rave culture*, stressing that young British people display increasing interest in the pursuit of a non-pagan religiosity. York's analysis, especially in its second part, provides a clear introduction to the innovative approach adopted by Michael Corsten in his essay, which discusses the 'techno' phenomenon as constituting the symbolic and proto-religious practice of modern urban youth. Corsten argues that the 'youth scene' is comparable to the rites of passage indispensable to achieve salvation, and that it is a life phase that will become an increasingly important part of youth culture in the future.

Tadeus Doktór also analyses alternative religions, citing data to show that NRMs are most widespread in Eastern Europe among social groups most sensitive to religious change, especially young people and the well-educated, who are the most susceptible to both secularization and religious renewal. The high percentages of young people who believe in para-science, para-religion, telepathy and reincarnation constitute relatively strong movements in whose birth the fall of communism has been a major factor.

Doktór shows that esotericism and orientalism invade the social fabric, especially in Russia, and help to detach groups from the traditional symbolic universe. This view is shared by Mikhail F. Chernysh, as regards Russia, who claims that disenchantment with communist dogma has led young people in other directions, thereby creating the preconditions for the birth of alternative beliefs. William Swatos Jr. and Loftur Reimar Gissurarson, the authors of the final essay in the book, conduct detailed analysis of the neo-pagan revival in Iceland to show that it is the product of urban civilization. This revival embodies both localism and cosmopolitanism in a neo-pagan world view. The absence of dogma gives it considerable flexibility, so that the oral tradition is constantly adapted according to circumstances.

In conclusion to this introduction one may say that moral relativism – which makes every individual the paramount designer of the good (by now called 'value') – and the desire for eternity do not always find satisfactory responses in the structured religions. Sometimes, for fear of constrictions, the desire for eternity is parcelled out into small lots. And it is this feature that gives the gurus, the prophets, memory-less doctrines, belief in reincarnation their particular fascination.

Thus it is that the characteristic human desire for the sacred is expressed through everyday events and in the form of 'flashbacks' – often in contradictory manner – externally to the institutions and sheltered from dogmas. Increasingly, one notes the spread of traditional religious movements and the formulation of new cults which rotate around a charismatic leader intent on importing the spiritual and religious goods of his country of origin into the West.

Independently of the various explanations that can be offered, the novel characteristic of this *fin de siècle* is that the return to religion discussed in this book is taking place outside the ecclesiastical institutions. This is a universe with blurred and imprecise features, characterized by heterogeneity and syncretism, and in which individuals ground their identities on their own selves alone, on self-reflection, on the assertion of freedom. And its undisputed protagonists are young people.

One may therefore agree with Robert N. Bellah[30] that modernity is a new phase in the history of religion, and concur with Gordon Melton when he writes:

> This growth of so many alternatives religiously is forcing a new situation on the West in which the still dominant Christian religion must share its centuries-old hegemony in a new pluralistic religious environment.[31]

---

30   Robert N. Bellah, *Beyond Belief: Essays on Religion in a Post-traditional World* (New York: Harper and Row, 1976), p .39.
31   J. Gordon Melton, 'Modern Alternative Religions in the West', in John R.Hinnells (ed.), *A Handbook of Living Religions* (Harmondsworth: Penguin Books, 1984), p. 455; See also: J. Gordon Melton, *Encyclopedia Handbook of Cults in America* (New York: Garland, 1992); J. Gordon Melton and Robert L. Moore, *The Cult Experience: Responding to the New Religious Pluralism* (New York: Pilgrim Press, 1982).

1 The new religious paradigms and European youth

YVES LAMBERT

Introduction

Various historians and philosophers stress that certain periods in history have been crucial in developing techniques, political structures or world views which came to dominate the scene for the next centuries or millennia before they in turn were questioned and replaced, or altered and inserted into new systems. 'Man seems to have started again from scratch four times,' Karl Jaspers wrote in 1949: in the Neolithic age, with the earliest civilisations, with the emergence of universalist religions, philosophy and early science, and with modernity.[1] This is not to imply that everything was removed, only that each of these 'axial turns' produced a general reshaping of the 'symbolic field', to use Pierre Bourdieu's term, and especially a religious upheaval which led to disappearances, re-definitions and emergences. Thus, notwithstanding profound changes, only Judaism and Hinduism survived the preceding axial age. One may therefore assume that modernity, especially if it is about to be completed, stands as a major challenge against former creeds, as well as being an indisputable source of religious innovation. Moreover, the hypothesis of modernity as a new axial turn enables consideration in the very long term — that of civilisations — and comparative work to offer an interpretation which accounts not only for the disappearance of religions but also for their revivals, mutations and inventions. This is at odds with the secularization thesis. Of course, secularization is a fundamental feature of the modern landscape, but it is only one among others: it cannot be given primacy *a priori*, nor can it be considered more than a partial theory of religion in modernity.

Starting from the definition of modernity as a new axial turn, and from global analyses of modernity as a new religious stage, I shall propose a general model of the relationships between modernity and religion, emphasising distinctive religious features and new paradigms. My purpose especially will be to highlight the case of new religious movements (NRMs)

---

1 Karl Jaspers, *Origine et sens de l'histoire* (Paris: Plon, 1954), (German edn., 1949), pp. 37-8.

and parallel beliefs (astrology, telepathy, spiritism, positive and negative waves, cosmic energies, charms, and so on) in European youth, bearing in mind that the latter are much more widespread than NRMs (in France, telepathy is as pervasive as belief in God). Finally, I shall try to explain why these phenomena have blossomed in the past thirty years.

1. Modernity as a new axial period

The concept of 'axial age' used to be applied to the emergence of universalism, and in particular to the sixth and fifth centuries BC, which constituted a key stage in the process: Deutero-Isaiah, the century of Pericles, the Upanishads, Jaïn, Buddha, Confucius, Lao-tse.[2] This age is considered 'axial' because we are still its heirs and and live its legacy especially through the great religions. But there is in fact no reason for not considering each of these periods to be 'axial': the Neolithic age was axial for the Palaeolithic age, and so on. Jaspers himself regarded the onset of modernity in the nineteenth century as the harbinger of a probable 'second axial period',[3] and he *de facto* treated modernity as a new axial period. He was not entirely convinced on the matter, however, because globalization had not yet been accomplished (in 1949), although we can assume that it has been today. Jaspers identified modernity with four fundamental features: modern science, a yearning for freedom, the entry of the masses on the historical stage, and globalization. One may also add the growth of capitalism and of functional differentiation.

But are we not already in the post-modern age? I tend to agree with Anthony Giddens when he writes: 'rather than entering a period of post-modernism, we are moving into one in which the consequences of modernity are becoming more radicalised and universalised than before',[4] a period of 'high modernity', therefore, or of 'late modernity'. What defines post-modernity is far from displaying the fundamentally new traits that characterize an axial turn, and it can instead be explained in terms of off-shoots of generalized modernity, except for the possibility of mankind's self-destruction, although this too is a result of science. The hallmark of post-modernity – loss of confidence in the 'great narratives' or in constant progress – differentiates it only from the prior phase of modernity, from the

---

2   Robert N. Bellah, *Beyond Belief: Essays on Religion in a Post-traditional World* (New York: Harper and Row, 1976).
3   Jaspers, *Origine et sens de l'histoire*, pp. 38, 98.
4   Anthony Giddens, *The Consequences of Modernity* (Cambridge: Polity Press, 1991), p. 3.

mid-nineteenth century (industrial society, marxism, fascism, positivism) until the collapse of communism. The relativization of science and technology is not a new development: their excesses and dangers have always been denounced; they are merely becoming more serious because of their intensification (nuclear threat, pollution). One could continue in this vein and show that the changes of the past thirty or forty years are in fact in keeping with the distinctive features of modernity (while having their own specificity at the same time). I cite for instance the cases of permissiveness, the primacy of the self, feminism, increasing education, information and communication, computer technology – not forgetting the independence of former colonies, which is curiously overlooked by post-modernists. The same holds true for the selective revival of certain traditions, now that modernity has prevailed over tradition, or for the repeated appeals to local identities provoked by the creation of supranational entities and the weakening of the old nation-states.

Although we may consider modernity to be a new axial period, we are unable to know where we are in the process. We cannot even know whether this axial period will be followed by some sort of stabilization, as was formerly the case, since modernity is in permanent and even accelerating change, so that it will probably give rise to some sort of permanent shift. On the other hand, it is certain that no new worldly spiritual insight has spread on a wide scale. To date, the principal novel feature of the modern symbolic landscape has been the propagation of secular conceptions and world views (science, ideologies, ethics, human rights, and so on). One also observes fundamental changes in Christianity like demythization, the emphasis on mundane purposes, acceptance of individual freedom, and religious pluralism. 'I am reasonably sure,' writes Bellah, that 'even though we must speak from the midst of it, the modern situation represents a stage of religious development in many ways profoundly different from that of historic religion.'[5] Besides, as J. Gordon Melton puts it,

> during the twentieth century, the West has experienced a phenomenon it has not encountered since the reign of Constantine: the growth of and significal visible presence of a variety of non-Christian and non-orthodox Christian bodies competing for the religious allegiance of the public. This growth of so many alternatives religiously is forcing a new situation on the West in which the still dominant Christian religion must share its centuries-old hegemony in a new pluralistic religious environment.[6]

---

5   Bellah, *Beyond Belief: Essays on Religion in a Post-traditional World*, p. 39.
6   J. Gordon Melton, 'Modern Alternative Religions in the West', in Hinnells (ed.), *A Handbook of Living Religions* (Harmondsworth: Penguin Books, 1984), p. 455.

We may be in a phase of burgeoning evolution, of which 'quick fixes', syncretism, nomadism, subjectivism and pragmatism are also indicative signs.

2. Searching for the distinctive religious features of modernity

What can we learn from global analyses of modernity as a new stage in the religious history of humankind, or from those which consider the modernist challenge against religion as a whole? Jaspers restricted himself to some terse but insightful remarks: 'If a transcendent aid does manifest itself,' he predicted concerning full-blown modernity, 'it can only be for a free man and by virtue of his autonomy',[7] for 'he that feels free lets his beliefs fluctuate, regardless of any clearly defined dogma [...] in accordance with an unfettered faith, which escapes any specific definition, which remains unattached whilst retaining the sense of the absolute and seriousness, along with their strong vitality'; 'a faith,' he adds, which still has not 'found any resonance with the masses' and is despised by the representatives of the official, dogmatic and doctrinaire creeds. 'It is likely, therefore, that the Bible religion will revive and undergo modifications',[8] and this will emphasise the will to be free; indeed, Jaspers' definition fits rather well with contemporary views on *individualization*. Jaspers himself, moreover, exemplifies radical *demythization:* he believed neither in divine revelations nor in the incarnation and resurrection of Jesus, whom he considered only to be a spiritual genius. He was convinced, however, that there was a transcendent dimension in man to be found within the self, and expressed especially through the value attributed to life and effort after achievement. He thus singled out two further possible characteristics of religion in modernity, especially in new forms: *uniqueness* and *worldliness*.

Kitagawa emphasises three interrelated characteristic traits – *man as the centre, this-worldly soteriology* and the *search for freedom* – which resemble those identified by Jasper. He points out in particular 'that all classical religions tended to take negative attitudes toward phenomenal existence and recognized another realm of reality' which was more important, and that 'in this life, man was thought to be a sojourner or prisoner' yearning for the heaven or nirvana that would release him from suffering, sin, imperfection, finitude.

---

7 Jaspers, *Origine et sens de l'histoire*, pp. 278-9.
8 Ibid., p. 280-1.

A radical change has taken place in this respect in the thinking of modern people, in that they no longer take seriously the existence of another realm of reality. To be sure, they still use such expressions as paradise, Pure Land, Nirvana and the Kingdom of God. These terms have only symbolic meaning for the modern mentality [for which] this phenomenal world is the only real order of existence, and life here and now is the center of the world of meaning.[9]

Kitagawa describes 'the single cosmos of the modern man' which compels religions 'to find the meaning of human destiny in this world - in culture, society and human personality [...] in order to fulfill the human vocation'[10] (citing examples like Gandhi), and of a soteriology centred on this world within each religion.

According to Bellah,

the central feature of the change is the collapse of *the dualism* that was so crucial to all the historic religions [...] There is simply no room for a hierarchic dualistic religious symbol system of the classical historic type. This is not to be interpreted as a return to primitive monism: it is not that a single world has replaced a double one but that an infinitely multiplex one has replaced the simple duplex structure.[11] (emphasis added)

Bellah continues:

Behind the 96 per cent of Americans who claim to believe in God, there are many instances of a massive reinterpretation that leaves Tillich, Bultman and Bonhoeffer far behind [...] the dualistic worldview certainly persists in the mind of many of the devout, but just as surely many others have developed elaborate and often pseudo-scientific rationalization to bring their faith in its experienced validity into some kind of cognitive harmony with the twentieth-century world.[12]

This is due, he explains, to science and individualization, which reduce the distance between the human and the divine, the laity and the clergy. His emphasis on *individualization* is reminiscent of Jaspers: 'the symbolization of man's relation to the ultimate conditions of his existence is no longer the monopoly of any groups explicitly labelled religious';[13] 'now less than ever can man's search for meaning be confined to the church';[14] 'one might almost be tempted to see in Thomas Paine's 'My mind is my church' or in Thomas

---

9   Joseph Kitagawa M. (ed.), *The History of Religion. Essays on Problems of Understanding* (Chicago: The University of Chicago Press, 1967), p. 61.
10 Ibid., pp. 61-2.
11 Bellah, *Beyond Belief: Essays on Religion in a Post-traditional World*, pp. 39-40.
12 Ibid., pp. 41-2.
13 Ibid., p. 42.
14 Ibid., p. 43.

Jefferson's 'I am a sect myself' the typical expression of religious organisation in the near future';[15] 'each individual must work out his own ultimate solutions and the most the church can do is provide him a favourable environment for doing so, without imposing on him a prefabricated set of answers',[16] knowing that he will have an 'open and flexible pattern of membership'. 'Not only had any obligation of doctrinal othodoxy been abandoned by the leading edge of modern culture, but every fixed position had become open to question in the process of making sense out of man and his situation',[17] for 'culture and personality themselves have become to be viewed as endlessly revisable'. Hence we can speak of *flexibility* and *revisability*. Bellah observes, moreover, that 'the search for adequate standards of action, which is at the same time a search for personal maturity and social relevance, is in itself the heart of the modern quest for salvation',[18] which again relates to *earthly fufilment*.

Nakamura's analysis of 'modern religious attitudes' examines the features that we have already met, except the collapse of dualism. It also explores humanism more deeply and develops new aspects: pluralism, the movement toward equality, approach to the masses, which echoes Jaspers' emergence of the masses.[19] In what Nakamura calls the 'denunciation of religious formalism and stress on inner devotion' – a pure heart, pure mind, pure faith, with anti-ritualistic and anti-magic emphases – we recognize the Reformation, but he also stresses the typically modern *search for authenticity*, which can accordingly be added to the picture. He refers to this-worldliness in similar terms to Kitagawa's, evidencing the 'return to this-worldliness', the 'rise in popularity of worldly activity and vocational ethics'. He again echoes Kitagawa in his references to 'changing in the evaluation of man', 'man conceived as supreme and stress on human love', whence derives a new religious emphasis on 'service to people'. He underlines the 'increased lay tendency of religion' (lay roles, married priests, and so on) and its 'accelerated approach to the masses' (the use of vernacular language, services to people, and so on).

More than the other authors discussed, Nakamura develops the notion of the 'heightened movement toward equality of man and anti-discrimination' in its secular as well as religious forms, a notion which we may link with Jaspers' freedom and the emergence of the masses. He stresses the rise of the idea that

---

15 Ibid.
16 Ibid., pp. 43-4.
17 Ibid., p. 42.
18 Ibid., p. 43.
19 Nakamura Hajime, *A Comparative History of Ideas* (London: Routledge, 1986).

each religion is valuable, or in other words he points to acknowledgement *of pluralism* as a typical global effect of modernity. Interestingly, he shows that these various changes emphasise *positive and humanistic aspects of religion*, including the value of the body, in opposition to fear of damnation or asceticism, and that man's increased value has resulted in renewed emphasis on religious ethical norms.

We know that the secularization thesis leads to emphasis on religious *individualization, rationalization* and *privatization*. Starting from the secularization thesis, and not from the stages of religious history, various authors have conducted general analysis of modernity as a global challenge to religion. Peter Berger has emphasised the rise of *secular world views* and the *de-hierarchization, de-dualization* and *pluralization* entailed by science, individualism and democracy.[20] Danièle Hervieu-Léger had stressed *deregulation, bricolage, pragmatism, subjectivism* and the development of an *emotional community* type of religion which valorizes personal experience,[21] while Françoise Champion highlights *self primacy, worldliness, optimism,* alliance with *science,* and *love ethics.*[22] Jean-Paul Willaime has shown that the fundamental features of modernity (systematic reflexivity, functional differentiation, individualization, rationalization, globalization, and pluralism) may fuel both religious decomposition and recomposition – the latter especially in ultra-modernity because it reasserts the value of tradition, culture, meaning, and subjectivity.[23] Lester Kurtz examines the following: (i) *the substitution of religious traditions with rationalism, scientism and individualism*, (ii) *secularization*, (iii) the *revitalization* of traditional forms, (iv) the construction of *quasi-religious forms* like civil religion or ideologies, (v) the creation of new forms of religious beliefs and practices through processes of *syncretism*, underlining the fact that pluralism is able to produce revitalization as well as *relativization*.[24] Post-modern analysts, for their part, have highlighted *self-religion, bricolage, syncretism, pluralism, subjectivism, probabilism, mobility.*

---

20 Peter Berger, *The Sacred Canopy* (New York: Doubleday & Co., 1967).
21 Danièle Hervieu-Léger (with Françoise Champion), *Vers un christianisme nouveau?* (Paris: Cerf, 1986).
22 Françoise Champion, 'La croyance en l'alliance de la science et de la religion dans les nouveaux courants mystiques et ésotériques', *Archives de science sociales des religions*, n. 82, 1993, pp. 205-22.
23 Jean-Paul Willaime, *Sociologie des religions* (Paris: Puf, 1995).
24 Lester Kurtz, *Gods in the Global Village, The World's Religions in a Sociological Perspective* (London: Pine Forge Press, 1995).

3. The new religious paradigms against the background of a general model of the relationships between religion and modernity

Although the foregoing picture is probably complete as far as it goes, it is an assembly of features, not a systematic model of the relationships between religion and modernity. As a contribution to the construction of such a model I shall proceed as follows.

Firstly, Jaspers' features (science, freedom, emergence of the masses, and globalization) will be of close relevance to analysis of the religious effects of each of the distinctive components of modernity, but at least two more features should be added: the development of capitalism and functional differentiation. My analysis singles out four typical religious effects for each feature: decline, adaptation or re-interpretation, conservative reaction, and the flourishing of new religious insights. The way in which these factors have historically operated can explain the religious situation in each country.

Secondly, I shall address the combined effects of these features, or in other words, the global effects of modernity on religion, such as those listed above (worldliness, secularization, revitalization, pluralization, and so on). Here, account must first be taken of religion's place in the overall 'symbolic field'. Conversely, there are typical patterns of religion's influence on modernising factors and processes, but analysis of these would beyond the scope of this chapter.

As a brief summary of the analysis that follows, therefore, I shall first review the distinctive features of modernity and then examine its global effects, paying attention to new religious paradigms, parallel beliefs and NRMs.

It is perhaps superfluous to point out that *science* may engender atheism (scientism, materialism) as well as re-interpretations (de-mythization, for example), reactions (creationism) or innovations. The latter comprise the Church of Scientology, Christian Science, New Age movements, the para-sciences (notably parapsychology), and the most widespread parallel beliefs: astrology, telepathy, cosmic energy, waves, extra-terrestrials, which are perceived as scientific by the majority of their adherents. Indeed, science also conveys a pronounced empiricist attitude, whence derives the importance of personal experience, as in communication with the dead or near-death experiences. Borrowings from the human sciences have led to the development of new spiritual movements like human potential, Scientology (Dianetics) or Transcendental Meditation. Within ultra-modernity, the pervasiveness of science and its relativization (pollution, the nuclear threat) may favour both a return to religious traditions and the rise of para-scientific salvation (Scientology, New Age movements, extra-terrestrial beliefs). Françoise Champion has shown that contemporary mystical-esoteric adepts believe in a convergence between science and religion,[25] so that the new spirituality forges an alliance with pure science. Para-scientificity is a typically modern religious paradigm, of which the re-assertion of *holism*, especially in therapeutic and mystic groups, is another aspect.

Likewise, *individual freedom* may typically lead to the rejection of religion, to a more personal religion, to a reaction taking the form of the assertion of collective identity, or to the bricolages, syncretisms and inventions – especially in ultra-modernity – that enhance self-determination: all of these forms of behaviour can be observed in European youth.[26] Protestantism was the first religious expression of the will to freedom. We know that parallel beliefs are entirely free, since they are controlled by neither institutions nor orthodoxy and can be adopted and defined as the adherent wishes. One also observes that the most successful new religious movements among European youth are those which respect self-determination (New Age), or at least claim to develop personal potential (Scientology), while the most rigid and closed 'cults' are now in decline.

Mass movements, too, have contradictory effects according to the historical role played by churches in supporting or rejecting them (democracy, nationalism, socialism, communism, fascism, and so on), as David Martin has pointed out.[27] Ultramodernity has seen the collapse of communism – religion's worst enemy – the refutation of the 'great narratives', and the emergence of specific movements (counter-culture, feminism, ecology, peace, regionalism) which renew or undermine the role of religion according to this principle. Counter-culture movements were one of the main sources of NRMs in the 1960s and 1970s, and ecology is a significant concern for many of them (New Age and Scientology, for example), and not only in the form of spiritual ecology.

Similarly, *globalization* may give rise to the radical relativization of religions (whose truths are mutually incompatible), to pluralist re-interpretations (all religions are valid), to fundamentalist reactions (from protection to attempts at monopoly), or to innovations (syncretism, NRMs,

---

25 Champion, 'La croyance en l'affiance de la science et de la religion dans les nouveaux courants mystiques et ésotériques', *Archives de science sociales des religions.*
26 Roland Campiche (ed.), *Cultures jeunes et religions en Europe* (Paris: Cerf, 1997); Yves Lambert, Liliane Voyé, 'Les croyances des jeunes Européens', in Campiche (ed.), *Cultures jeunes et religions en Europe*, pp. 97-106.
27 David Martin, *A General Theory of Secularization* (Oxford: Blackwell, 1978).

parallel beliefs). Each of these effects grows increasingly acute in this phase of accelerated globalization.[28] For instance, according to the European Values Survey conducted in 1981, 22 per cent of 18-to-24 year olds thought that there was only one true religion, as opposed to the 52 per cent who believed that all the great religions offered interesting insights, and the 26 per cent who declared that no religion had any truth to offer. All specialist commentators point to globalization as one of the main factors behind the spread of NRMs, as well as of bricolage and syncretism.

The growth of *capitalism* bred both anti-religious materialism (besides socialism and communism) and a need for spiritual fulfilment or charitable help, but also a market-type religious structure oriented to consumption. However, data are lacking on this aspect, and also concerning the consequences of the present triumph of capitalism. It is not clear whether capitalism is in affinity with spiritual attitudes in so far as it is driven by invisible, abstract forces and mechanisms felt to be purely human, although they may have uncontrollable consequences on individual life-conditions.

Functional differentiation (state-building, the differentiation between the public sphere and the private sphere, autonomization as opposed to religion) may foster the marginalization of churches as well as their liberation from state-legitimation, and the development of associative activities (care, social welfare, human rights, and so on). To the extent that this signifies pluralism, it encourages the development of new religions and NRMs.

There are, moreover, *industrialization* and *urbanization*, which are typical features of modernity but mainly as a consequence of science and technology, which are both highly ambivalent: primarily de-Christianizing but also favourable to new patterns of religious life and organisation.

As to the global effects of modernity on religion, a first finding is that religion has lost its monopoly over the 'symbolic field' structured by both religious and *secular systems* (science, philosophies, ideologies, value-systems). Although the latter are not anti-religious, indeed they are associated with religion, they foster more autonomous attitudes towards religion or within it. In ultra-modernity, values (human rights, for example) gain increasing importance because they are the most universal coordinates and those most suited to pluralism: they can be appropriated by religious or secular systems, which gives even more freedom and flexibility to personal constructions and interpretations.

---

28 Peter Beyer, *Religion and Globalization* (London: Sage, 1994).

I shall now discuss a number of paradigms consequent on modernity, laying no claim to exhaustiveness, however, and only briefly touching on *secularization,* since this has been widely analysed elsewhere.[29]

Worldliness has already been mentioned. It is a consequence of principally of science, freedom, mass movements and capitalism. Worldliness may detract from religion as well as re-interpret it. The importance of other-worldly salvation has collapsed. In the course of my own research in a Breton parish, I have observed that Catholicism has been *de facto* re-interpreted for the purpose of worldly fulfilment, the function of the after-life being to save from eternal damnation; an after-life whose existence was asserted by a significant proportion of young Europeans in 1990 (European Values Survey). New millenarianisms, too, propose fulfilment on earth (Jehovah's Witnesses, Mormons). In ultra-modernity, worldliness is both more persuasive (since never has man had so many means to achieve realization on earth) and highly precarious, because of the nuclear or environmental threats as well as of unemployment, so that it may entail a retreat from religion, a need for spiritual comfort, or a search for salvation from these new evils. Numerous parallel beliefs and NRMs, and especially the most successful of them, have mundane purposes, examples being Scientology, New Age (which promises future harmony on earth) and Human Potential. The belief in reincarnation now increasingly widespread in the West is usually nothing more than a replay of the game of life with no notion of karma. Of course, as Wallis has shown in his typology based on the attitude towards the world,[30] not all NRMs are world-affirming. Yet world-rejecting movements are less successful, and Wallis predicts a better future for the former.

It seems more appropriate to speak of the *oneness of the cosmos* rather than the collapse of dualism, which is only its extreme form. This more specifically relates to the monotheist context since the oriental religions tend to be monist. Of course, science has undermined the hierarchical dualist universe that opposed the earth inhabited by humans against the heavens inhabited by God, which is even less plausible in the era of space conquest. The results are either disbelief or a reconciliation between human and the divine, or the adoption of monist beliefs. One observes this rapprochement from early Protestantism to the Catholicism of Vatican II (which says 'thou'

---

29   Karel Dobbelaere, Wolfgang Jagodzinski, 'Secularisation and Church Religiosity' (chapter 4), 'Religious Cognitions and Beliefs' (chapter 7). 'Religious and Ethical Pluralism' (chapter 8), in Jan W. Deth and Elinor Scarbrough (eds.), *The Impact of Values* (Oxford: Oxford University Press, 1995).
30   Roy Wallis, *Elementary Forms of New Religious Life* (London: Routledge, 1984).

to God) and especially in Pentecostalism and Charismatism, which experience the 'God within' (the Spirit) and are the most rapidly growing strands of Christianity. God is increasingly defined as a spirit or vital force, rather than as a personal God: the origin or the architect of the universe, the energy, the divine within each creature, the cosmic consciousness, and so on. Monism is spreading in the West through esoteric groups (the micro-macro cosmos), oriental religions (the Divine Light Mission, the International Society for Krishna Consciousness, the Rajneeshees, for instance), while numerous NRMs (New Age, Scientology, Human Potential) and parallel beliefs (astrology, telepathy, 'waves', 'energies', are sustained by a scheme of oneness or direct communication between humans and the planet).

If there is no God who rewards or punishes, nor is there karma, is this to say that good and the evil are no longer sanctioned? There is, in fact, a sense of *immanent responsibility* that has developed on the basis of the human sciences, self-determination, worldliness and oneness. The primary senses of good and the evil are defined according to whatever helps or hinders self-realization in congruence with self-realization by the partner, the family, close friends, colleagues, and under the guarantee of reciprocal trust, with the consequence that *authenticity* towards oneself and others becomes a fundamental value. In the broadest sense, good and evil are whatever increases, or otherwise, divine love, universal harmony, cosmic consciousness, and so on. In between lie laws, norms and rights. There is a belief that one's life-chances improve (and others' as well) if one takes advantage of God's love, Jesus's message, the Spirit's help, or of astrology, energizing, communication with the inner self, release from engrams, and the like, and largely without the concept of a perfect system such as a judge-God or a mechanical karma, with their after-life consequences, which characterised the former axial period. Prevalent among Christians is the perception that sin detracts to a greater or lesser extent from God.

Pluralism is a consequence of science (which undermines the literal understanding of the scriptures), of the will to freedom (personal religious choice), of democracy, globalization and functional differentiation. It may give rise to a radical relativization of religion as a product of the imagination, stimulate competition in the religious market, encourage ecumenism, favour bricolage or syncretism, facilitate the adoption of new religious beliefs and practices, or provoke defensive or aggressive reactions – as already pointed out concerning globalization, which is closely linked to pluralism. Indeed, NRMs have benefited greatly from pluralism, which is a condition for their consolidation, especially if they are negatively perceived.

Mobility, flexibility, revisability – typically ultra-modern attitudes, as we have seen – are related to freedom, pluralism and accelerated change. NRMs display these features very markedly, as Eileen Barker has pointed out when discussing the Moonies, of whom only one in twenty were still members after two years.[31] Some NRMs are intentionally very loosely-organised, so that they resemble spiritual supermarkets, as in the case of New Age and the 'mystic-esoteric nebula',[32] for which self-determination is sacred.

Also to be stressed are other effects: perhaps most notably the alternation of religious *decline* with phases of revival, a phenomenon probably due to the rhythm of the stages in symbolic reconfiguration.

4. Why have parallel beliefs and NRMs burgeoned in the past thirty years?

Explanations for the rise of NRMs and parallel beliefs have pointed to a variety of causes: the counter-cultural rebellion against materialist, technical, consumerist and individualist society (fuelled by the Vietnam War and the decline of civil religion in the USA)[33] and many others, the rejection of established institutions by the baby-boom generation and the deregulation of churches; the rise of globalization and pluralism, the quest for identity and community in an impersonal, functional and bureaucratic world,[34] the relativization and de-utopization of modernity,[35] the decomposition of religion. The authors cited usually mention several causes.[36]

I conclude my analysis by tackling the issue another way. The usual reaction to the phenomenon is surprise, particularly in the former context of the predominant thesis of secularization. If we view modernity as a new axial shift, the question is rather why the NRMs did not arise earlier and on a

---

31 Eileen Barker, 'Religious Movements: Cult and Anti-cult since Jonestown', *Annual Review of Sociology*, 12, 1986, pp. 329-46.
32 Champion, 'La croyance en l'affiance de la science et de la religion dans les nouveaux courants mystiques et ésotériques', *Archives de science sociales des religions*, 82, 1993, pp. 205-22.
33 Charles Glock and Robert Bellah (eds), *The New Religious Consciousness* (Berkeley: University of California Press, 1976).
34 James Beckford, 'Holistic Imagery and Ethics in New Religious and Healing Movements', *Social Compass*. 31, 2-3, 1984, pp. 259-72.
35 Hervieu-Léger (with Champion), *Vers un christianisme nouveau?* (Paris: Cerf, 1986).
36 James Beckford, *New Religious Movements and Rapid Social Change* (London: Sage, 1986); Thomas Robbins, *Cults, Converts and Charisma: The Sociology of New Religious Movements* (London: Sage, 1988); Eileen Barker, *New Religious Movements, A Practical Introduction* (London: Horne Office, 1989); John Saliba, *Understanding New Religious Movements* (Grand Rapids: Eerdmans, 1995).

broader scale. Why are the pre-modern religions still so strong? I shall seek to answer these provocative questions and then return to the former one: why in the past thirty years?

Of course, as various commentators have pointed out, the emergence of new religious insights and groups is a phenomenon of long standing,[37] of which the rise of revivalist sects can be seen as the first expression, followed by the flourishing of non-Christian movements especially in the second part of the nineteenth century. Yet the recent proliferation is unprecedented, as Melton has shown in the case of the United States (more than two hundred NRMs compared with around thirty at the end of the last century). Without considering parallel beliefs, which are much more widespread, I would draw attention to the following two points: (i) if the distinctive feature of religion is that it goes beyond the objective limits of humanity and nature, modernity has aggressively competed against religion through the contemporary relativization of science, progress and ideologies; (ii) the great religions, as universalist religions, have so far been able to adapt and resist but are themselves relativized.

Modernity has been able to take humanity beyond its former limits through the development of science, technology, freedom, democracy, and economics. It promised more than it could deliver, as Danièle Hervieu-Léger has stressed, but progress seemed to be endless and hopeful despite its drawbacks, with some ideologies even promising a superman or a perfect society. The experience of fascism, the collapse of communism, the radical menace of nuclear destruction, the everyday threats of pollution or unemployment have undermined this confidence. Is it that the great religions have won the game? To be sure, they can rest assured *vis-à-vis* science or ideologies. However, they may be suspicious of globalization because, although they are universal in principle, they are not so in fact. Moreover, although human rights may be currently the most universalistic system, they do not provide the ultimate meaning. As we know, Christianity is decreasing in Europe. In France, the belief that there is only one true religion diminished from 50 per cent in 1952 to 15 per cent in 1981. Hence both modernity and Christianity have weakened in Europe. Christianity is stronger in the United States but it is more strongly challenged by new religions and NRMs.

To return to the initial question – why the proliferation of NRMs and parallel beliefs – I would place the causes within this very long-term frame of evolution, stressing the fact that a relativization of both modernity and religions has occurred in the past thirty years. This has thrown open the door

---

37 Glock and Bellah (eds), *The New Religious Consciousness*.

for new paradigms, new beliefs and new practices, although we are obviously still only in the initial phase of any powerful new spiritual movement to come. In Europe, the abandonment of the institutional churches is much more marked than entry to NRMs, which rate no more than 1 per cent. Indeed, to date the most salient phenomenon has not been NRMs but the silent spread of new spiritual paradigms through what I have called 'parallel beliefs'.

Conclusion

Are these parallel beliefs preparing the ground for new spiritual agencies? If we try to foresee possible developments, not seeking to predict the future but merely as a heuristic exercise, we may imagine several scenarios. Recall first the four main trends observed among European youth: (i) an erosion of Christianity since the mid-1960s; (ii) a minor revival of Christianity; (iii) a shift towards pragmatism, probabilism and relativism; (iv) the spread of NRMs and especially of parallel beliefs – all against the background of a symbolic field increasingly dominated by criteria expressed in terms of values. We may imagine a combination between this axiological basis and mainly parallel beliefs, a combination between axiological landmarks and Christianity or other great religions or NRMs, the primacy of Christianity or the other great religions or NRMs, the rise of new spiritual agencies, or probably the coexistence of several religious forms, of religious and secular systems, of several scenarios, with a great degree of self-determination.

2 The new perspective of youth: religion in Europe towards the end of the millennium

LUIGI TOMASI

Introduction

The crisis of Churches has proceeded *pari passu* with the proliferation of new forms of religiosity, and new religious movements have become one of the principal features of social change. As a consequence, the most significant aspect of these last years of the century is the liberation of the sacred, which partly evades the control of those organizations that have traditionally regulated it.

The sacred permeates the secular realm. It competes with the ritualization of everyday life and gives impetus to change. Religion explodes, multiplies, and must comply with the law of competition. Religion is forced to give itself credibility and desirability, for it is unable to impose itself by fiat: it must be sold to customers who are not obliged to accept it. Thus the religious institutions become, on occasion, market agents, while religious traditions turn into consumption goods. Hence the development of the sacred displays the fluctuations and contradictions of modernity in well-defined patterns.

While the sacred spreads though the realm of the profane, the secular insinuates itself into the religious sphere. The production and management of the sacred scatters and diversifies, and the supply of meanings multiplies. Churches are subjected to conflicting pressures: those for 'adaptation' which urge openness to modernist demands, those that envisage a 'return to integrity', doctrinal and liturgical; those that assert a 'revitalization of faith and a charismatic renewal'; those that 'restore a liberating thrust to religion'. The religious institutions are riven by these forces; their control over tradition is weakened and they are forced to revive its meaning, its symbols and its rituals.

The multiplicity of supply manifests in the realm of the sacred the abundance of the new that it generated: Christians of dissidence and syncretism who often form sects; centres of mobilization inspired by the most diverse of doctrines; therapy groups which utilize the power of the sacred and of ritual. Modernity produces unforeseen outcomes: religious innovation seeks to adjust to present situations by introducing personal means of expression which off-set the factors of 'depersonalization' and which combine values that are in part traditional. There is not lack of critical assessment centred on the individual and on his/her demand for sense and values, and which accuses the new religions of exacerbating self-centredness and of fostering a 'narcissistic' society.

This demand for sense requires absolute answers, whether of acceptance or rejection. The former explains not only submission or complete passivity but also a return to conservative and authoritarian Christianity. The latter are directed towards inner conversion achieved within groups. Both seek to transfigure everyday experience, to restore meaning to it within the plurality of realities engendered by modernity.

In modernity, the believer or the religious group is caught up by an irremediable tension between presentation of their identity, individual or communitarian, and assertion of the universal meaning of the message of which they claim to be privileged bearers. It is against this background that the attitudes of young people to religion should be viewed.

Examination of recent developments in the various European countries as regards religious issues and churches prompts a number of considerations. At a general level, the position of the European churches must be compared with the ongoing process of the secularization of states, although one should bear in mind that all societies undergo alternating process of sacralization and desacralization. The situation of the dominant religions tends to give way to one of pluralism which requires the introduction of a certain degree of secularity. In actual fact, this is an attitude more pragmatic than doctrinal; and one must take note of a commitment declared by a part of the population, whether in the majority or minority, and draw the consequences.

One may accordingly measure the significance of the religious recession, in both beliefs and practices, that has continued without interruption in recent decades. Moreover, the enfranchisement of ethics from religion has created a context in which the Church's authority in applying moral norms has weakened.

It seems that the crisis of religion has a different meaning. It is no longer a matter of the distancing of people from the Church as an institution but of the decline of a cultural identity defined by the heritage of Christianity.

The analysis that follows refers to young people in Western Europe, omitting discussion of youth in Central-Eastern Europe, a topic which requires separate treatment in view of the cultural complexity in which they live. The culture of young people in that part of Europe, in fact, is the product of a past that dates back to 1989 but more specifically of the present, and of the necessity to plan or to intuit the future. The projects of East European youth tend less and less to abide by established rules and grow increasingly individualized. These are young people characterized by a marked orientation to the sphere of the private and the self and attracted by Western hedonistic ideology. They are weak, easily influenced, open to any proposal as long as it is immediately realizable, endowed with a culture shaped largely by circumstances and which expresses itself wholly in action. For practical reasons, the analysis here deals with youth in Western Europe, focusing in particular on Italy, Ireland, England and France, although its findings can be applied to European youth as a whole.

1. The youth of Western Europe and religion

I begin with Italy. A recent national survey, 'La religiosità in Italia',[1] has shown that 'among young people, who in some way presage the future, as levels of schooling have increased so forms of popular religion have declined, although the more 'essential' form of religiosity tied to the liturgy (mass and communion) has increased'.[2] Cesareo's conclusion is matched by Lanzetti's observation concerning secularization and young people: 'young people aged 18-21 worship more regularly than do their immediate elders'.[3]

Lanzetti goes on to say: 'Young people, and especially graduates, have abandoned the ascribed forms of religious expression, which are more impersonal in character. By contrast, the desire to achieve inner clarity through prayer is a religious attitude characteristic of younger and more educated people'.[4] This finding is borne out by the 3rd Iard Report, 'Giovani anni '90', which reports that 'religious observance shows a slight tendency to increase among young people in the nineties, compared with previous generations'.[5]

---

1 Vincenzo Cesareo, Roberto Cipriani, Franco Garelli, Giancarlo Rovati, *La religiosità in Italia* (Milan: Mondadori, 1995); Clemente Lanzetti, 'I comportamenti religiosi', in Cesareo, et al., *La religiosità in Italia*.
2 Vincenzo Cesareo, 'Introduzione' in Cesareo et al., *La religiosità in Italia*, pp. 3-17.
3 Lanzetti, 'I comportamenti religiosi', in Cesareo, et al., *La religiosità in Italia*, p. 76.
4 Ibid., p. 92.
5 Alessandro Cavalli, Antonio De Lillo, *Giovani anni 90. Terzo rapporto Iard sulla condizione giovanile* (Milan: Il Mulino, 1993), p. 83.

These results confirm those of a previous study on 'Giovani e religione',[6] which clearly shows the gradual recovery in Italy of both faith in God (faith in God and the importance of God in one's life) and of religious practice (prayer, church attendance, acceptance that birth, marriage and death should be celebrated with religious rituals). Although young people live in a society fraught with contradictions, and although they are surrounded by messages at odds with their religious beliefs, they show a willingness to embrace religious values, even though these are sometimes expressed in an individualized manner.

The figures show that the opinions of Italian young people about the Catholic Church's action regarding the most serious social issues (disarmament, the Third World, racial discrimination) are positively and homogeneously distributed at the national level, and their concern stems from reflection on the anthropological aspects of Christian doctrine. In this specific regard, Italian young people display a global vision and greater trust in the teachings of the Church, although they tend to reject whatever does not offer a concrete solution to humankind's problems.

One sometimes discerns, especially in northern Italy, a non-dogmatic religion which discriminates among the traditional verities of Catholicism. The clearest example of this is the marked disbelief among young people in the devil, in hell, in paradise, in the resurrection of the dead, and in the life after death, which signals that Catholic eschatology is continuing to lose credibility.

The culture of subjectivity, which is mainly manifest in 'sexual morality' (extramarital affairs, homosexuality), is well-established. In certain areas one notes almost a dichotomy between the teachings of the Church and the attitudes of young people. Whereas in the south of Italy one finds a high degree of acceptance of the sexual morality preached by the Church, young people in the centre and north of the country assert the value of sexual freedom and resist the precepts of religious authority. These differences of attitude also emerge when young people are asked to assess the Church's action on the problems of family life, although this should be set in relation to concrete issues that interviewees view as important.

Italian young people (with higher percentages among the better educated) pass generally positive judgement on the aspects of Catholic morality which concern what one may call 'intermediate morality' (abortion,

---

6   Luigi Tomasi, 'I comportamenti religiosi', in Renzo Gubert (ed.), *Persistenze e mutamenti dei valori degli italiani nel contesto europeo* (Trento: Reverdito, 1992), pp. 539-78.

euthanasia). These issues have been the centre of heated debate for a number of years, and young people consider them to be predominantly social in character. Young people with levels of schooling and in employment tend to conduct a personal search, and so too do those who live in the towns and cities of northern and central Italy most exposed to disaggregating conflict. Religious experience finds one of its moments of maximum expression in worship, especially in the form of ritual celebrations. This phenomenon is most evident in small communities and, sometimes, among subjects with lower levels of schooling. Despite the north/south divide in Italy as regards religious practice in general, one may say that young people are strongly committed to religion, although they exhibit considerable diversity in their attitudes to morality and are dubious of Catholic eschatology.

Finally, one notes a marked normative pluralism and moral relativism deriving from a pronounced emphasis on the subjective aspect of human existence. This tends to orient Italian young people to an arbitrary use of their lives and of their bodies which is not always open to the communitarian dimension. As a result, young people internalize and hierarchize values on the basis of experience and thus develop their own codes of behaviour.

There is a strong orientation to the 'quotidian' and to the culture of subjectivity. Personal conscience frequently serves as the benchmark of what is good and bad. However, these same young people, so often indifferent to the positions taken up by the Church doctrine and moral questions, accept its teachings when they concern peace, human rights, justice, and so on.

These findings prompt reflection on the fact that the public lives of Italian young people are no longer regulated by shared collective values. The social bond – the religious bond as well – is no longer established *a priori* but arises from personal choice; a choice which gives rise to flexible, reversible and personalized belongings. Young people fashion their identities from a set of elements drawn from the different groups or subgroups with which they feel an affinity. This also explains why, from the religious point of view, groups and movements arise which, although they declare themselves Catholic, invent their own ritual and symbols in order to transmute their experience as believers – in other words, to establish their identities.

These, therefore, are young people who pursue numerous paths in expressing their religious experience, who rediscover certainties even if they discriminate among values, who assert greater subjectivity. They are young people who live in a society characterized by widespread and composite religiosity, highly problematic, which is influenced by the times – i.e. by the present socio-cultural context – and distinguished by a detachment from the past and uncertainty as regards the future.

It should be pointed out that, although speaking and writing about young people is always an arduous undertaking, in a heterogeneous and fragmented society like that of today it is unlikely that strong identities will be born and develop. It is more probable that fragile personalities will be formed. The cultural humus surrounding the young Italian prevents him or her from developing a definite identity, which springs instead from personal experience as pieces from many and different puzzles are fitted together without any unitary pattern.

Young people today live in an uncaring society which breeds a sentiment of distance, often of alienation. They therefore have to cope with a society of contradictions, of membership, of endless desires, and characterized by individualism and efficiency. Obviously, a society of this kind produces great uncertainty in young people; uncertainty that engenders a crisis of identity, or better, a lack of purposiveness. In concrete terms, this entails the socially coerced renunciation of any project to construct the future. Young Italians are therefore destructured as persons and possess contradictory and constantly evolving identities. The problem is exacerbated by the ongoing crisis of politics in Italy which is reflected in the inability of society to furnish the younger generation with models that meet their needs.

Turning to another European example – that of Ireland,[7] where 95 percent of the population is Catholic – one finds a generally positive attitude to the surrounding culture. Irish Catholics are more tolerant than they were sixty years ago and endorse the unification of Catholics and Protestants.

As regards sexual morality, the young people of Northern Ireland differ greatly from their parents and from the previous generation of young people, given that only 11 percent of young Catholics and Protestants aged between 16 and 34 regard premarital sexual relations as always wrong – as opposed to 59 percent of subjects with stronger convictions – in what is the most religious population in Europe.

Ireland as a whole has the highest percentages of Christian faith and practice in Europe, probably in the entire Christian world, and certainly among islands or nations with populations of more than 5 million. Half the population of the Republic of Ireland (3.5 million inhabitants) is aged under 28. The figures on faith and religious practice reveal two trends: a significant decline in religious practice among young people in the 18-to-35 age group (88 percent twenty years ago, 78 percent today) and a persistently high overall

---

7   John Fulton, 'Mutamenti valoriali e religiosi fra i giovani in Gran Bretagna e Irlanda', in Luigi Tomasi (ed.), *La cultura dei giovani europei alle soglie del 2000. Religione, valori, politica e consumi* (Milano: Angeli, 1997), pp. 78-80.

level of religious practice; a substantial decline in worship in the cities, where less than half the young adult population attends church.[8] However, it is worth noting that studies by Greer and Francis suggest that attitudes to sexuality, life and self are more closely tied to a person's profound Christian convictions than to his or her amount of church attendance or personal prayer. The great majority of young workers are 'non-churchgoers'.[9]

The situation is different in England,[10] where young people display progress-oriented, non-traditionalist attitudes to a broad set of values. Three principal ideologies can be identified: hedonism (obtaining satisfaction), materialism (having), post-materialism (being).

It seems that generosity and tolerance are increasing among English young people. Crude hedonism, risk-taking, and 'living on the edge' peak among 18-to-24 year olds and decline noticeably in the 30-to-34 age group, remaining at the same levels for all subsequent age groups.

The failure of parents to transmit religious values and practices to their children is a central element in the decline of religion. The group in which this decline is most evident are young people, the Irish of the second and third generation, and people inhabiting urban areas. The figures provided by Francis and Kay[11] show that abandonment of the Anglican Church declines as age increases. Levitt[12] offers several explanations as regards young people, notably that parental expectations of church attendance by their children are not particularly high. What we might call a 'life-commitment' to religious participation and practice does not exist. Church attendance and involvement in parish associations and youth activities are viewed simply as one aspect of the general education of young people. Once this process has been completed, church membership and attendance are no longer regarded as important. Among young people in general, religious beliefs are still strong, but it should also be noted that their convictions extend beyond the boundaries of Christianity and encompass eastern religions, spiritualism and other practices that fall under the heading of 'supranatural'.

---

8 Ibid.
9 Leslie J. Francis, John E. Greer, 'Catholic Schools and Adolescent Religiosity in Northern Ireland: Shaping Moral Values', *The Irish Journal of Education*, 1990, 24, pp. 40-7.
10 John Fulton, 'Mutamenti valoriali e religiosi fra i giovani in Gran Bretagna e Irlanda', pp. 78-82; Helen Wilkinson, Geoff Mulgan, *Freedom's Children: Work, Relationships and Politics for 18-34 Year Olds Today* (London: Demos, 1995), p. 21.
11 Leslie J. Francis, William K. Kay, *Teenage Religion and Values* (Wright Books: Gracewing Fowler, 1995).
12 Mairi Levitt, *Nice When They Are Young: Contemporary Christianity in Families and Schools* (Aldershot: Avebury, 1996).

Socialization imparts a way of life which is easily preserved when a person moves to another village or small town, because these replicate the cultural patterns and rituals of the birthplace. Urbanization and modernization have dismantled this model of communitarian interaction. The official church in Great Britain is no longer able to maintain the link between religion and communitarian culture, because in the expanding cities the face-to-face communitarian relations that controlled individual behaviour have ceased to exist.

As regards France, the last country discussed here, in a survey conducted in 1994 by Guy Michelat, Julien Potel and Jacques Sutter,[13] 53 percent of the young people interviewed declared themselves to be Catholics and 36 percent that they had no religion. Conversely, the values for subjects aged 65 and over were 79 percent and 14 percent respectively. The overwhelming majority of French 'Catholics' have become 'heirs without a legacy',[14] that is, individuals without an inherited system of explanatory beliefs and symbols.

In France, beliefs, as the cognitive framework of attitudes, are decisive factors in ongoing social change. They have a legitimizing force, and as such they have been theologically instituted by history to form an essential part of the cultural heritage. It is this for reason that they today constitute a crucial arena of conflict. One certainly discerns here a generational effect which conditions, or embodies, the progressive abandonment of beliefs inherited from Christianity.

Above all, the evolution of societies impedes the transmission of the Christian heritage. Suffice it to mention the breakdown of the family, social instability and mobility in the current economic context, the prolongation of formal education, change in the nature and functioning of authority, the prioritization of relations internally to each generation.

Young people are the first to be affected by these phenomena of change. Yet, besides these conditionings an even more fundamental factor is at work. In explaining the decline of religion, it is pointless to draw a dualistic opposition between religion and reason, demonizing the latter and confining the former to an exclusive domain. It is not at this level that the question

---

13 Survey conducted by the CSA Institute, from 17 to 21 January 1994, for 'Le Monde', 'La Vie', *Le Forum des Communautés Chrétiennes and L'Actualité Religieuse dans le Monde*, on a sample of 1014 subjects aged 18 and over. All the results have been published in *L'actualité religieuse dans le Monde* (ARM), no. 122, 15 May 1994. The survey has given rise to numerous articles and a book. Jaques Sutter, 'I giovani francesi e la deriva delle religioni', in Tomasi (ed.), *La cultura dei giovani europei alle soglie del 2000*, pp. 21-56.
14 Monique Le Corre, 'L'athéisme', in Michel Clévenot (ed.), *L'état des religions dans le monde* (Paris: La Découverte Le Cerf, 1987).

The new perspective of youth 39

should be addressed, but at that of legitimating beliefs which have lost their plausibility and which are therefore no longer able to produce sense. The meaning of beliefs is not confined to beliefs themselves, isolated from any cultural context, and in relation to the symbolization process that derives from them. Symbolic language comprises a significance that goes beyond primary and immediate sense, a latent self-awareness, a spirituality. This language which enables people to reconstitute their unity, taking account of their different levels of perception, is designed for the exploration of the invisible, for the discovery of the hidden side of humankind, to grasp the divine. Religion, and beliefs in particular, are inscribed in the space created between the symbol and the concept.[15]

In the search for meaning, the process of symbolization that derives from experience of the world, of gesture and of the word, begins upstream of belief. A breakdown thus occurs because reified and fossilized beliefs are unable to express the symbols of life. It is consequently the evolution of culture in all its components of science, ethics, aesthetics, and so on, that gives fluidity of reference to religious phenomena, of which young people are not only the principal witnesses but also the promoters.

2. The theory of materialism/postmaterialism

There is a tendency among sociologists to argue that religion has lost most of its impact on social life. Following Max Weber, some of them cite the rationalization and disenchantment of the world, while others stress the crucial role played by improvements in material conditions and living standards.[16] Yet others point to the diminished importance of religious institutions, activities and modes of thought relative to social differentiation and specialization, viewing the latter as the most powerful forces of modernization.[17]

Because of social and cultural differentiation, people in contemporary societies participate in different universes of meaning, each governed by its own values. Modernity divides every human life into a multiplicity of segments, each with its own rules and specific forms of behaviour. Thus work

---

15 Max Horkheimer, Theodor W. Adorno, *La dialettica dell'illuminismo* (Turin: Einaudi, 1996).
16 Ronald Inglehart, *Culture Shift in Advanced Industrialized Societies* (Princeton: Princeton University Press, 1990).
17 Wilson, *Religion in a Sociological Perspective*, (Oxford: Oxford University Press, 1982).

is separate from leisure, private life from public life, the collective from the personal. Although most theories on the declining impact of religion claim general validity, one should bear in mind that the diminution of religion's influence on other aspects of social life is not a uniform process.[18]

If religion has gradually declined and lost its influence on other social values, especially public ones, an important question arises: what 'new' system of values can replace the religious beliefs now disappearing? Of relevance here is Ronald Inglehart's well-known theory of cultural change, according to which unprecedented economic development, the rise of the welfare state, improved educational levels and spread of the mass media have gradually changed values concerning politics, the family, the environment, social and moral themes. These changes should be interpreted as a shift from materialistic values to postmaterialistic ones.

The emergence of postmaterialism therefore signals a broad process of cultural change which is presumably reshaping contemporary Western culture. Together with the transition from materialism, it is further supposed that the importance of the institutional religions is diminishing. In this sense one can view Inglehart's theory as partly a theory parallel with that of secularization, and partly as one additional to it, because it envisages an emerging pattern of a new hierarchy of values which is likely to replace religious attitudes in decline.

In its basic assumptions, Inglehart's theory is open to the core of value change. Whilst materialistic values seem relatively coherent with the central importance of economic and physical security, postmaterialistic values seemingly comprise a wide range of beliefs, but apparently lack an evident intrinsic common denominator or a motivational base.[19] Postmaterialistic values are therefore associated with a wide spectrum of themes; a spectrum probably too wide to be analysed as a unitary whole, which makes it difficult to identify the precise relation between postmodernism and the other social values. At the same time, it should be noted that self-expression and personal freedom are often deemed to constitute the nucleus of the postmodernist value-system.

---

18 Goran Therborn, *European Modernity and Beyond* (London: Sage, 1995), p. 213.
19 Thorleif Pettersson, 'Culture Shift and Generational Population Replacement: Individualization, Secularization and Moral Change in Contemporary Scandinavia', in Thorleif Pettersson and Ole Riis (eds.), *Scandinavian Values. Religion and Morality in the Nordic Countries* (Uppsala: Acta Universitatis Upsaliensis, 1994). Thorleif Pettersson, 'Profili valoriali dei cattolici e dei protestanti', in Tomasi (ed.), *La cultura dei giovani europei alle soglie del 2000*, pp. 103-7.

According to Inglehart, the decline of religion and of its influence on moral norms can be explained by three processes: (i) an increased sense of security has reduced the need for the absolute rules imposed by churches; (ii) the particular functions of religious morality have lost importance; (iii) when people compare their world-views and everyday experiences with traditional religious beliefs, they find incoherences.[20]

Moreover, according to Inglehart, the connection between the emergence of the postmodern and the decline of traditional religious orientations is conditioned, not intrinsic: even though traditional religious beliefs are in constant decline, there is growing sensitivity to the meaning and purpose of life.

The decline of religion and the rise of postmodernism can be viewed as resulting from the increased levels of security made possible by the institutionalization and development of the modern welfare state and of material well-being. In contemporary societies one observes a gradual shift from the absolute importance of economic and physical security to a greater emphasis on belonging, expressiveness and the quality of life. In other words, in the more developed countries postmaterialism will be accompanied by changes in the social values and traditional morality hitherto influenced by the churches, whereas in the less developed ones religion will continue to be an important source of morality, and postmaterialism will be less developed.

Although a number of criticisms, both conceptual and empirical, have been brought against Inglehart's theory,[21] one may conclude that it nevertheless sheds useful light on the youth/religion relationship in Europe.

Conclusion

The foregoing discussion of the end-of-century attitudes of young people to religion prompts the following five observations.

Firstly, emphasis should be placed on the prolongation of youth, which passes through a series of intermediate stages between dependence and autonomy. This phenomenon, which is common to all the young people of Western Europe, disrupts traditional schemes and expresses a profound social ambiguity. Researchers have grouped the ways in which this prolongation of

---

20 Inglehart, *Culture Shift in Advanced Industrialized Societies*, pp. 117-79.
21 Elinor Scarbrough, 'Materialistic-postmaterialistic Value Orientations', in Van J. Deth, Elinor Scarbrough (eds.), *The Impact of Values* (Oxford: Oxford University Press, 1995), p. 156.

youth occurs into two principal models, which can be further subdivided. The 'Mediterranean' model comprises a prolongation of formal education, delayed entry to the labour market, prolonged cohabitation with the parents, and marriage shortly after the young person has left home. By contrast, the 'Nordic' model consists of early detachment from the family of origin, belated marriage and children, and therefore a period of life as a more or less stable couple or as a single person.[22]

When the style of life changes, the relationship between young people and their families is thrown into relief. In France, for example, one is struck by the increasing numbers of young people living alone, especially females from the upper and middle classes. In Italy, by contrast, at the age of 29 almost half of males and a quarter of females still live with their parents – the highest percentage in Europe.

This phenomenon can be explained by the greater modernity of the Italian family, which has given rise to a better and more balanced relationship between the generations living under the same roof. In Germany, where huge structural changes have followed reunification of the country, there has begun a process often described as 'social individualization' because it accentuates precocious socio-cultural independence among young people as a dialectic governing their personal life-orientations. The family thus consists of two generations of adults, that of the 'parents' and that of the 'young people', a feature which has a close bearing on the problem of religion.

Secondly, one notes in contemporary Europe the spread of religious worship based on the 'spontaneity of individual and collective religious expression', which tends to superimpose itself on forms based on strict observance of ecclesiastical doctrine. The general evolution of religiosity is the consequence of a change in religious sensibility due mainly to cultural change in people's universes of meaning. This means that the religious institutions finds it difficult to impose – primarily on the faithful, and on young people in particular – an orthodox system of organized meanings associated with an array of obligatory practices. Religion is viewed as 'fluctuating symbolic capital' on which young people freely draw to construct their religious frame of reference.

Thirdly, this evolution of the sacred should be viewed in terms of 'modernization'. Although on the one hand this process has engendered major socio-structural renewal in society, economics and science, on the other it has brought changes in the values, beliefs and attitudes of traditional

---

22 Alessandro Cavalli and Oliver Galland, (eds.), *L'allongement de la jeunesse* (Arles: Actes Sud, 1993).

societies, on which structural modifications have inevitably had their effects, producing a new type of consciousness and culture. One may therefore attribute to modernization the twofold meaning of socio-structural and cultural change. Both senses highlight the erosion and disappearance of old communities and ancient reference systems, and the birth of new orders characterized by high levels of differentiation, fragmentation and rationalization. This situation directly influences the present, sometimes frenetic, endeavour to reconstruct a communitarian identity.

Fourthly, youth culture should be viewed as a specific expression of the 'differentiation process' that has given greater complexity to the overall structure of society, and to its subsystems as well; the process whereby religion has become an individual choice in modern society. This suggests that in the Europe of today, although young people may greatly emphasise diversity, they simultaneously conduct a distinctive and shared search for a religiosity determined by a culture held together by a specific, albeit highly varied and personalized, values system.

My final observation concerns the 'spirit of the times' which influences the breakdown in the observance of religious precepts and explains the proliferation of beliefs and practices which remained on the margins as long as the sphere of belief was strictly controlled by the institutions.

Overall, it seems that the fluctuating religiousness that today characterizes the young people of Western Europe can be viewed as the outcome of a partial indifference to, or rejection of, inherited religion, but also as the continuing manifestation of a form of spirituality. This is indubitably the outcome of the conflict between religious doctrine and ongoing circumstances, as well stemming from the difficulty of transmitting the religious message in contemporary society.

3 New Age: re-enchantment of the world?

FRANZ HÖLLINGER

Introduction

The term 'New Age' has been introduced into the social sciences to denote a large number of heterogeneous groups which aim to transform modern Western society by developing and promoting a new spiritual consciousness.[1] As Berger, Berger and Kellner have pointed out in their book *The Homeless Mind*, the feature shared by these groups is their rejection of the preponderance of functional rationality in modern Western society. They all strive for emotional experience, sensitivity and intuition as a counterweight to pure rational thinking, searching for natural ways of life as a counterbalance to artificial environments, for natural healing methods as alternatives to pharmaceutical medicine, advocating 'holistic' views of the world as alternatives to the over specialized modern sciences.[2] New Age overlaps with other new social movements and cannot be clearly distinguished from them. It overlaps with the ecology movement, since both movements propound more natural ways of living, as well as with certain currents of feminism in so far as both maintain that 'female' qualities, such as sensitivity and intuition, should be given more weight in our society. There is also a connection between New Age and the psychotherapy movement, since for both the development of the 'inner self' by means of emotional and sensual experience is a paramount goal. And New Age overlaps with the new religious movements: a criterion which to a certain extent helps to distinguish between them being the more individualistic engagement in esoteric, occult and magic practices on the one hand, and the more collective pursuit of new forms of religious experience on the other. After the new esoteric and religious movements started to spread

---

[1] In his book *New Age und moderne Religion* (München: Chr. Kaiser, 1994), Christoph Bochinger has investigated the history of the term 'New Age'. The vision of a 'New Age' dates back to ancient and mediaeval messianic movements. In the present century, this term was first used in the late 1960s by American counter-culture literature, and in a book about the Findhorn community in Scotland. In the German-speaking world it became popular only when a leading publishing company began publishing a book series on esoteric literature entitled *New Age* in 1980.

[2] Peter Berger, Brigitte Berger, Hansfried Kellner, *The Homeless Mind* (New York: Random House, 1973).

through Western Europe in the 1970s, for more than a decade social scientists did not pay a great deal of attention to this new social phenomenon. Most of them who embraced the ideals of Enlightenment and scientific rationality had been convinced of the irreversibility of the process of secularization and disenchantment with the world. They considered the new esoteric and religious revival to be a marginal phenomenon, as a transitory reaction against the ongoing expansion of enlightened rational thought and forms of behaviour. Closer scientific interest was paid to these phenomena only when they proved not to be of transitory character, and were found to be influencing a considerable part of the population of Western societies.

In spite of the scientific ideal of objectivity, discourse on the new religious movements contains a strong evaluative component. Studies on New Age by authors who sympathise with its ideas and methods tend to stress the positive effects they may exert on the emotional state of individuals and on society at large.[3] Scientists with a Christian background (working in religious research institutions) and academic psychologists or psychiatrists have focused on the dangers raised by esoteric groups and sects for the young generation (and for churches!).[4] The majority of social scientists still largely ignore the esoteric and religious revival, however, and when they do talk or write about it, they give unmistakably negative evaluations. I had a striking personal experience in this regard when participating in an international research team constructing a cross-national comparative questionnaire on religion. It took a great deal of effort on my part to convince these researchers that magic and esoteric practices should be included in a sociological research project on contemporary religious attitudes and behaviour. In the end a few questions were included in the questionnaire. The topic, however, was always referred to as 'superstitious beliefs'.

The revival of religious, esoteric, occult and magic ideas and methods has prompted social scientists to coin the expression 're-enchantment of the world'. Most of them consider re-enchantment to be a step back from the high standards of modern, enlightened rationality towards the irrational modes of

---

3   Examples of positive but not uncritical studies of new religious and esoteric movements are the following: Meredith B. McGuire, 'Ritual, Symbolism and Healing', *Social Compass* 34/4, 1987, pp. 365-79; Danièle Hervieu-Léger, 'Present-Day Emotional Renewals. The End of Secularization or the End of Religion?' in William H. Swatos, Jr. (ed.), *A Future for Religion?* (London: Newbury Park, 1993), pp. 129-48; Bochinger, *New Age und moderne Religion. Religionswissenschaftliche Analysen*.

4   I can cite only examples in Germany: Wilhelm Haack, *Europas neue Religionen. Sekten - Gurus - Satanskult* (Wien: Deutscher Taschenbuchverlag, 1993); Gunter Klosinski, *Psychokulte. Was Sekten für Jugendliche so attraktiv macht* (München: C.H. Beck, 1996); Hansjörg Hemminger (ed.), *Die Rückkehr der Zauberer. New Age. Eine Kritik* (Reinbek bei Hamburg: Rewohlt, 1987).

thought and action of former times. In my opinion, the argument for characterizing the adepts of new esoterism as rational or irrational should not depend on judgements as to whether or not the theoretical premises of the methods that they employ are compatible with modern natural-scientific thinking. The criterion should instead be the instrumental rationality of esoteric methods. Thus, the central questions addressed by this article are: (i) what are the goals of the new esoteric movements, what methods do they use, and to what extent are their goals achieved?; (ii) what are the intended and unintended effects of new esoterism on the social behaviour of New Age adepts?

1. Enchantment and magic

Before examining new esoterism itself, I shall briefly discuss how 'magic' and 'enchantment' has been analysed and understood by modern Western science, and what Max Weber meant by his thesis of the 'disenchantment of the world'.

James Frazer's 'law of sympathetic magic' is a characteristic example of how magic was perceived by late nineteenth-century scientists. According to Frazer, all magic rituals are based on the assumption that a symbolic action will produce the same result in reality: for example, sticking a needle into a doll representing the enemy will cause the enemy to fall ill or die. Frazer concludes that, since such rituals are based on false causal assumptions, they can be considered as no more than wishful thinking, as superstitious and irrational beliefs.[5] The majority of scientists until the present day would pass similar judgment on magic, esoteric or occult phenomena. Weber and Durkheim, however, warned against unreflecting denunciation of primitive magic thought as 'irrational': when seen from the subjective perspective of the actor, magical techniques can be downright rational; they are irrational only when looked at from a different perspective on reality.[6]

The core of Max Weber's thesis of the 'disenchantment of the world' runs as follows: the more people are able to control the essential processes that guarantee and threaten human life by means of rational calculation and techniques, the more they will desist from believing that these processes are

---

5   James Frazer, *The Golden Bough* (New York: Basic Books, 1964, [1890]).
6   Emile Durkheim, *Die Elementaren Formen des Religiösen Lebens*, (Frankfurt: Suhrkamp, 1981, [1912]), p. 48; Max Weber, *Wirtschaft und Gesellschaft* (Tübingen: Rohr, 1985, [1922]), p. 245; Frank Robert Vivelo, *Handbuch der Kulturanthropologie*, (Stuttgart: Klett-Kotta, 1991), p. 161.

caused by supranatural forces, spirits and gods, and the more they will desist from magical techniques in order to influence and to control spiritual powers.[7] Enchantment is characterized as a belief in supranatural forces and the use of magic techniques in order to control supranatural forces. Weber does not assert, however, that magic methods are devoid of all instrumental rationality. Although he considered himself to be *'religiös unmusikalisch'* (a person with no talent for religion), more than most other sociologists he understood that religion is above all a matter of spiritual experience, not of beliefs. According to Weber, the common roots of both magic and religion lie in the 'discovery' by primitive society that certain persons have uncommon 'magical' abilities – such as the capacity to forecast future events or to heal – which can be provoked and reinforced by means of ecstasy-generating techniques. Since it was evident to Weber that any kind of ecstasy can provoke uncommon states of consciousness and uncommon energies, he did not doubt that persons with particular abilities, and who in addition have undergone systematic training, when in a state of ecstasy can perform acts which those unable to produce such phenomena take to be miraculous.[8]

Weber did not conduct further exploration of magical techniques and their practical effects. Magical ecstasy techniques were important for him only in so far as they provided a starting-point for his analysis of the process of rationalization of religious mysticism and asceticism. Both magical and mystical ecstasy are based on the production of uncommon psychic states by controlling the functions of the body. Indian mystical ecstasy techniques, however, differ from magical ones in that they do not rely on drugs as a means to induce ecstasy, and in that the techniques of asceticism and body control have been more systematized. The effects of mystic techniques are easier to control and to predict than the effects of magical ones. Consequently, according to Weber, Indian mystic techniques are more rational than magical ecstatic techniques *in regard to* achieving a more stable state of mystic contemplation.[9]

---

[7] See for example, 'Wissenschaft als Beruf', in *Gesammelte Aufsätze zur Wissenschaftslehre* (Tübingen: Mohr, 1988, [1924]), p. 594.

[8] Weber ibid., pp. 245-6. See also Max Weber, *Hinduismus und Buddhismus, Gesammelte Werke zur Religionssoziologie* Band II (Tübingen: Mohr, 1978, [1916-20]), pp. 167-70.

[9] The argument that all advanced techniques of religious asceticism and mysticism are rationalized derivatives of magical ecstasy techniques frequently recurs in the three volumes of Weber's writings on sociology of religion. A more systematic account is given in his famous 'Zwischenbetrachtung: Theorie der Stufen und Richtungen religiöser Weltablehnung', in *Gesammelte Aufsätze zur Religionssoziologie*, Band I, pp. 536-42.

In summary of this short discussion of Weber's 'disenchantment' thesis, we can conclude that it was not his intention to imply that all historical forms of magic are based on false causal assumptions. He only thought that human societies abandon methods which are less efficient in achieving a given purpose as soon as more efficient ones become available. Under this interpretation, the 're-enchantment of the world' should not be considered as simply a return to irrational ideas and forms of action. It can also be viewed as the rediscovery of knowledge systems which have been abandoned in the course of modernization because they proved to be less efficient than modern science and technologies in many respects, but which may still be useful for certain purposes and certain human needs.

2. The goals and results of esoteric practices

Magic and esoteric methods were used in the past to manipulate every kind of natural phenomenon. There is no doubt that primitive societies overestimated the power of magicians and esoteric schools to manipulate nature by means of spiritual energies. For good reason, human societies dispensed with the questionable abilities of the rain-maker as soon as they developed more reliable methods of giving fertility to the soil by means of irrigation. The great majority of present-day esoteric methods no longer seek to influence inanimate nature. Their principal purpose is to influence the psycho-physical state of human beings, to cure human diseases and to enable human beings to lead better lives by becoming aware of their abilities and spiritual potential.

While Western dualism distinguishes between matter and mind as two different qualities, magic and esoteric thought consider all the phenomena of the world to be parts of one original energy. Reality is not divided between material objects and energies (or processes), there is a fluent transition between material objects and (spiritual) energies. All the parts of reality are related to each other and influence each other. For example, methods like Tarot and I Ching start from the assumption that the person consulting the cards or the I Ching will subconsciously choose the card or pictogram which corresponds to his/her momentary psychic state.

Magic and esoteric thinking assume that there exists a higher 'spiritual' energy in addition to normal mind-energy. This energy was called '*mana*' by primitive societies and '*chi*' in Chinese science. All human beings, as well as all material phenomena, are influenced by this higher spiritual energy, but only certain persons are able to gain access to it and to manipulate it. A fundamental goal of all magic and esoteric methods is to train the ability to gain access to higher spiritual energies, or in other words, to achieve a state of 'higher consciousness'.[10]

Western scientific thought finds these assumptions difficult to accept. The criterion for considering a phenomenon trustworthy is that it can be verified and reproduced intersubjectively, which is certainly not the case of magic and parapsychological phenomena. Esoteric schools themselves do not claim that these phenomena can be produced and understood by everybody; on the contrary, throughout history esoteric knowledge has been kept secret, being revealed only to persons considered able to use it correctly. In defence of esoterism one may argue, however, that many modern technologies can be understood and reproduced only by the small community of specialized scientists. The majority of individuals can only believe that it is today possible to destroy the entire planet by means of hydrogen bombs, but they could never prove that this is actually true.[11]

The logic and the effects of magic and esoteric techniques are easier to understand when considered as symbolic action.[12] A central function of magic and esoteric rituals is to lead the human mind – and thus also human behaviour – in a certain direction by means of symbols and symbolic actions. Marcel Mauss and Claude Lévi-Strauss have provided numerous examples of the powerful effects of magic rituals in primitive societies. In his anthropological studies, Mauss found various cases of persons who died some weeks after a magical curse had been placed on them. He gives the following explanation for the phenomenon. Not only the cursed man but the entire community to which he belonged believed strongly into the magic curse. The community broke off all social ties with the cursed man and treated him as if he were already dead. The experience of being considered dead reinforced the man's own belief in the curse, he fell sick and finally died. Thus when health, sickness or death is the object, magic rituals can in fact produce the desired effect, if the persons concerned strongly believe in the magic ritual.[13] Lévi-

---

10 Edmund Runggaldier, *Philosophie der Esoterik*, (Berlin: Kohlhammer, 1996), pp. 35-61.
11 Max Weber noted that modern technologies are by no means more rational (i.e. easier to understand) for most members of modern society than the techniques applied by magicians were for members of primitive societies (see: 'Wissenschaft als Beruf', in *Gesammelte Aufsätze zur Wissenschaftslehre*, p. 449-50). The argument that there is a great deal of 'magical' thinking in our use of modern technologies has also been put forward by Carlo Mongardini: 'Über die soziologische Bedeutung des magischen Denkens', in Arnold Zingerle, Carlo Mongardini (eds.), *Magie und Moderne* (Berlin: Gudrian & Hoppe, 1987), p. 37, and by Hans-Jürgen Fraas, *Die Religiosität des Menschen* (Göttingen-Zürich: UTB, 1990), p. 124.
12 Runggaldier, *Philosophie der Esoterik*, pp. 62-75; Alfred Lorenzer, *Das Konzil der Buchhalter* (Frankfurt: Fischer, 1992), pp. 23-48.
13 Marcel Mauss, 'Theorie der Magie', *Soziologie und Anthropologie* 1, 1974, pp. 124ff.

Strauss asserts that shamanistic healing can be explained in a thoroughly rational way when one takes account of the emotions evoked by symbolic action. By 'summoning' bad spirits, or by symbolically acting like a bad spirit, the shaman evokes images and strong emotions in the client, thereby enabling the latter to re-experience a psychic trauma, which is the precondition for the recovery of the sick. The crucial point, according to Levi-Strauss, is not whether the healer and his client believe that the spirits really 'exist'. It is the visualization of the spirit as a symbol for the psychic conflict. Levi-Strauss concludes that the logic and effects of shamanistic healing rituals are similar to those of psychoanalytical therapy.[14]

Both in Freudian and Jungian psychoanalysis, symbols occur in the unconscious state of night dreams; but also symbols and symbolic actions in daytime life are considered to be important movers of psycho-emotional processes. It is a basic principle of psychoanalysis that the client is assisted by the therapist to change his/her (neurotic) behaviour by finding out how the symbols of his/her dreams relate to his/her behaviour. According to Jung, a certain category of symbols – what he calls 'archetypes' – are of particular importance, since they are symbolic representations of universal human experiences, such as birth, death, sexuality, and so on. These symbols play a central role in all religious and esoteric traditions. By analysing the symbolic meanings and psychodynamic functions of archetypes from the perspective of modern psychology, Jung made an important contribution to bringing esoterism and humanistic psychology closer together.[15] Today, numerous schools of humanist psychology regard symbols and symbolic actions as important means with which to influence the psychic state of human beings. The method of performing symbolic actions which represent a psychic conflict (for example, beating a pillow which represents the father) in order to resolve this conflict, is method used by many forms of psychotherapy. As the understanding of psychic processes in humanistic psychology is similar to esoteric assumptions in many respects, two movements have increasingly approximated each other place in the last decades. Many psychotherapists, trained in modern psychotherapy and who first worked with these methods only, have incorporated elements of spiritual and esoteric technique – such as meditation and breathing techniques, ecstasy techniques, reincarnation therapy – into their work as their careers have progressed.

---

14 Claude Lévi-Strauss, *Strukturale Anthropologie* (Frankfurt: Suhrkamp, 1977), pp. 224-55.
15 Hans-Jürgen Ruppert, 'Altes Denken auf neuen Wegen: New Age und Esoterik', in Hemminger (ed.), *Die Rückkehr der Zauberer*, pp. 86ff.

The concept of symbols as carriers and transmitters of energy also aids understanding of the practical effects of esoteric healing methods like homeopathy or Bachblüten therapy, and 'divination methods' like Tarot and I Ching.

Homeopathic medicine is produced by the so-called process of powering: one part of the healing substance is mixed with ten parts of a neutral liquid; then one part of the resulting liquid is again mixed with ten parts of neutral liquid. This process is repeated up to thirty, fifty or even three hundred times. Since in higher-powered medicine even the last molecules of the healing substance have disappeared, according to modern natural science it is impossible for this kind of medicine to have any causal effect. Homeopathic doctors, however, do not claim that their medicine works in the same way as modern Western medicine does. For homeopathy, the healing element is not a material substance but the transmitted immaterial information. Thorwald Dethlefson, a prominent New Age author, illustrates this principle with the example of information-transfer by means of print media.[16] The book – as a material object – is only the carrier of the information it contains. The information itself exists independently of the carrier and can be transmitted in different forms. Healing achieved by homeopathy can be explained to a certain extent also by the social process of the treatment itself. It is well known that the consultation of the client is a central part of the homeopathic treatment. Homeopaths take more time than 'orthodox' physicians to consult their clients in order to find out what the physical, psychic and social determinants of the disease may be, and accordingly choose the appropriate medicine. They not only prescribe a medicine but also discuss with their clients which of their habits to change, which food to eat or to avoid, and so on, in order to get well again. Homeopathic treatment may thus have a positive effect on health also because the client changes his or her habits according to the doctor's advice. The function of the medicine is symbolically to reinforce the self-healing-power of the client.[17]

Tarot cards and I Ching work on a similar principle of influencing the human mind by means of symbols. Rather than methods of divination, they are methods to achieve better knowledge of the psychic drives behind one's own behaviour and that of others. Tarot cards and I Ching pictograms are symbols which represent essential dimensions and problems of human life. Unlike the words of human language, which have rather precise cognitive

---

16 Thorwald Dethlefson, *Schicksal als Chance* (München: Bertelsmann, 1979), p. 159.
17 Runggaldier, *Philosophie der Esoterik*, pp. 143-6.

meanings, pictures are symbols with complex meanings.[18] Whatever the pictograms chosen, the person interpreting them will perceive and focus (only) on those aspects of their complex symbolic meaning which are relevant to his/her momentary psychic state. According to the 'theory' of Tarot and I Ching, the pictograms by no means mechanically predict what will happen in the future. As 'archetypical' symbols, they contain information about elementary processes of human and social life, indicating what will be the consequences of a given form of behaviour. They thus help those able intuitively to interpret these symbols correctly to see the consequences of certain actions more clearly and thereby find a way to solve the problem at hand.[19]

3. Intended and non-intended consequences of new esotericism

As a conclusion to the preceding analysis of some esoteric methods we may say that they do exert an influence on the mind and on the behaviour of individuals by transmitting information via symbols or symbolic actions. The effects of practising esoteric methods can be compared to those of reading books. Reading a single book in most cases will not change our personality. But if people read certain kinds of book regularly, they will eventually develop a personality different from that of people who read no books at all. In the same way, esoteric methods – (only) when taught by an experienced teacher and constantly practised – can help people to achieve more profound consciousness of themselves. Every kind of meditation, but also methods like Tarot and I Ching, when practised in that way, can have positive effects on the personality. They increase awareness about the psychic motivations and unconscious drives of a person's social behaviour. Thereby they are also able to improve sensitivity to the social environment. On the other hand, throughout history esoteric and mystic traditions have tended to favour withdrawal from the world and indifference to the social environment. The main concern of the esoteric search for 'holistic' consciousness is personal well-being, not the well-being of others.

---

18 The differences between verbal and non-verbal symbols have been analysed by the German philosopher Ernst Cassirer and his student Susanne Langer. With reference to Cassirer and Langer, the German sociologist and psychotherapist Alfred Lorenzer, in his book *Das Konzil der Buchhalter. Die Zerstörung der Sinnlichkeit*, discusses the importance of non-verbal symbols and rituals for the psychic well-being of human beings and their integration into society.
19 Runggaldier, *Philosophie der Esoteric*, pp. 121-3; Ruppert, *Altes Denken auf neuen Wegen: New Age and Esoterik*, pp. 95-7.

The new esoteric movement has doubtlessly had positive effects in the area of medicine. By concentrating almost exclusively on the physical determinants of health, modern Western medicine has long neglected the fact that psychic and social factors, too, have a powerful impact on people's well-being. What gives many people greater confidence in a homeopath than in an ordinary physician is that the former spends longer on consulting the client in order to discover the possible physical, psychic and social causes of his/her illness. It is not the goal of homeopathy to make clients believe that the medicine will automatically heal disease. This is more the case of orthodox medicine. On the contrary, the ideal of homeopathy is to enable the client to become aware of his or her own self-healing potential. What has been said here about homeopathy also applies to other esoteric methods. The assertion that those who employ these methods necessarily believe in magic effects is not true.

It is true, however, that there are many people who *mistake* esoteric methods for 'magical' ones. Throughout history, there have existed two forms of magic: popular and professional. Popular magic is in fact based to a large extent on the belief or hope that performance of a ritual will mechanically produce the desired result. Professional magic and esoteric methods, by contrast, are based on techniques of arousing, manipulating and controlling psychic forces. In order to prevent esoteric techniques from being employed wrongly or dangerously, in all former societies esoteric knowledge was transmitted only to persons considered as qualified and who were willing to undergo long and demanding training. The New Age movement has broken with this principle by revealing esoteric methods in simplistic bestsellers and instruction courses open to everybody. New Age authors justify the popularization of esoterism by arguing that humanity today is in need of a new consciousness, and that everybody should be given a chance to achieve higher forms of spiritual experience. A characteristic feature of many New Age adepts, however, is that they do not go deeply into one particular esoteric method. Instead, they jump from one method to another, reading a little bit about everything, experimenting with numerous methods at the same time, or one after the other.[20] This approach to esoterism may not be as dangerous as some critics have claimed. However, as in the case of other techniques, the dilettante use of esoteric techniques will produce results very different from those achieved by a skilled and well-trained expert. This is the case of people

---

20 Bochinger, *New Age and modern Religion*, pp. 495-98; Hubert Knoblauch, 'Das unsichtbare Zeitalter. "New Age", privatisierte Religion und kultisches Milieu', *Kölner Zeitschrift für Soziologie und Soziologie und Sozialpsychologie*, vol. 41, 1991, p. 517ff.

who, after attending a few workshops on yoga, chromotherapy or Bachblüten therapy, consider themselves able to practise these methods and teach them to others. This, of course, also happens when people with only superficial knowledge of Tarot cards base their decisions on the outcome of the 'oracle'.[21] Many New Age adepts overestimate the effects that can be achieved by esoteric methods. There is no doubt that our emotional states are to a certain degree influenced by colours, but this does not mean that chromotherapy is a proper means to cure any kind of disease at all. Esoteric therapy methods may indeed be dangerous when they are viewed as radical alternatives to modern Western medicine.

Dialogue between orthodox medicine and alternative therapies has long been hampered by the claims of both sides that their methods are the more reliable means with which to secure human well-being. Meanwhile, a gradual approximation between the two sides has taken place. Ordinary physicians increasingly accept homeopathy, acupuncture and psychotherapy as complementary methods. The question is no longer whether the one or the other method is more reliable in general, but which method is more suited to a specific problem.

New social movements become popular when and because there is a social need for them. However, whenever social movements become mass movements, the ideals of their founders are diluted and sometimes even distorted into their opposite. Christianity took the form of the Inquisition in the Middle Ages. Marxism, when translated into the reality of Communist regimes, proved to be much less satisfactory for the people living in those societies than had been foreseen by Marx. Nevertheless, in many respects, Christian and socialist ideals all over the world have exerted and still exert a positive influence on society. Like all utopian ideals, also those of New Age can be realized only to a very modest degree. In spite of the claim by some New Age prophets that the 'holistic consciousness' will change all the spheres of modern society, the majority of New Age adepts do not doubt that modern science and technology are indispensable to solution of many of the problems afflicting complex modern societies. They do not seek to achieve a radical transformation of modern science and society, only to improve their *individual* well-being. There are indications that esoteric practices, when used properly, can help in accomplishing this goal.

---

21 Critical comments in this regard are made by almost all social-scientific studies on New Age: see, for example, Bochinger, *New Age and Modern Religion*, pp. 496-505; Ruppert, *Altes Denken auf neuen Wegen: New Age and Esoterik*, pp. 98-103; Fritjof Capras, 'Moralisches Unternehmen und die New Age-Bewegung', *Kölner Zeitschrift für Soziologie und Sozialpsychologie*, Sonderheft 33, 1933, pp. 249-70.

4 The abstract image of God: the case of Dutch youth

JACQUES JANSSEN

Introduction

By the end of the 1970s, the Netherlands had taken the lead in the European secularization process, and church membership in the country is now the lowest in the whole of Western Europe. Studies by Dutch sociologists show a steady decline in religious organizations, opinions and behaviour.[1] The figures seem clear and unambiguous. In 1945, 40 percent of the Dutch population were Catholics; in the year 2000 this percentage will have been halved. For the Protestant denominations, the figures are even more telling: in 1945 their percentage was above 40; in the year 2000 it will be below 15. The percentage of non-church members was 15 in 1945, in the year 2000 it will be approximately 62, and it is predicted to rise to 75 in 2020.[2]

When we add to these facts and predictions the trend in all European countries for the younger generation to score substantially lower on almost all aspects of religious behaviour than older people,[3] we may deduce that Dutch youth is at the summit of secularization. Indeed, a national survey of Dutch youth (1991, mean age 23.9) conducted by the present authors found that 61 percent were not members of a church.[4] The European Values Study of 1990 reported a somewhat lower percentage of 53 (18-to-29 age group),[5] which is nevertheless the highest in Western Europe.

---

1 James Becker and Rene Vink, *Secularisatie in Nederland 1966-1991* (Rijswijk: Sociaal en Cultureel Planbureau, 1994).
2 Ibid., pp. 175-80.
3 Campiche, (ed.), *Cultures des jeunes et religions en Europe* (Paris: Cerf, 1997).
4 Joep de Hart and Jacques Janssen, 'Jongeren en politiek' in Arjan Dieleman, Frans van der Linden and A. Perrijn, *Jeugd in meervoud* (Utrecht: Uitgeverij De Tijdstroom bv., 1993).
5 Campiche, (ed.), *Cultures des jeunes et religions en Europe*, p. 52.

Several other studies show similar or even substantially more negative results.[6] In parishes and church organizations, all programmes designed to attract the young appear to fail.[7] The churches are losing contact with the younger generation, and in the years to come the results of this mutual estrangement will become more and more visible in participation and opinion indexes.

In Europe as a whole the consequences of secularization are more marked in predominantly Protestant countries where participation in church and church-related organisations is falling more rapidly.[8] In the Netherlands this is reflected in the steep decline over the past decades in the largest Protestant group ('Hervormden'), but since the 1960s the Catholics have had to cope with the most turbulent development.[9] Their numbers have diminished considerably, and while in the whole of Europe the Protestants score lower on religious indexes, in the Netherlands it is the Catholics who show the lower scores: they go to church less, they are less interested in religion, pray less, pay less, and so on.[10] It has even been claimed that 41 per cent of the Dutch Catholics should be labelled as 'non or weak believers',[11] and this applies *a fortiori* to Catholic youth. Even the most active of them – those who participate in church choirs – express doubts on every kind of religious issue and display the same religious profile as rank-and-file members.[12]

In European studies,[13] the exceptional position of the Dutch Catholics is related to the debate between the Dutch Catholic Church and the Vatican in the 1960s. However, this may very well be only a symptom of a much more

---

6 Frans van der Linden, *Groot worden in een klein land. Feiten en cijfers uit het onderzoek naar de leefwereld van jongeren tussen 12 en 21 jaar* (Nijmegen: ITS, 1989); Joep de Hart, *Levensbeschouwelijke en politieke praktijken van Nederlandse middelbare scholieren* (Kampen: Kok, 1990); Hans Alma, *Geloven in de leefwereld van jongeren* (Kampen: Uitgeverij Kok, 1993); Hans van der Ven and Berdine Biemans, *Religie in fragmenten: een onderzoek onder studenten* (Weinheim/Kampen: Deutscher Studien Verlag/Kok, 1994); Jos W. Becker, Joep de Hart and Jann Mens, *Secularisatie en alternatieve zingeving in Nederland* (Rijswijk: Sociaal en Cultureel Planbureau, 1997).
7 Ton Bernts, *Meer stem voor jongeren: een onderzoek naar jongerenkoren, religiositeit en kerk* (Nijmegen: ITS, 1995); Hans van der Ven, 'Het religieus bewustzijn van jongeren en de crisis van het jongerenpastoraat', *Praktische theologie: Nederlands tijdschrift voor pastorale wetenschappen, 22 (3)*, 1995, p. 342.
8 Campiche, *Cultures des jeunes et religions en Europe*, p. 52.
9 Gerald Dekker, Joep de Hart and Jan Peters, *God in Nederland, 1966-1996*, (Amsterdam: Anthos, 1997).
10 Ibid.
11 Jan Peters, Martin van Hemert, Ton Bernts and Louis Spruit, *Geloven in deze tijd. Onderzoek en perspectief* (Den Haag: Kaski, 1996), p. 20.
12 Ton Bernts, *Meer stem voor jongeren: een onderzoek naar jongerenkoren, religiositeit en kerk* (Nijmegen: ITS, 1995), p. 99.
13 Campiche, *Cultures des jeunes et religions en Europe*, p. 54.

complicated issue, in which a major role is played by the docility of the Dutch Catholics that once made them an example of obedience. In the first half of the twentieth century, deviant opinions and criticism were not tolerated within the strictly hierarchical Dutch Catholic Church. The successful emancipation of the Dutch Catholics on the social, cultural and political levels can be attributed to this strategy of unity. However, the drawbacks became apparent in the second half of the twentieth century. When the authority of the church was challenged, it faded overnight and the internal motivation of its adherents proved to be weak. On leaving its shepherds, the flock went astray.[14]

The secularization process is often depicted as an ongoing, one-way decline in religion. This line of argument can be criticised by pointing to the complexity and multi-dimensionality of the secularization process in the Netherlands.[15] While the above-mentioned facts will not be questioned as such, there is much more to say on religion than simply regarding it as a fading phenomenon. Generally, only a very few young people reject religion explicitly or prefer atheism. They still possess religious identity, but this has become a private affair, insecure, non-specific and abstract. This is manifest inside as well as outside the churches. In European studies, Dutch youth – the group with the lowest number of church members – score rather high (fifth place among sixteen countries) when religion is measured not by membership but as an individual characteristic indicated by church attendance, prayer and the salience of religion in one's life.[16]

To elaborate this point, we shall first show that there is no such thing as *the* religion of Dutch youth: there are instead several religions and religious practices. Moreover, it should not be forgotten that non-religious people also differ fundamentally on several existential issues and practices. To depict the full range of the Dutch youth, religious as well as non-religious, we shall have to distinguish nine different groups. Secondly, numerous studies have reported the low participation by young people in church affairs, and they also show that the young have hardly any knowledge of institutional religion. A large proportion of the Dutch population, regardless of educational level, does not know what Easter is about, let alone Pentecost or Ascension Day. Of course, there is a problem in what the young do not do and do not know, but we are more interested in what they actually do and what they actually know. We also want to hear it expressed in their own language, and as a consequence

---

14 Jan Roes, *In de kerk geboren. Het Nederlandse katholicisme in anderhalve eeuw van herleving naar overleving*, (Nijmegen: Valkhof Pers, 1994).
15 Jacques Janssen, 'The Netherlands as an Experimental Garden of Religiosity. Remnants and Renewals', *Social Compass*, 45 (1), 1998, pp. 101-13.
16 Campiche, *Cultures des jeunes et religions en Europe*, p. 59.

our research has been predominantly based on the analysis of open-ended questions. The multiple choice method employed by several surveys can be useful in some cases, but it has shortcomings when the intention is to gain full understanding of how young people construct their religion. In general, open-ended questions are to be preferred to closed ones when the behaviour and concepts of people are subject to constant change and reconstruction. If this is the case, old concepts soon lose their validity and new concepts must be explored. Besides, we are living in an age of cultural change, marked by individualization and differentiation, in which people must construct their own concepts. In a certain sense, they must be inventors. Religious beliefs and practices are increasingly shaped outside the traditional institutional churches and become more and more individualized and diverse.[17] To understand the religious practices of today's youth, we must study their thought processes, and not just the outcomes of this process.[18] Using open-ended questions is therefore the best – if not the only – way to gain insights into the contemporary religious practices of youngsters. Accordingly, we asked young people to tell us about their religious feelings in their own words. By using open-ended questions, we also avoided the problem of alarming the young respondents with words and images on the subject of religion. For instance, the word 'God' seemingly has an intimidating effect on youngsters: when asked straight out whether they pray to God, only 11 percent say that they do, but when asked how they pray, in an open-ended question, 30 percent of respondents spontaneously mention God as the direction of their prayer (see below). Hence, asking a question does not always yield the answer, whereas not asking the question does. Polonius's famous advice to his servant Reynaldo: 'by indirections find directions out' (Shakespeare, *Hamlet*, Act II, Scene I) certainly applies here.

The research was carried out in 1991.[19] The sample consisted of 687 Dutch youngsters with an average age of 23.9 years (male 44 percent, female 56 percent; 62 percent of subjects attended full-time education, 57 percent of them at university). The answers to the open-ended questions were analysed using a computerized technique called Textable,[20] a computer program which can handle texts, categorize them and link them with data from closed

---

17 Dekker, Joep de Hart and Peters, *God in Nederland. 1966-1996*.
18 Bernard Spilka, Ralf W. Hood and Richard L. Gorsuch Jr., *The Psychology of Religion: An Empirical Approach*, (Englewood Cliffs: Prentice-Hall, 1985), p. 69.
19 Joep de Hart and Jacques Janssen, 'Jongeren en politiek' in Arjan Dieleman, Frans van der Linden, and Sandra Perrijn, *Jeugd in meervoud*, (Utrecht: Uitgeverij De Tijdstroom bv., 1993).
20 Jacques Janssen, *Tekst-tabel*, (Nijmegen: University of Nijmegen: Department of Psychology, 1990).

questions. One of the advantages of Textable is that it enables interaction between open and closed information processing, while also making it possible to continuously control and adapt the category system and return to the original answers at any point in the analysis.

1. The diversity of the religiosity of Dutch youth

The Netherlands is a plural country in both name and in character. It has for long been a country of several religious minorities living harmoniously together in what has been called a 'pluralized' society. In the 1960s this plural society grew even more pluralized as a result of the processes of secularization and individualization, and the emergence of new religious movements, here summed up by the term 'New Age'.[21] In order to construct a category system for religious involvement, we made use of traditional sociological variables like 'church membership' and 'church attendance' (more or less than three times a year). But in order to categorize the non-religious youngsters, we also had to use personal variables. We opted for the variable 'praying' (regularly or sometimes, versus never), because this seems to be the most persistent religious element in a secularised society,[22] and the variable 'engagement in New Age activities', since New Age is the most successful recent movement, as well as including various activities and capturing the process of individualization and change in religious concepts.

By combining these sociological and personal variables, we were able to distinguish nine religious groups (Table 4.1).

---

21 Janssen, 'The Netherlands as an Experimental Garden of Religiosity. Remnants and Renewals'.
22 Campiche, *Cultures des jeunes et religions en Europe*, p. 59; Jacques Janssen, Maerten H. Prins, Cor J. Baerveldt and Jan van der Lans, (under review), *The Structure and Variety of Prayer. An Empirical Study of Dutch Youth.*

Table 4.1: The construction of a category system for religious involvement. N=687

	Varieties of religious involvement	Church Membership	Praying	Church attendance	New Age activities	%	N
1	Orthodox	member	praying	church attendance		4	26
2	Calvinist	member	praying	church attendance	3	7	46
3	Reformed	member	praying	church attendance		7	46
4	Catholic	member	praying	church attendance		11	79
5	Marginal	member				9	60
6	New Age		praying		6 activities	15	106
7	Ex-member	ex-member	praying		#6 activities	17	119
8	Doubter		praying		#6 activities	9	60
9	Non believer					17	119
	No category					4	26

The first distinction is the traditional one between church members and non-church members. This sociological variable still works, albeit for a decreasing segment of youth. Our research found that 39 per cent of youngsters were still members of a church. Within this group we discerned *Orthodox Protestants* (4 percent), *Calvinists* (7 percent), *Reformed Protestants* (7 percent) and *Catholics* (12 percent). It was known from previous research that these groups show a decreasing measure of participation and conviction.[23] Furthermore, there are those who, although they consider themselves members of a church, either never attend church or never pray. We labelled these *Marginals* (9 percent).

For the remaining 61 percent who were not affiliated to a church, we devised a new heuristic scheme. This group is not usually differentiated

---

23   Jan Peters and Otto Schreuder, *Katholiek en Protestant* (Nijmegen: ITS, 1987); Joep de Hart, *Levensbeschouwelijke en politieke praktijken van Nederlandse middelbare scholieren,* (Kampen: Kok, 1990); Bert Felling, Jan Peters and Otto Schreuder, *Dutch Religion. The Religious Consciousness of the Netherlands after the Cultural Revolution* (Nijmegen: ITS, 1991); Dekker, de Hart and Peters, *God in Nederland. 1966-1996.*

further, but in our opinion this is a mistake: apostasy is as multicoloured as conversion, and disbelief is as complex as belief.[24]

Besides, non-denominational people are also individualized and construct their own particular ways of life. First we distinguished the *New Age* youngsters, who participated in a considerable number of New Age-related activities (16 percent). We presented a list of twelve fields of interest: yoga, reincarnation, astrology, extraterrestrial civilizations, parapsychology, macrobiotics, anthroposophy, homeopathy, the New Age movement, Buddhism, Zen and holism.[25] Youngsters not affiliated to a church who participated in activities related to six or more of these issues were considered to be 'New Age-minded'. The seventh group was made up of former members of churches (*Ex-members*), whose only religious activity was praying (18 percent). The eight group, labelled *Doubters* (9 percent), had never been affiliated to a church but nevertheless prayed at least sometimes. The last group comprised the *Non-believers* (18 percent), who lacked any kind of religious involvement whatsoever. They were in Max Weber's words 'religiös unmusikalisch', tone-deaf to religion.

We predicted beforehand that this heuristic category system for religious involvement would reflect a rank order of orthodoxy. Pearson-R and ETA are represented in every table: when the Pearson-correlation is high and the ETA does not substantially differ, the rank order model that we predicted holds.[26] As regards variables directly related to religion, this prediction was indeed strongly validated. When the respondents were asked about the importance of being a good Christian (V57), whether they agreed that conciliation with death is only possible by having faith in God (V534), and the importance of being close to God (V84), the correlations were very high (.70 to .72) and linear (the ETA hardly diverges). The definition of a higher reality (V418) also correlated strongly (.68) and was linear. The most religiously involved youngsters – the orthodox Protestants – believed that there is a God. The less religiously involved the youngsters were, the more they tended to answer that there is a higher being, or that they did not know, and most of the non-believers stated that God does not exist (Table 4.2).

---

24 Paul W. Pruyser, *Between Belief and Unbelief* (New York: Harper and Row, 1974).
25 Joep de Hart and Jacques Janssen, 'New Age als paracultuu', *Voorwerk*, 1, 1992, pp. 14-24.
26 Pearson's R measures linear relationships. The correlation ratio, ETA, is sometimes termed the 'coefficient of curvilinear correlation'. When a relationship is linear, R equals ETA; in curvilinear relationships, the degree to which R is less than ETA is a measure of the extent to which a curvilinear relation exists. A perfect curvilinear relationship (ETA = 1.0) may even have an R of zero.

Table 4.2: Scores of the nine religious groups on variables directly related to Christian religion

V84 The importance of being close to God; V534 Conciliation with death is only possible by trusting God and surrendering to Him; V57 The importance of being a good Christian; V418 Definition of a higher reality. Range V84 and V57: 1= very important, 5= very unimportant; V534: 1= agree totally, 5= do not agree at all.

	V84	V534	V57	V418				
	Close to God	Trust God in death	Good Christian	Definition of a higher reality %				
Religious involvement	mean score	mean score	mean score	God	higher being	don't know	doesn't exist	total
1. Orthodox	1.8	2.1	1.9	87	13	0	0	4%
2. Calvinist	1.8	2.0	1.8	70	24	7	0	7%
3. Reformed	2.0	2.2	1.9	72	20	9	0	7%
4. Catholic	2.9	2.9	2.6	41	43	14	1	12%
5. Marginal	3.5	3.5	3.1	29	41	29	2	9%
6. New age	4.2	4.4	4.1	5	47	42	6	16%
7. Ex-member	4.3	4.5	4.3	6	24	48	22	18%
8. Doubter	4.4	4.5	4.3	4	44	28	25	9%
9. Nonbeliever	4.8	4.9	4.7	1	10	43	46	18%
Total	3.7	3.8	3.6	16	31	30	23	N=687
Pearson -r	.72	.71	.70	.68				
Eta	.74	.74	.73	.69				

At this point rank order is evident, but there are three clear break points. There is a substantial gap between active church members (group 1-4) and non-church members (group 6-9) which is filled by those who considered themselves members but did not attend church: namely the marginals (group 5). Their position is as predicted and, compared to the non-church members, they place relatively greater weight on being good Christians and faith in God when faced with death, but they differ from church members in that they place less importance on being close to God in daily life. The latter aspect is also reflected in their definition of a higher reality: marginals shift away from an image of God to a more abstract higher being, and 29 percent of them are in doubt.

A second break point occurs in the bottom half of the scale. In the non-membership groups (6-9) the figures are as predicted, but there is an evident leap between marginals (group 5) and non-members (group 6-9). The non-members (and especially the non-believers) were more opposed to religious interpretations and placed little importance on Christian values. The word

'God' was almost completely rejected. Differences among New-Age, ex-members, doubters and non-believers are small, but clearly linear.

Within the groups of active church members (1-4), a third breaking point is visible between the Protestant groups (1-3) and the Catholics (4). The Protestant respondents believed it very important to be close to God and to be a good Christian (mean score about 2), whereas the Catholics took up a somewhat ambiguous position (mean score about 3): they clearly less often defined the higher reality in which they believed as 'God', a lot of them preferring expressions like 'higher being' or 'higher power'.

This highlights the rather precarious situation of Catholicism, particularly in Dutch society: we shall meet this feature again when we look at other variables. Catholics, moreover, seemed generally to be less religiously involved than Protestants.

Caution is necessary, however. Catholics and Protestants differ not only in a quantitative but also in a qualitative sense. The Protestant religion emphasises God as an exterior force and prefers a dialectical image of God, one in which God is 'radically other than' the world.[27] Catholics, on the other hand, have a predominantly analogical or sacramental image of God in which God is made present in and through the world and interpersonal relationships. Therefore Catholics are more inclined to see God as a symbol; they more often doubt the existence of an actual higher being or of God; and they more strongly endorse an autonomous, inner-worldly meaning of human life.[28] Consequently, when orthodoxy is measured by asking about the importance of being close to God, faith in God and the importance of being a good Christian (as in Table 4.2), Protestants are bound to score higher than Catholics.

The difference between the Catholic and the Protestant modes of belief has been nicely described by Umberto Eco, using a computer analogy. In this view, Macintosh computers are Catholic and DOS computers are Protestant:

> [T]he Macintosh is cheerful, friendly, conciliatory, it tells the faithful how they must proceed step by step to reach – if not the Kingdom of Heaven – the moment in which their document is printed. It is catechistic: the essence of revelation is dealt with via simple formulae and sumptuous icons. Everyone has a right to salvation,

---

27 Andrew M. Greeley, *The Catholic Myth: the Behavior and Beliefs of American Catholics* (New York: Scribner's, 1990).
28 Greeley, *The Catholic Myth*; Felling, Peters and Schreuder, *Dutch Religion. The Religious Consciousness of the Netherlands after the Cultural Revolution*; Jan Peters, Martin van Emert, Ton Bernts and Leo Spruit, *Geloven in deze tijd. Onderzoek en perspectief* (Den Haag: Kaski, 1996), p. 20.

whereas

> DOS is Protestant, or even Calvinistic. It allows free interpretation of scripture, demands difficult personal decisions, imposes a subtle hermeneutics upon the user, and takes for granted the idea that not all can reach salvation. To make the system work you need to interpret the program yourself: a long way from the baroque community of revellers, the user is closed within the loneliness of his own inner torment.[29]

Hence Catholics are not necessarily less religious than Protestants – just as a Macintosh PC is no less a computer than a DOS PC – but they are religious in a different way.

A second set of variables relating to religious behaviour contained weaker correlations (.31 to .71) but which were still linear (the ETA does not differ substantially). These variables concerned the meaning of life, dying and death, and interest in religious matters. The stronger the religious involvement, the more the subjects disagreed with the proposition that people themselves must give meaning to life (V528). Those most closely involved in religion disagreed that, at the moment of dying, they must face death by relying on their own strength (V526) and, as we have seen in Table 4.2, seek conciliation with death by having faith in God and surrendering to Him. Stronger religious involvement was also associated with the belief that death is not the end (V529), but that there is a heaven or paradise (V536). And finally, stronger religious involvement meant closer interest in religious information transmitted by television, radio, articles and conversation about religious matters (V405, V407, V408) (Table 4.3).

---

29 Umberto Eco, *La bustina di Minerva*, Umberto Eco's back-page column in the Italian news weekly *Espresso*, 1994, September 30.

Table 4.3: Scores of the nine religious groups on variables related to religious attitudes and activities

V528 It is people themselves who give meaning to life; V526 At the moment of dying, we must face death by relying on our own strength and not trust any religion; V520 There is life after death; V536 I believe in a heaven or paradise after life; V405 Reading articles on religion; V407 Listening to religious radio programmes or watching religious television programmes; V408 Talking about religion. Range V528, V526, V534 and V536: 1= agree totally, 5= do not agree at all.

Religious involvement	V528 Self meaning life	V526 Own power when dying	V520 per cent Life after death	V536 Heaven paradise	V405 per cent Read articles on religion		V407 per cent Radio TV religion		V408 per cent Talk about religion	
					regularly	never	regularly	never	regularly	never
1. Orthodox	3.5	4.4	84	2.0	62	4	27	39	54	0
2. Calvinist	3.6	4.3	88	1.9	41	14	14	16	47	4
3. Reformed	3.1	4.2	88	2.0	27	15	23	17	40	6
4. Catholic	2.4	3.6	79	2.3	17	29	3	45	21	7
5. Marginal	2.0	3.3	60	2.8	7	48	3	53	10	27
6. New age	2.0	2.8	62	3.7	7	33	4	43	19	14
7. Ex-member	1.9	2.7	33	4.1	5	47	3	50	13	18
8. Doubter	1.8	2.6	37	4.1	3	54	2	58	9	20
9. Nonbeliever	1.6	2.1	24	4.6	2	61	0	66	5	31
Total	2.2	3.1	54	3.4	13	16	6	39	19	47
Pearson -r	-.49	-.55	-.50	.65	.43		.31		.35	
Eta	.53	.56	.53	.67	.46		.36		.38	

The differences within the Protestant groups were small, but linear as expected. The only apparent exception was in the strikingly low percentage of orthodox and especially Calvinist youngsters who watched religious television programmes, but this exception proves the rule since some of them were not allowed to watch television at all, according to the precepts of their religious creed.

Again we find a rather sharp contrast between the Protestant groups (1-3) and the Catholics (4). Catholic youngsters were more similar to non-church members: they agreed that people themselves have to give meaning to life, and that at the moment of dying people must face death by relying on their own strength, whereas the Protestant groups placed emphasis on trusting in God, especially at the moment of dying but also, as we have seen in Table 4.2, in daily life as well. One also notes that the Catholics were much less interested in information regarding religious matters.

The possibility of life after death was considered plausible by all active church members (groups 1-4, about 80 percent) and the marginals (60 percent), but also by New Age youngsters (62 percent). However, only the church members believed in a heaven or a paradise, while for the New Age group life after death took the form of reincarnation, as we shall see later in in Table 4.4.

Overall, our predictions were corroborated. The scale we devised for measuring religious involvement reflected a clear rank order. The strongest items focused on being close to God, being a good Christian, and trusting God in the face of death. Differences within the Protestant groups were small but in line with our predictions. For the Protestant respondents it was very important to be close to God and to be a good Christian. They labelled a higher reality almost always as 'God' and they often talked about religious matters. The Catholics differed remarkably from the Protestant groups, they less often defined the higher reality in which they they believed as 'God' and were less in agreement that being a good Christian or being close to God is important. They were less interested in religion: they much more rarely read articles, listened to the radio or watched television.

The New Age group displayed a greater interest in religion than the marginals, but more closely resembled the non-members on the other variables. The group of non-believers – representing a significant proportion of Dutch young people (about 17 percent of the population) – rejected any reference to God and Christianity and was not interested in religious matters.

The group of youngsters engaged in New Age-related activities deserves closer attention. New Age is an increasingly popular movement characterized by a broad variety of traditions, practices, techniques, therapies and organizations.

The core beliefs of New Age can be summarized in the following assumptions: apart from sensory reality, there is an invisible and spiritual reality that, in principle, can be accessed by everyone; there is a holistic coherence in nature; by way of transformation and reincarnation everything and everyone is in continuous growth towards a higher spiritual level; and a new era and a new world order – the 'age of Aquarius' – is imminent.[30]

On several items we found curvilinear correlations (indicated by the fact that Pearson's R is substantially smaller than the ETA).

---

30 Horst Stenger, 'Der "okkulte" Alltag', *Zeitschrift für Soziologie*, *18 (2)*, 1989, pp. 119-135; Wouter Hanegraaff, *New Age Religion and Western Culture: Esotericism in the Mirror of Secular Thought* (Leiden: Brill, 1996); Jos W. Becker, Joep de Hart and Jann Mens, *Secularisatie en alternatieve zingeving in Nederland* (Rijswijk: Sociaal en Cultureel Planbureau, 1997).

Table 4.4: Some special characteristics of the New Age group

V112 Importance of spending a lot of time on art and literature; V113 Importance of experiencing beauty; V80 Importance of self-development; V489 Importance of getting acquainted with Eastern wisdom in relation to the meaning of life; V538 Belief in reincarnation; V280 Vote for green/left political party; V299 Willingness to participate in a political demonstration; V512 Importance of own psychological problems in relation to the meaning of life. Scales V112, V113, V80, V489, V538, V512 range from 1 (strongly agree) to 5 (strongly disagree).

Religious involvement	V112 Art and literature	V113 Beauty	V80 Personal development	V489 Eastern wisdom	V538 Reincarnation	V280 per cent Political party green left	V299 per cent Participation in demonstrations	V512 Psychological problems
1. Orthodox	3.2	2.6	1.6	3.5	4.4	19	32	3.0
2. Calvinist	3.2	2.6	1.7	3.8	4.3	16	24	3.1
3. Reformed	3.3	2.8	1.7	3.9	4.4	9	25	3.4
4. Catholic	3.2	2.6	1.6	3.4	3.5	4	22	3.3
5. Marginal	3.5	2.6	1.7	3.8	3.6	13	22	3.1
6. New Age	**2.6**	**2.0**	**1.3**	**2.8**	**3.0**	**28**	**52**	**2.4**
7. Ex-member	3.0	2.4	1.6	3.5	4.3	24	46	2.9
8. Doubter	3.0	2.6	1.5	3.6	3.8	19	32	3.0
9. Nonbeliever	3.0	2.4	1.5	3.6	4.1	24	43	3.3
Total	**3.0**	**2.5**	**1.6**	**3.5**	**3.9**	**19**	**36**	**3.0**
Pearson -r	-.12	-.08	-.07	-.04	-.01		-.14	-.01
Eta	.23	.21	.19	.28	.39		.24	.22

On the items in Table 4.4, the New Age youngsters scored higher than both the orthodox and the non-believer respondents. They were more interested in art and literature (V112), in experiencing beauty (V113), and they placed greater emphasis on personal development (V80). They were more interested in oriental wisdom (V489) and believed more strongly in reincarnation (V538). Politically they were left-oriented (V280), and they were more revolutionary in their political opinions and actions (V299). Furthermore, they reported that personal psychological problems had an important bearing on the meaning of life (V512) (Table 4). These results correspond with those obtained by Baerveldt,[31] who found that people for whom New Age constitutes a philosophy of life have a drive to personal development and personal growth, are engaged in social affairs and are

---

31 Cor Baerveldt, 'New Age-religiositeit als individueel constructieproces' in Martin Moerland (ed.), *De kool en de geit in de Nieuwe Tijd: wetenschappelijke reflecties op New Age* (Utrecht: Van Arkel, 1996).

politically active (moderately left-wing). Baerveldt also found a second group of people who participated in New Age activities in order to solve psychological problems. This group lacked the social and political involvement of the first group and for them New Age functioned rather as an individual therapy and not as a form of religiosity.[32]

To sum up: on the basis of the linear and curvilinear correlations found in Tables 4.2, 4.3 and 4.4, our index of religious involvement based on historical and individualised variables is highly precise and valid. It takes account of historical and recent developments, social structure and individual behaviour. However, given the validity of our scale, all the more striking is the fact that it does not correlate in the least with all the various opinions, ideals and forms of behaviour that matter in the daily lives of young people. When the respondents were asked about the role played by partners, parents, the environment, injustice, sex, health, work, education, love, music and politics in giving meaning to life, we found not a single substantial correlation with religious involvement (Table 4.5).

---

32 Ibid.

Table 4.5: Scores of the nine religious groups on various variables related to daily life

V106 Having a partner/life companion; V101 Getting along with one's parents; V124 Protecting the environment; V123 Fight injustice, poverty and suffering; V68 Having a good sexual relationship with one's partner; V97 Having good health; V73 Giving work priority in life; V491 One's upbringing in relation to the meaning of life; V471 Love in relation to the meaning of life; V499 Musical experiences and events in relation to the meaning of life; V477 Political protest actions or attempts to change society in relation to the meaning of life. Range scale: 1 = very important, 5 = very unimportant.

Religious involvement	V106 Partner	V101 Parents	V124 Environment	V123 Injustice	V68 Sex	V97 Health	V73 Work	V491 Upbringing	V471 Love	V499 Music	V477 Politics
1. Orthodox	2.2	1.8	2.2	2.4	1.6	2.2	3.2	2.2	1.9	2.5	1.9
2. Calvinist	2.2	1.8	2.1	2.1	1.6	1.6	3.1	2.3	2.1	2.4	2.3
3. Reformed	2.5	1.6	2.0	2.1	1.9	1.7	3.0	2.3	2.3	2.4	2.0
4. Catholic	2.4	1.6	2.2	2.5	1.8	1.6	3.1	2.3	2.0	2.4	1.9
5. Marginal	2.1	1.5	2.2	2.6	1.7	1.4	2.7	2.3	1.7	2.5	1.9
6. New age	2.7	1.8	2.0	2.2	1.6	1.8	2.9	2.1	2.0	2.3	2.0
7. Ex-member	2.6	1.9	2.3	2.8	1.5	1.8	2.9	2.5	2.0	2.7	2.2
8. Doubter	2.5	1.6	2.3	2.6	1.7	1.6	2.9	2.4	1.8	2.5	1.9
9. Nonbeliever	2.6	1.8	2.2	2.6	1.6	1.6	2.9	2.3	2.0	2.8	2.4
Total	2.5	1.7	2.1	2.5	1.6	1.7	2.9	2.3	2.0	2.5	2.1
Pearson -r	.11	.05	.05	.15	-.05	-.04	-.06	.05	-.03	.08	-.02
Eta	.18	.16	.14	.24	.17	.20	.11	.12	.13	.08	.16

The differences are small and it is unclear how to interpret them. Variables concerning daily life do not exhibit a link with religious involvement such as those found earlier: there is no linear nor any curvilinear correlation or coherence.

The only (weak) correlations between religious involvement and behaviour in daily life lie in the realm of *rites de passage*. The degree of religious involvement proved to be a weak structuring force in the passage from adolescence to adulthood in some cases. We looked for a relation between the categories of religious involvement and the age at which people are allowed to do certain things, or are expected to think about things and be responsible. It turns out that such a relation exists only in the case of marriage, dancing courses and the age of first sexual experience (Table 4.6).

Table 4.6: The mean age of the nine religious groups for various life-events

At what age did you or do you expect to: V20 get married; V16 participate in a dancing course; V39 have the first complete sexual experience with another person; V12 make your first independent holiday trip; V28 be considered by youngsters as an adult; V26 first realize the limits of what people can achieve; V36 start worrying about your future; V35 drive your first own car; V38 for the first time think about the meaning of life and death. Mean age of respondents: 23.9 years.

Religious involvement	V20 Marriage	V16 Dancing course	V39 First sex	V12 Self holiday	V28 Seen as adult	V26 Limits on achievement	V36 Worry about future	V35 Drive own car	V38 Meaning of death
1. Orthodox	24.6	19.0	20.8	18.7	20.7	17.0	18.9	22.2	16.7
2. Calvinist	24.2	19.6	19.7	18.2	20.1	15.6	20.1	22.2	16.8
3. Reformed	24.4	16.4	19.2	18.2	20.4	16.1	20.0	22.0	16.1
4. Catholic	24.1	15.8	19.3	18.2	19.4	16.7	20.2	22.3	16.5
5. Marginal	24.6	16.0	18.3	18.0	20.8	17.2	18.9	21.6	16.5
6. New age	25.9	15.8	18.2	17.3	19.9	15.9	18.7	22.9	16.5
7. Ex-member	26.3	16.4	19.2	17.8	19.5	15.3	19.4	22.0	16.4
8. Doubter	27.8	16.3	18.2	17.7	20.3	16.4	19.5	21.8	16.9
9. Nonbeliever	25.1	16.1	18.2	17.3	19.7	15.3	19.2	21.8	16.8
Total	**25.2**	**15.1**	**18.8**	**17.7**	**19.9**	**16.0**	**19.3**	**22.1**	**16.6**
N	313	455	565	623	503	352	402	381	464
Pearson -r	.24	-.20	-.19	-.14	-.07	-.07	-.05	-.03	.02
Eta	.34	.28	.27	.17	.17	.15	.14	.13	.06

The closer the religious involvement, the later in their lives the youngsters participated in a dancing course (especially the orthodox Protestants and the Calvinists) (V16), went on holiday by themselves (V12) and had sex for the first time (and it is the orthodox in particular who postpone this moment) (V39).

Conversely, the closer the religious involvement, the sooner they expected to get married (V20). Hardly any differences emerged among the moments when our respondents realized the limits to what men and women can achieve (V26), contemplated the meaning of death (V38), worried about their futures (V36), were seen as adults (V28) or drove their own car (V35).

Religious involvement thus has a rather small effect on daily life.

Other studies have obtained the same results.[33] As Fuchs[34] concluded for German youth, so we can conclude for the Dutch: namely that religion seems to have no structuring value for everyday life. But again caution is required. The mean scores in Table 5 are rather high. Hence, while there is no difference among the religious groups, overall young Dutch people consider daily life to be an important source of meaning. As van der Linden[35] concluded from a national survey of Dutch young people: 'The terminology of the young without belief strongly corresponds with what believers say about giving meaning to life'. Understanding of this feature requires more profound study of the religion of youth, not just as a sociological variable but as everyday practice.

2. What young people do and think: prayer and the image of God

In Europe, church membership varies substantially from country to country, and Dutch young people occupy a prominent place, but there are striking similarities among the opinions of all young people, including the Dutch. In countries like England,[36] Germany,[37] France[38] and Belgium[39] social researchers have concluded that young people lack interest in official, institutional religion but at the same time they have found that only a small minority prefer atheism.[40] Youngsters have a primarily experiential and experimental outlook on religion. Religion is 'home-made' from personal

---

33 Liliane Voyé, 'Les jeunes et le corps stigmatisé' in Roberto Cipriani and Maria I. Macciotti, *Omaggio a Ferrarotti* (Rome: Siares, Studi e Recerce, 1988); Frans van der Linden, *Groot worden in een klein land. Feiten en cijfers uit het onderzoek naar de leefwereld van jongeren tussen 12 en 21 jaar* (Nijmegen: ITS, 1989); Hans Alma and Gerben Heitink, 'Having Faith in Young People's Worldview and their Lifepattern', *Journal of Empirical Theology*, 7 (2), 1994, pp. 52-74.
34 Werner Fuchs, 'Konfessionelle Milieus und Religiösität', *Jugendliche + Erwachsene '85*, Band 1, (Leverkusen: Leske and Budrich., 1985), pp. 265-304.
35 Frans van der Linden, *Groot worden in een klein land. Feiten en cijfers uit het onderzoek naar de leefwereld van jongeren tussen 12 en 21 jaar*, (Nijmegen: ITS, 1989), p. 120.
36 Adrian Furnham and Barrie Gunter, *The Anatomy of Adolescence. Young People's Social Attitudes in Britain* (London: Routledge, 1989).
37 Heiner Barz, *Religion ohne Institution? Jugend und Religion* (Opladen: Leske + Budrich, 1992).
38 Pierre Cousin, Jean-Pierre Boutinet and Michel Morfin, *Aspirations religieuses des jeunes lycéens* (Paris: L'Harmattan, 1985); Yves Lambert and Guy Michelat, (eds.), *Crépuscule des religions chez les jeunes? Jeunes et religions en France* (Paris: L'Harmattan, 1992).
39 Dirk Hutsebaut and Dominic Verhoeven, 'The Adolescents' Representation of God from Age 12 until Age 18: Changes or Evolution?', *Journal of Empirical Theology*, 4, 1991, pp. 59-73.
40 Campiche, *Cultures des jeunes et religions en Europe*.

experiences of important life events. Prayer in particular is a widespread and important individualized ritual for the young: while only 39 percent of Dutch youth state that they are members of churches, 82 percent say they pray at least sometimes. In European studies[41] Dutch young people occupy third place after Ireland and Italy (among 16 countries) on prayer. And this time – and this is exceptional – there is hardly any difference with respect to the elder generation (18-29 years: 61 percent; 60 years and older: 68 percent). Central to understanding the religiosity of today's youth is knowing what their prayer is about. We asked our respondents to tell us in their own words what prayer is, why they pray, when they pray, and how they pray. At the basis of prayer by young people, as our analysis shows, is the well-known tripartite structure of the ritual: when in trouble (mostly concerning other people) people undertake an activity (mostly asking or hoping) to cope with the trouble (mostly on an emotional level): thus we have a need, an action, and an effect (see Table 4.7).

Table 4.7: Frequencies in a model of praying practices by modern young people. N=687

1. Need (408)	2. Action (561) ⟶	4. Effect (398)
(negative (346), others (207))	(ask/hope (201), meditate (197))	(emotional (286))
	3. Direction (330) (God (207))	
	5. Time (385) (at night (223))	
	6. Place (403) (in bed (215))	
	7. Method (394) (eyes closed (119), hands joined (104))	

Furthermore, although the young respondents were not asked about the direction of their prayer, most of them spontaneously mentioned a direction, an addressee, whom most of them called God. We shall discuss later the image of God for these youngsters. For the time being we shall focus on the need, action, direction and effect, in an attempt to distinguish among different types of prayer. Depending on the centrality of one of these four elements, we predicted four kinds of prayer. If the emphasis is on the effect (wanting to be cured), we have 'primitive' prayer; if the emphasis is on the direction (God) we are dealing with 'religious' prayer; if the action of praying as such is central, the prayer is 'meditational' and if the need, the coping element, is paramount, we have 'psychological' prayer. However, factor analysis

---

41 Ibid., p. 52.

showed that in our sample of Dutch youths primitive and religious prayer are empirically the same; consequently, we summarized the two as 'religious'. It also turned out that every instance of prayer is a combination of these three types of prayer. It is therefore more appropriate to speak of three aspects of prayer: successively religious, meditational and psychological.

An unexpected finding is the importance of method, time and place. Every type of prayer has its own set of adjuncts. Young people who pray at any time and anywhere say a meditational prayer. Religious prayer is said quietly, at fixed moments in church and often uses formulaic expressions. Psychological prayer is done at night, lying in bed with hands joined and eyes closed. Hence place, time and method are much more important than was foreseen, and they are not just (adverbial) adjuncts loosely connected with a sentence of more central importance. Durkheim[42] emphasised passim the importance of religion in structuring time and place. In the Middle Ages, the time of day was named after the prayer that was said (for instance, compline and vespers), but also today times and places are structured by religion.

Religious involvement determines the way in which youngsters pray. We found that the more religiously involved of our young respondents prayed more often and gave more complex and richer definitions of prayer. The Protestants showed more expertise than the Catholics, and the latter more than the non-believers. There was a close correlation between the nine categories and the prevalence of religious praying elements: Pearson R .40,[43] and also between praying frequency and the number of structural elements mentioned. Competence and experience gave rise to a more complete and more extensive prayer. The Protestant and the Catholic prayers also differed with respect to content and style. The Catholic respondents used more formulas, and the Protestants more often prayed with their eyes closed and their hands joined.[44]

The characterization once given to Catholic and Protestant prayer by psychologist James Bisset Pratt still holds: a Catholic priest, Pratt pointed out, prays in silence, alone, mumbling and repeating formulas. A Protestant minister prays openly, loudly and clearly, in front of an audience, hands joined and eyes closed. He seeks to formulate 'the most eloquent prayer ever addressed to a Boston audience'.[45]

---

42 Emile Durkheim, *Les formes élémentaires de la vie réligieuse. Le système totémique en Australie* (Paris: Alcan, 1960, [1912]).
43 Jacques Janssen, Joep de Hart and Cecile Draak den 'A Content Analysis of the Praying Practices of Dutch Youth', *Journal for the Scientific Study of Religion*, 29, 1990, pp. 99-107.
44 Ibid.
45 James Bisset Pratt, *The Religious Consciousness. A Psychological Study* (New York: Macmillan, 1920), pp. 297-8.

These differences notwithstanding, there is a close similarity among the prayers of the young, especially as regards the meditational and psychological aspects, neither of which is correlated with religious involvement. Overall, we can characterize prayer by the young as psychological in nature: when confronted with specific and painful events, in particular the death of relatives, young people pray in order to find the strength to continue. The problem is concrete, but it cannot be solved, so that the desired effect is a psychological change within the person doing the praying. The action is meditational in that youngsters do not communicate or talk, but ponder and think. Only a small proportion of young people add religious elements to this structure of prayer: they thank God or they ask for real effects. Even when youngsters ask for real effects, they use their prayer as a concentrated motivation.[46] Youngsters typically pray when examinations are imminent, but they do not ask for good results; instead they ask for the ability to concentrate and to study well. However, for the majority of young people praying is a coping mechanism, a kind of non-directional therapy which they apply in order to keep their lives in balance.[47]

It is when they must cope with important problems that people turn to religion. Young people are confronted for the first time in their lives with problems that are by their very nature insoluble, like the death of loved ones. Several studies have shown that experiences of death, and in particular the death of personal acquaintances, are the major causes of reflection by young people on the meaning of life, or the onset of religious experiences.[48] However, young people today do not turn to institutionalized religion, preferring private religious practice instead: they pray – as we have seen – when they are alone, in bed, at night, with their eyes closed (see Table 7). Both time and place are significant. In today's hectic life, no time is left for silence and meditation. In bed, people are finally on their own and can contemplate the day in silence and solitude. The paramount reality of everyday life is interrupted and, between active thought and deep sleep, brain activity is reduced to a mode of passive receptivity whereby the person 'turns inward' and meditates on the contradictions of daily life.[49]

---

[46] Janssen, de Hart and Draak, 'A Content Analysis of the Praying Practices of Dutch Youth', 1990, pp. 99-107.

[47] Janssen, Prins, Baerveldt and Lans, (under review), *The Structure and Variety of Prayer. An Empirical Study of Dutch Youth.*

[48] Joep de Hart, *Jongeren na de middelbare school. Levensbeschouwelijke opvattingen, waardeoriëntaties en sekseverschillen* (Kampen: Uitgeverij Kok, 1994).

[49] Bernard Spilka, Ralph Hood, and Richard Gorsuch Jr., *The Psychology of Religion: An Empirical Approach*, (Englewood Cliffs: Prentice-Hall, 1985); Janssen, de Hart and Draak den 'A Content Analysis of the Praying Practices of Dutch Youth'.

Interpreting these findings, Liliane Voyé[50] has described the prayer of the young as an individualized, do-it-yourself confession. We find this to be an interesting and appropriate interpretation. In prayer, feelings of guilt, disappointment and deficiency are coped with, and new intentions and plans are formulated. Prayer, therefore, has important psychological functions in the construction of identity. It is meant, as St. Augustine pointed out, not to instruct God but to construct oneself: 'ut ipsa (mens) construatur, not ut Deus instruatur'.[51] Prayer is a mechanism with which to draw up an inventory of daily events and to learn acceptance of the inevitable.

Although the young pray privately, in darkness and in bed, they are not alone. They spontaneously mention an addressee of their prayer who in most cases is termed 'God'. But who is 'God' for people the majority of whom state that they do not belong to a church? To answer this question we conducted a separate study.[52] Again we used open-ended questions and analysed the texts of the young respondents' replies. Comparison of our results with some of the findings by European values studies highlighted the importance of allowing the young themselves talk about religion in answer to minimal questions. When the young Dutch respondents were asked whether they prayed, many of them answered in the affirmative, and there was hardly any difference between them and older respondents (61 percent versus 68 percent). But when they were asked whether they prayed to God, the number decreased considerably and a sizeable difference with respect to their elders appeared[53] (11 percent versus 42 percent). At the same time, when talking about their own religious practices the young spontaneously used the word 'God', and they did so rather often (Table 4.7).[54] We must consequently conclude that the word assumes different meanings in different contexts.

The word 'God' in questionnaires is related to institutional religion; in their own language, the young re-invent the word as a label for a central element which they cannot define in any other way. Young people have their own 'native religious grammar'.[55]

---

50   Campiche, *Cultures des jeunes et religions en Europe*, p. 141.
51   Augustinus Aurelius, *Oevres completes. Librarie de Louis Vives. 1877-1873*, Epistola CXL, caput XXIX, p. 69.
52   Jacques Janssen, Joep de Hart and Marcel Gerardts, 'Images of God in Adolescence', *The International Journal for the Psychology of Religion*, 4, 1994, pp. 105-21.
53   Campiche, *Cultures des jeunes et religions en Europe* (Paris: Cerf, 1997).
54   Jacques Janssen, Joep de Hart and Marcel Gerardts, (1994). 'Images of God in Adolescence', *The International Journal for the Psychology of Religion*, 4, 1994, pp. 105-121; Janssen, Prins, Baerveldt and Lans, (under review). *The Structure and Variety of Prayer. An Empirical Study of Dutch Youth*.
55   Lindbeck in Hans van der Ven, 'God in Nijmegen: een theologisch perspectief: over het empirisch onderzoek naar de "sensus fidei", respectievelijk "sensus fidelium"', *Tijdschrift voor Theologie*, 32 (3), 1992, pp. 225-49.

When the young respondents were asked to describe the 'God' that they talked about, they used a wide variety of words and metaphors. It seemed as if they were constructing their own definitions 'on the spot'. A Belgian panel study by Hutsebaut and Verhoeven[56] found that there is no correlation between the definitions of God given by young people at the age of 12 and the age of 15: like our respondents, they apparently lacked a common stock of words and metaphors. In a Dutch study, youngsters reported that they were unable to give answers to the well-known Vergote/Tamayo questionnaire on the image of God because, in their view, the items were not suitable (any longer) to describe God.[57] Traditional images of God have lost their credibility, and young people prefer a vague and abstract representation. They devoutly practise the mission set by Jim Morrison's *An American Prayer*: 'Let's reinvent the Gods'.

Since the traditional concepts and representations of God seem to have fallen out of use, and new ones are still in construction, we were forced to ask our respondents to talk about their God in their own words. We consequently used open-ended questions. On looking for the common concepts used by the young use to describe God, we found first that God was described more often as an activity than as a being. In 32 percent of their definitions the respondents said 'God is'; in 75 percent of their texts they said 'God does'. The most frequently mentioned activities of God were wielding power and supporting people. We further found that the images of God are difficult to specify in parental terms or in those of gender. Although God was generally referred to as 'he' (82 percent of the texts), God was called a man in only 6 percent of the texts, and father or mother figures were rarely used as images of God. When forced to choose, the majority of respondents called God a man (52 percent) and a father (28 percent), but in their further commentaries they explicitly referred to traditional pictures and stories: God is a man, so says the Bible, and he is generally depicted as such in paintings and drawings.[58]

---

56 Dirk Hutsebaut, and Dominic Verhoeven, 'The Adolescent's Representation of God from Age 12 until Age 15', *Proceedings of the fourth symposium on the psychology of religion in Europe* (Nijmegen: University of Nijmegen, 1989), pp. 147-56.
57 Karin Mischke, and Maaike Wittenberg, *Godsbeelden. Een analyse op een steekproef van Nederlandse studenten met gebruikmaking van de Semantic Differential Parental Scale (SDPS) van Tamayo and Vergote*, Intern rapport (Nijmegen: Katholieke Universiteit Nijmegen, Vakgroep Cultuur- en Godsdienstpsychologie, 1990).
58 Janssen, de Hart and Gerardts, 'Images of God in Adolescence'.

As European studies show, the majority of the Dutch youth define God as a spirit or force, not as a person.[59] We conclude that Dutch young people primarily use indefinite, impersonal and abstract terms to describe God as someone or something exercising some sort of power over people: we do not know him but see his acts.[60] The idea of God, as Pratt[61] puts it, 'has a large pragmatic element'. Or, in Leuba: 'God is not known, he is not understood, he is used'.[62] God is reinvented on the basis of daily practice.

Conclusion

'Our time is a time of religious decline. The once enduring vitality of the religious is in decay. [...] Youth is in open conflict with the established society and with the authority of the past. They experiment with eastern religions and techniques of meditation. The greater part of mankind is affected by the decay of the times'.[63] There is no doubt that the religious landscape of Europe is in turmoil and that it will change dramatically in the next decades. The differences between the young and older people are great, and they point especially to the decreasing salience of traditional, institutional religion. Today, even the core believers among the young embrace ideas and practices that deviate fundamentally from official prescriptions, and they differ substantially from those of the elder generation. However, the pessimistic view of culture and the state of religion quoted above was written in the late first century AD by Tacitus, and it refers to the state of the ancient Hellenistic world. In all ages, younger generations have deviated from the footsteps of their predecessors, who regret and criticise this deviation. 'Rade volte risurge per li rami - L'umana probitate' ('Rarely does human worth rise through the branches') Dante lamented in *Purgatory* (VII,121-122); and in *Paradise* (VIII, 93) he despairingly wonders: 'Come uscir può di dolce seme amaro' ('how from sweet seed may come forth bitter'). Social scientists may share Tacitus' and Dante's concern without borrowing their moralistic

---

59 Campiche, *Cultures des jeunes et religions en Europe*, p. 108; Hans van der Ven, 'God in Nijmegen: een theologisch perspectief: over het empirisch onderzoek naar de "sensus fidei", respectievelijk "sensus fidelium"', *Tijdschrift voor Theologie*, 32 (3), 1992, pp. 225-49.
60 Janssen, de Hart and Gerardts, 'Images of God in Adolescence'.
61 James Bisset Pratt, *The religious consciousness. A psychological study* (New York: Macmillan, 1920), p. 207.
62 Henry James, 'Content of the Religious Consciousness', *The Monist*, 11, 1900-1, pp. 536-73.
63 Bruno Borchert, *Mystiek. Het verschijnsel, de geschiedenis, de nieuwe uitdaging*, Second, revised print (Haarlem: Gottmer, 1994).

overtones. Dante, as a matter of fact, also accepted that young people must go their own way (*Paradise* VIII, 127-135). We do not know why; they do not know how. For the time being they grope in the dark; let us say they wander in a dark wood. They doubt, they hesitate, they advance by trial and error.[64]

In contemporary society the problems described by Tacitus and Dante coincide: culture is changing rapidly and resists transfer from one generation to the next as a complete 'package'. Achieving culture has become increasingly a process of construction, of actively acquiring a personalised set of beliefs, values and behavioural norms. This pragmatic way of thinking and constructing meaning by trial and error is shared by the young participants in today's youth culture, who must constantly construct their culture and thus their religion: that of modern youth is a 'do-it-yourself-culture'.[65] Youngsters are really 'bricoleurs', according to Lévi-Strauss' famous dictum;[66] they are not 'ingenieurs' who draw up plans and sketches and share a history as professionals. These 'bricoleurs' are amateurs who act on concrete bases, inventing by re-combining what is present in their daily life situations. They have no history: life starts afresh every day. They cannot be pinned down to their plans and intentions, for they have none. The drawing of their buildings can only be made when the buildings are finished. Moreover, they do not wish to be members of fixed groups; they try to evade common formulas and do not want to be labelled. The concept of social groups is elusive because youngsters themselves hardly ever use conceptions of social groups or categories.[67] Even an outright punk, who knows perfectly well that others have no choice than see him as a punk, has a tendency – as research has shown[68] – to say that he is not a punk. He is primarily himself, unique and undefinable.

Like their culture, the religion of young people is in flux, unstable, changing, reinvented from day to day. Beliefs and practices are adrift in a process of eclecticism and bricolage.[69] Only a minority see the bright light of atheism, only a minority carry the blinding torch of fundamentalism. Young

---

64   Campiche, *Cultures des jeunes et religions en Europe*, p. 144.
65   Jacques Janssen, *Jeugdcultuur. Een actuele geschiedenis* (Utrecht: De Tijdstroom, 1994), p. 37.
66   Claude Lévi-Strauss, *Le totemisme aujourd'hui* (Paris: Puf, 1962).
67   'Social Identities and Social Groups' in Sue Widdicombe and Robin Wooffitt (eds.), *The Language of Youth Subcultures. Social Identity in Action* (Hertfordshire: Harvester Wheatsheaf, 1995).
68   Jacques Janssen and Maerten Prins, 'Jeugdsubculturen binnenstebuiten: een onderzoek naar de homologie van jeugdsubculturen', *Jeugd and Samenleving*, 2/3, 1991, pp. 194-212.
69   Jean-Louis Schlegel, 'Du christianisme au bouddhisme: les practiques religieuses aujourd'hui', *L'Esprit*, 6, 1997, p. 29.

people more often construct a personal framework of meanings, choosing among the religious and ideological ideas currently available in the 'spiritual marketplace'.[70] In this eclectic process, religious institutions have lost their monopoly, and although the young still draw on religious traditions, they use them more as 'a toolbox of symbols than a sense of community or belonging'.[71] As Van Baal pointed out:

> new symbols are not found, they are created and creating is exceedingly rare. [...] Modern man is not even able to create a single new word. Whenever we need a new term or expression, we borrow words from a foreign language, reshape them a bit and thus we make a new term. We make it, but do not create. [72]

In this manner, young people today borrow symbols and create their own religion: the religion of the majority of young people is an open-ended question *par excellence*. Many of them assert that they do not believe but that they have an idea of God; many others state that they believe but have no idea of God. The prayer of one of our respondents can be taken as exemplary of the religion embraced by the young: 'I pray to God, in whom I don't believe, that He will help my friend who does believe in Him, if he exists'.[73] How could one be more honest to God?

The rise of the New Age movement ties in with this modern attitude towards religion. New Age can be viewed as a prototypical form of a 'do-it-yourself' religion.[74] Whereas the traditional churches are characterized by membership and a clear structure and organization, New Age is not. It organizes people not into groups but into networks; consumption not membership is central. Increasing numbers of young people reject religious doctrines, adopting instead an exploratory and experimental attitude towards their philosophies of life. Although the motivation of some New Age adherents lies in the realm of individual therapy, there are others for whom New Age activities provide a means to give meaning to their lives.[75] New Age is not a ready-made belief system which replaces traditional religion; it is vague, undefined and constantly changing. Which indicates that a shift is

---

70 Bert Felling, Jan Peters, and Otto Schreuder, *Dutch Religion. The Religious Consciousness of the Netherlands after the Cultural Revolution* (Nijmegen: ITS, 1991).
71 John Fulton, 'Modernity and Religious Change in Western Roman Catholicism: Two Contrasting Paradigms', *Social Compass, 44 (1)*, 1997, pp. 115-29.
72 Jan van Baal, 'Changing Religious Systems, in Pieter Vrijhof and Jacques Waardenburg (eds.), *Official and Popular Religion. Analysis of a Theme for Religious Studies* (The Hague: Mouton Publishers, 1979).
73 Janssen, de Hart and Gerardts, 'Images of God in Adolescence', pp. 105-21.
74 Baerveldt, 'New Age-religiositeit als individueel constructieproces' in Moerland (ed.), *De kool en de geit in de Nieuwe Tijd: wetenschappelijke reflecties op New Age.*
75 Ibid.

taking place, not from belief to disbelief, but from belief to 'seekership', as Campbell puts it.[76] This 'seekership' can be placed in the context of advanced industrial society, as Inglehart does when he discerns a postmaterialist worldview emerging among the younger generation, with relatively greater concern for the meaning of life and renewed emphasis on the sacred, although this is 'sacred in nature rather than in churches'.[77]

The religion of young people is not just their affair. It is embedded in our culture: perhaps it is the herald of the future, perhaps it tells us something about the essence of religion. The international journal *Esprit* has characterized our times as 'les temps des religions sans Dieu' ('the times of religions without God'). There is a general tendency to define God in unspecific, abstract and impersonal terms, and if this is a variation on atheism, it may be a wholesome one. Bruno Borchert[78] has stressed the religious dimension of today's atheism: 'it does not arise out of scepticism and indifference but out of a loss of faith in old images and an inability to find new ones. This lack of contact with God can prove to be a good breeding ground for a fresh form of mysticism'. We share the optimistic view of Roland Campiche[79] and Ronald Inglehart (1990) that the individualized religion of the young is not just a sign of de-Christianization, it may be the basis for the re-founding of religion.

---

[76] Eileen Barker, (ed.), *New Religious Movements: A Perspective For Understanding Society* (New York: Edwin Mellen Press., 1982).
[77] Inglehart, *Culture Shift in Advanced Industrial Society*, p. 433.
[78] Bruno Borchert, *Mystiek. Het verschijnsel, de geschiedenis, de nieuwe uitdaging*, Second, revised print, (Haarlem: Gottmer, 1994), p. 165.
[79] Campiche, Alfred Dubach, Claude Bovay, Michael Krüggeler and Peter Voll, *Croire en Suisse(s)*, (Lausanne: L'Âge d'homme, 1992).

5 New religious movements and youth culture in Great Britain

MICHAEL YORK

In my day as a youth, 'youth culture' itself was understood as that which automatically excluded anyone over the age of thirty. And I have tended to assume that 'youth culture' has essentially remained as the particular province of young people who traditionally distrust anyone over thirty. In this sense, 'youth culture' becomes a mobile set of attitudes, fashions and behaviours belonging to an ever-changing base population. For those of us over the age of thirty, whilst we may understand the circumstances and problems faced by individuals – at least in as much as we remember the same situations from the times when we were ourselves young – a 'true' understanding of 'youth culture' may be precluded, and the culture itself could well remain something which is forever an enigma.

It is of course a mistake to identify all contemporary youth with what we designate as 'youth culture'. In looking at the latter in Britain, we are not considering the evangelical movement as it manifests itself among the young – except to the degree that Christian-rock music has on occasion been appropriated into pentecostal forms of worship. 'Youth culture', at least as I am using the term here, is a designation for a subcultural manifestation within British culture which at the same time has international or transnational expressions in other countries or societies as well.

The most viable forms of culture are religious and linguistic. With the emergence of the nation-state, national culture has become something with a territorial component. But even the culture of the political state can often be subsumed within, or at least has links with, lingual and religious cultures that extend beyond the nation-state.

But then too, in today's multicultural and interactive world of commerce, communication and migration, the contemporary nation-state is more often than not a pluralistic society of different ethnicities. This is increasingly the case of Britain to which its imperialistic legacy has bequeathed a rich mix of diasporas from the Indian subcontinent, from Africa, from the West Indies and elsewhere.

Sociology has come to speak in terms of the mainstream culture or the mainstream society. Whilst the latter becomes increasingly difficult to identify and localize, the difficulty is compounded when a philospher such as Jean-François Lyotard declares the end of the meta-narrative. The grand narratives of Marxism, Freudianism, Darwinianism, Roman Catholicism, Anglicanism or so forth have been replaced, according to Lyotard's deconstructive thinking, by the many small-narratives of locality and subcultural orientation. It is therefore perhaps most profitable to consider 'youth culture' as a 'counter-narrative' within whatever might be identifiable as the dominant 'mainstream-narrative' of the host society.

Peter Lerner[1] considers it important to distinguish youth culture as a subcultural form rather than as a synonym for a counter-cultural underground. Its transient norms, values and lifestyles question various aspects of established hegemonic modes, but Lerner sees this as a product more of 'diffuse youthful energy' than as a 'conscious hostility to accepted adult values'. In part a fabricated target for the Western consumer industry, youth culture is in general a vehicle for the expression of an identity which remains variously subordinate and quasi-contentious. In the heyday of the post-1960 new religious movements (NRMs), many youth were attracted to such groups as the Children of God, est, Hari Krishnas, the Moonies and so forth. As the membership of these movements has matured and the attraction of the groups themselves continues to decline, NRMs have ceased to occupy the predominant attention of today's youth.

Youth culture' in Britain and beyond is no longer exclusively restricted to the under-thirties. The dress, language, music and patterns of consumption which constitute contemporary British youth culture is more broadly known as 'rave culture'. All the same, the 'acid house' parties which are central to rave culture include an influential, albeit comparably small, number of aging hippies from the counter-cultural days of the 1960s. Fraser Clark, founder of numerous rave-centred organizations and participant in San Francisco's legendary 1967 Summer of Love, describes himself as a 'zippy' which he explains as a midway position between the hippy drop-out and the yuppy entrepreneur. Describing a quasi-spiritual paradigm, according to Clark, the zippy is someone who seeks to balance his or her right- and left-brain hemispheres; someone who endeavours to harmonize his or her role as a technoperson of the late twentieth century with the hippy values of spontaneity, here-and-now presence, self-autonomy, mysticism and detachment. To the degree that elder zippies like Clark are instrumental to the

---

1 Peter S. Lerner, 'Youth Culture', in Alan Bullock, Oliver Stallybrass & Stephen Trombley (eds.), *The Fontana Dictionary of Modern Thought* (London: Fontana Press, 1988), p. 915).

formulation of rave culture, they serve in a capacity akin to that of the priest. However, the description of the zippy applies frequently to many of the rave youth themselves, for whom the older designations of 'straight' and 'alternative' are no longer accurately applicable. In Clark's words, 'A zippy could be a businessman taking a yoga class or a Rainbow lady setting up her own little hemp stall business at a rave'.[2]

Rave culture is centred on a particular form of rock music – drawing its origins from disco (particularly gay disco) of the late 1960s/early 1970s followed by new wave, break dancing, electric boogie, hip hop and rap music including ganster rap. The distinguishing feature of rave is called 'techno' in the sense of being seamless. Music is studied to determine stimulation of individual and collective emotions, and, after careful analysis of what sound does to one physically, the musical beats are then selected. The 'seamless' musical track behind the rave activity is then purposively employed in an effort to achieve a hyper-trance state. Nothing is left to chance. Having similarities to neuro-linguistic programming, the musical cadence attempts to match the rate of the human heart beat. This is then increased by small increments.

Rave music began in Chicago as 'acid house' music. This presumably had less to do with the ingestation of LSD by participants than it did with the practice of pouring acid onto a music track to produce a different effect. From Chicago, the music moved to Ibiza where London disco aficiandos picked it up and brought it to Britain. Here, it was mixed with the drug ecstasy, another import fom America. The initial explosion of the rave scene then occurred in the cities of London and Manchester in 1986. Fraser Clark[3] clearly identifies rave culture as a continuation or resurgence of the 1960s counter-culture and one which he understands as growing in all developed countries and in others as well.

Consequently, in attempting to assess the dynamic between new religious movements and contemporary 'youth culture', it behoves us to recognize that 'youth culture'/rave culture is itself a new form of religiosity - one with New Age, neo-pagan and 'technoshaman' affinities. So whilst the modern British evangelical/pentecostal movement continues to draw adherents from the nation's younger population[4] and/or continues to employ

---

2   Fraser Clark, 'Rave Culture Means The End of The World as We Know It', *Towards 2012* Part III (special edition on Culture & Language), (Leeds: Unlimited Dream Company, 1997), p. 81.
3   Ibid., p. 79.
4   E.g., the London Church of Christ, the Birmingham Church of Christ, and the Baptist Jesus Fellowship Church among others.

rock music and other contemporary 'youth culture' forms in some of its worship (e.g., the now discredited 'Nine O'Clock Service'), and whilst more established new religious movements continue to appeal to some segments of British youth (e.g., Iskcon, Brahma Kumaris, the Western Buddhist Order, the New Kadampa Tradition, The Family and Scientology),[5] 'youth culture' is itself a decentred, segmented yet integrated network which interconnects primarily with the New Age, neo-pagan (e.g., Wicca and Druidry), Human Potential and Goddess Spirituality movements.

Rave culture has become a clearly established phenomenon in the last eight years. It can be recognized as a primary manifestation of the 'new age' cooperative culture which is believed to be replacing the more traditional and established competition culture of capitalism. A prevailing view is that now that the inappropriate world culture of communism has reached its demise, that of capitalism will be the next to go. As a religious movement, 'youth culture'/rave culture obviously involves youth, but this is a youth of all ages. Its salient feature is doubtlessly its own style of music and dance, and this form of expression brings together people from different backgrounds and different identities. In this sense, the rave serves as a meeting point which fuses diversity. It is non-hierarchial. There are no permanent leaders or huge stars. Its ethos is ecological and nature-oriented, and it seeks large gatherings – preferably in the non-urban countryside. On the dance floor in particular, everyone is equal, whilst cooperation is the rule which is followed in the setting-up and maintenance of the rave proper. Apart from the *ad hoc* rave itself, rave clubs are found more permanently in the larger cities of Britain. These expressions are augmented through the various festivals which occur throughout the summer months (e.g., the Glastonbury Festival and the Big Green Gathering near Salisbury).

Consequently, rave culture is a counter-development to that of punk culture, which is essentially cynical, apathetic and negative. The Generation X is opposed to materialism and the systemic corruption of present-day society, but the 'grunge' values of Kurt Cobain are in themselves non-transformational. Instead, contemporary 'youth culture' in its rave manifestation is an affirmative stance whose closest parallel is to that of the hippy movement of the late 1960s and early 1970s. It includes a political

---

5   Other New Religious Movements active in Britain include Ananda Marga, the Centres Network (formerly est), Maharaji's Elan Vital (formerly Divine Light Mission), Osho International (Rajneeshism), Nirmala Devi Srivastava's Sahaja Yogi, Sai Baba, Soka Gakkai, Maharishi Mahesh Yogi's Transcendental Meditation, and Sun Myung Moon's Holy Spirit Association for the Unification of World Christianity (formerly the Unification Church).

perspective, an ecological love of nature and a personalized spiritual orientation which is best described as shamanic. From the political viewpoint, rave considers both communism and capitalism to be 'fundamentally user-unfriendly'. Rave culture also advocates a reduced consumerism along with an expanded ecological consiousness. It is, however, the rave itself in which ego is transcended or dissolved, where shamanic consciousness-alteration occurs and where a re-balancing trance state is achieved.

Dance is central to rave culture. It is what connects the movement with the African *rhythms* so central to Voodoo, Santeria and American jazz. In colloquial expression, it is 'hot' rather than 'cool'. As a culture, a key moment for rave occurred when it interconnected with 'New Age travellers' and their festivals and thereby reaffirmed a counter-cultural root that leads from the 1960s. Through its literature, its therapeutic massage techniques, workshops and lectures, rave culture is not just a dance phenomenon but a wider spiritual movement which Matthew Fox recognizes as a new form of prayer. In Britain, it is not uncommon for members of one or more of the various druidic orders to appear during a rave and perform a short ritual before the resumption of the dance music. In London rave clubs such as Megatripolis, druids, wiccans and/or chaos magicians occasionally invoke the four directions at the beginning of the evening, which often then concludes with a spiral dance. With its affirmation of nature and the ethos of cooperation, its predilection for the countryside, and its emphasis on the experiential, rave religiosity belongs to the same relatively amorphous but expanding spiritual network that includes the New Age and contemporary pagan movements – both themselves descendants of San Francisco's Haight-Ashbury hippy culture. In the rave itself, the disc jockey serves as the 'techno shaman' who blends the music together and chooses when to change the mood of the dance floor. Alcohol is not the fashion in the contemporary rave.[6] Ecstasy and marijuana or hashish are in general the drugs of choice, but the key direction of energy is the dancing until dawn when the rave culminates with a greeting of the rising sun. Its ritual and grounding in nature have been formatted in such a way that British 'youth/rave culture' constitutes in itself a new religious movement which can be recognized as powerful through the many laws that have been passed against it.

---

6   For this reason, rave organization has been vehemently opposed by police, the judicial authorities and Masons in the English brewing centre of Luton. The agitation for this opposition was spearheaded by the local pubs, which reported a dramatic increase in Saturday night attendance once the raves were outlawed and discontinued.

In addition, there is a short line of connection between rave culture and the emphasis within 'youth culture' on the erotic-spiritual path spearheaded by Body Electric, Joseph Kramer and his EroSpirit Research Institute, and Rajneesh and his Osho Foundation. In the words of Ryam Nearing, author of *Loving More* (apud Gynan Nisarg),[7] 'Our goal is new kinds of relationships based on unconditional love, continuing spiritual growth, respect for our diversity, equality among partners, telling the truth about our deepest desires, and accepting personal responsibilty [...] together we explore the total transformation of love, sex, and the family'. In 'youth culture', sacred sexuality is moving from the confines of traditional monogamy into the innovations of spiritual polyfidelity. In Britain, the organizations which promote sexual sacrality include The Art of Being (UK) in Kent, and the London-based associations of The Ecstatic Being, the Osho Multiversity London, and New Paradigm Productions Ltd. (representing the Human Awareness Institute of San Francisco). The emerging trend within 'youth culture' is toward what is termed 'responsible non-monogamy'. Sexual spirituality is considered to promote 'a sense of love, security and personal empowerment'.[8] Polyfidelity, along with Earth First and other eco-political activities, is part of what British youth refer to as the 'direct action scene'.

The cult of youth has come to be elevated in mainstream focus in a virtually unprecedented manner. A young sound now dominates the music industry. But the so-called 'generation gap' has encouraged youth toward an autonomy to 'do its own thing'. Youthful arrogance, finding its chief support through the financial clout of the music industry, expresses a collective wish to topple all taboos. But whether a positive or negative influence, 'youth culture' both musically and semi-politically is so far proving to have a staying-power which has surpassed expectations. Along with the 1960s counterculture, the influences of Elvis Presley, the Beatles and the anti-war protests concerning Vietnam are considered direct influences on what the young perceive as today's situation of relative 'peace'. The 'follow the money' sort of proof, which protects 'youth culture's' appropriation of the music industry, reappears in the cinema. The film industry appears to aim its car-chase crash and pin-ball machine vacuous sequences of bang-bang, pop-pop, top box office, cheap thrill toward adolescent consumption. Despite its anti-capitalistic sentiment, it is this proof of numbers which supports contemporary 'youth culture' as a viable market.

---

7   Gyan Nisarg, 'Communal Sex-Lib', Towards 2012 Part III (special edition on Culture & Language), (Leeds: Unlimited Dream Company, 1997), p. 47.
8   Ibid., p. 51.

The raving with music into the night appears to be commensurate with youthful energy. This abundance leads to a joyful excess of jumping, swaying bodies in which mental faculties fade into the insistent beat of ceaseless albeit incrementally changing rhythms. In the intoxicating result, feelings of time and gravity are said to fall away before the augmenting power of pleasure found in a large gathering united through sound and movement. The rave is considered an exercise in the experience of non-verbal meaning. As one proponent of 'youth culture' put it to me, 'The fact that older folk find all this pointless, if not harmful, and make it illegal only further enhances the reveller's knowledge that to grow old is to become dumb and narrow-minded. Therefore, we become determined to rave on with a vengeance'. The creation of a group body remains the current thrust of British rave culture.[9] In this communal effervescence, the participants act as a single unity – a supraphysical organism.[10]

---

9   In Ireland, rave culture has yet to appear. There is a small interest in the drug ecstasy. In general, however, Irish youth culture focuses on international music (Boys Own, the Spice Girls) but with an Irish dimension. Unlike Britain, football culture in Ireland has more family attendance for match performances. Consequently, Ireland is without the football hooliganism which has become so prevalent among British youth in soccer attendance. Otherwise, Ireland follows Britain in seeing an erosion of traditional churches. Michael Garde of Dublin's Dialogue Centre claims, however, that with no scientific study and only anecdotal evidence in place of concerted research, there is little in the way of statistics for the Irish situation. He surmises that Ireland has followed Quebec in a drop from 90 percent of traditional religious practice to approximately 11 percent over the last twenty years. Garde also reports that with NRMs representing only 1 to 1.5 percent of the Irish population, the numbers of people involved are only approximately 50,000. In a group like Iskcon, the youth aspect is now peripheral, as the membership has shifted from one of sannyasins to that of families. The Unification Church in Ireland has also faced a drastic decline. Previously there were three or four centres, but in April of 1997, Reverend Moon disbanded the only one remaining. Meanwhile, the Church of Scientology claims an Irish membership of 200 even though it has a mission status only. Whilst most of its members fall within the 18-25 age range, Garde estimates that there may be only 40 active members. Apart from a detectably growing interest in Buddhism and in particular Tibetan Buddhism - mostly centred in Dublin - the Dublin Church of Christ is the one group which is having some degree of success in Ireland at present. Concurrently, whilst 91 percent of Irish young people attended the Roman Catholic Mass in 1987, the number had declined to 64 percent by 1991. Garde guesses that the figure would now be in the 50 percent range.

10   There is currently some argument that the rave scene in Britain is already finished. It is being replaced by what is termed 'drum-and-bass' intellectualism. In many respects the dance atmosphere remains the same, but the music track is occasionally briefly spliced with classical music such as an excerpt from Stravinsky's *Rite of Spring* (Sacre du Printemps) or with intrusions of traditional jazz. Whilst the drug ecstasy is still in vogue, there is apparently an increased usage of cocaine and amphetamine. The psychic effect is for more internalization within the individual and less the dissolving of individuality into a collective self typical of the rave. One youth argues that this allows for a stronger 'group mind' through individual diversity. On the other hand, another informant insists that whilst drum-and-bass has certainly grown massively, it has by no means replaced techno-and-trance.

In conclusion, it appears that British youth culture is largely and currently rave culture with much of its salient forms and features deriving from both the gay and black sub-cultures. The rave is nevertheless counterbalanced yet connected to the Road Protest Movement, despite the latter's largely anti-technology stance. Camps such as the Pollock Free State or the anti-Newbury by-pass protest are central expressions of British youth's environmental activity. The rave and the anti-road campaign may both be seen as instances of an emergent ecology-based quasi-spirituality – part of a 'development movement' in which the unifying goal, based on environmental studies, is termed 'appropriate tech' in contrast to 'high tech' or 'non-tech'.[11]

The NRMs of the 1960s and 1970s, whilst still flourishing to some extent in the British Isles, continue to decline in overall appeal and impact. Scientology and Buddhism (Friends of the Western Buddhist Order, the New Kadampa Tradition) to some extent appear to be the major exceptions to this general trend. Whilst the New Age movement increases in scope, influence and numbers, as in Ireland, it is more an adult than a youth phenomenon. Instead, the British young reveal a growing interest in and pursuit of neo-pagan religiosity: vernacular folk practice, Gardnerian and Alexandrian Wicca, Shamanic Craft, the various orders of Bards, Oviates and Druids, Ásatrú and Odinists, ceremonial magic, chaos magick, Goddess spirituality, and such 'eco-magickal' organizations as Dragon.[12] It is this neo-pagan or quasi-pagan orientation which interfaces with increasing numbers of British youth and furnishes a spiritual basis for much of both rave culture and eco-political activity. In addition, the funeral of Princess Diana drew from throughout the United Kingdom predominantly youthful mourners to London who expressed the need for direct and personal expression of bereavement.

The accompanying unprecedented breaking of protocols and the beginning signs of an emergent 'cult of Diana' may come to serve as a historic watershed in the evolution and acceptance of youth culture and its ecological, emotional and spiritual values by the wider society.

---

11 There are, however, few direct links between rave culture and direct action protest culture. For the most part, rave is purely hedonistic and highly commodified. The best example of cross-over is to be found in Reclaim the Streets in which techno sound systems are used as part of the roadblock strategy to disrupt car culture. On the other hand, writers such as George McKay maintain that there is indeed an increasing connection between protest and rave.

12 As part of the growing neo-pagan and New Age religiosity, increasing numbers of young people now express a belief in reincarnation. The techno-religious element within this spiritual spectrum has undoubtedly been influenced in Britain by the airing of such programmes as *The X-Files*, *Star Trek*, etc.

6 Ecstasy as 'this-worldly path to salvation': the techno youth scene as a proto-religious collective

MICHAEL CORSTEN

Introduction

Since 1989, year by year, the techno youth scene has expanded enormously into an important and large movement in re-united Germany. But also in other European countries, and in some developed societies on various continents (e.g. Australia, Japan, United States), similar music-dance cultures can be observed. Especially during so-called street parades, these 'scenes' attract huge numbers of young people aged between 15 and 25, who come together purely to dance and express themselves. Moreover, visiting 'techno clubs' and 'open-air raves' has become one of the most popular activities among adolescents in modern urban cultures.

In both dimensions, the Berlin techno scene especially has gained global prominence. Techno disc jockeys ('deejays' and 'deejanes') from all over the world perform in clubs like *Tresor* or *E-Werk*. Young adults from various countries have participated in the 'Love Parade', with between half a million and one million visitors in the last two years.

How can the attraction and global representation of such local youth scenes be analysed sociologically? This article seeks to reconstruct techno as the symbolic and proto-religious practice of a modern urban youth scene. Section 2 discusses the sociological theory of scenes as stabilized local audiences, according to recent approaches of (sub)cultural analysis. The methodological standpoint, the design chosen and the methods used are described in section 3. The main results of interpretative analysis of talks with insiders of the Berlin techno scene are given in section 4, and discussed in the light of the theoretical assumptions in section 5. Conclusions are drawn in the final section.

1. Theoretical considerations: scenes as 'cool places' for young people

1.1 Scenes: a sociological definition

The first task is to give more precise theoretical definition to scenes as social circumstances. In sociology, the term 'scene' has predominantly been used as a concept – for example in the symbolic interactionist[1] or structural-functionalist approaches[2] – to describe behaviour that complies with certain rules or action schemes, or phenomenologically to explain the concept of the situation through analogy with scenes in the theatre.[3] But when we talk about 'scenes' in everyday life, we refer to groups of people who can be taken to be the more or less stable audience of orderly reproduced local events – for example, a group of people who regularly visit art exhibitions. This meaning of 'scene' has been employed by some recent sociological studies of youth[4] and of life styles.[5] Schulze[6] especially has elaborated a rather different sociological definition. Scenes presume 'a local public: persons who come together at the same place at the same time'.[7] But a scene is not constituted only by one gathering at a certain time. It requires the reproduction of 'gatherings'[8] by a limited group of people experiencing specific events in specific places. Therefore, a scene is constituted by the stabilization of three symbolic assignments/meanings: the experience of scene-specific events; the definition of typical places (scene locations); the identification of an audience as a scene public.

---

1   Herbert Blumer, *Symbolic Interactionism: Perspective and Method* (Englewood Cliffs: Prentice-Hall, 1969); Erving Goffman, *The Presentation of Self in Everyday Life* (Garden City: Doubleday, 1959).
2   Talcott Parsons and Edward Shils (eds), *Toward a General Theory of Action* (Cambridge/Mass.: Harvard University Press, 1951).
3   Erving Goffman, *Frame Analysis: An Essay on The Organization of Experience*, (Cambridge, Mass.: Harvard University Press, 1974); Alfred Schutz, *Der sinnhafte Aufbau der sozialen Welt: eine Einleitung in die verstehende Soziologie* (Frankfurt a.M.: Suhrkamp, 1974).
4   Will Straw, 'System of Articulation, Logics of Change', *Cultural Studies*, 5, 1991, pp. 368-388.
5   Gerhard Schulze, *Die Erlebnisgesellschaft: Kultursoziologie der Gegenwart* (Frankfurt a.M.: Campus, 1992).
6   Ibid.
7   Ibid., p. 461.
8   Erving Goffman, *Behaviour in Public Places: Notes on The Social Organization of Gatherings* (London: Macmillan, 1963).

1.2 Experience of scene events

A scene is formed by the emergence of attributions concerning the experience of events regarded as typical of the scene. Basically, these attributions are known and shared by the participants in scene activities, but in the case of well-known scenes they are also common to outsiders (with respect to the scene) or 'normal people'. 'Local knowledge'[9] about such 'micro-cultures' enables persons to identify certain events as scene-events and associate them with a specific style of experience and activity. Schulze argues that the symbolic schemes (alltagsästhetische Schemata) of scenes can be taken to be 'opportunities of experiences' (Erlebnisangebot).

Schulze's and Straw's views on scenes share features in common with the 'Birmingham approach' to youth groups as 'subcultures'.[10] The main similarity lies in the reconstruction of scene-specific styles of experience and activities as the core element of collective self-identification. But Schulze's and Straw's views are not restricted to a perspective on cultural struggles between age groups as social classes. The 'distinction of cultures' is not interpreted as determined strictly and predominantly by social stratification, as in neo-Marxist approaches to culture like the Birmingham studies based on Gramsci's concept of cultural hegemony, or recent British youth studies[11] which argue with Bourdieu's terms of distinctive taste and symbolic capital.

Schulze's main interest lies in explanation of the possibility of scenes as a specific mode of a collective unity. This has much in common with Hitzler's view of modern lifestyle collectives, which he interprets as 'post-traditional forms of *Vergemeinschaftung*'.[12]

Therefore the basic task of analysis is to give a 'thick description'[13] of the store of symbols used by a scene group to identify individual experiences and activities as specific to their scene.

---

9   Clifford Geertz, *Local Knowledge: Further Essays in Interpretive Anthropology* (New York: Basic Books, 1983).
10 John Clarke, et al., 'Subcultures, cultures and classes' in Stuart Hall and Tony Jefferson (eds.), *Resistance Through Rituals* (London: Routledge, 1993); Paul Willis, *Profane Culture* (London: Routledge, 1978); Dick Hebdige, *Subculture: The Meaning of Style* (London: Methuen, 1979); Michael Brake, *Comparative Youth Culture: the Sociology of Youth Cultures and Youth Subcultures in America, Britain and Canada* (London: Routledge, 1985).
11 Sarah Thornton, *Club Cultures. Music, Media and Subcultural Capital* (Cambridge: Polity Press, 1995).
12 Ronald Hitzler, 'Sinnbasteln' in Ingo Mörth and Gerhard Fröhlich (eds.), *Das symbolische Kapital der Lebensstile* (Frankfurt a.M.: Campus, 1994), pp. 75-92.
13 Clifford Geertz, *The Interpretation of Cultures: Selected Essays* (New York: Basic Books, 1973).

1.2.1 Locality: time-spatio arrangements and social atmosphere of scene events One of the most important identifying aspects is the spatial arrangement and the specific atmosphere of scene events (Whyte;[14] for more contemporary scenes[15]). The spatial order of scene locations could be interpreted as a part of the opportunity structure of scene events. They offer a limited range of experiences. A scene event cannot happen in any place at any time. The place should symbolically fit specific styles of outward appearance and of inner arrangements. Scene events are time-located and time-limited. They usually start at certain times and have an average duration, and the sequence of activities follows a dramatic pattern. The specific time and spatial location of events effects a scene-shared atmosphere, the felt meaning of the 'place'.

1.2.2 Audience: the social characteristics of persons at scene events Not everyone takes part in scene events. But in general, scene events are viewed as public practices open to all-comers. Although exclusion exists above general age limits (you have to be 'old enough' to participate at a multitude of public events) set by the law, there are few strict criteria as to how and whom to exclude.

Therefore the mixture of persons at a scene may be more or less socially homogeneous or heterogeneous. Audiences may differ internally according to social characteristics such as age, educational level, income, job position, status, political influence, and so on, but they share the same scene-specific style. On the other hand, homogeneity – at least in the form of the evidence and significance of audience-specific characteristics – makes it possible to re-identify a scene.[16] This raises the question of the correspondence between individual and social selection.

---

14   William Foote Whyte, 'The Problem of Cornerville', in *Street Corner Society* (Chicago: University of Chicago Press, 1943).
15   Phil Cohen, 'Subcultural Conflict and Working-Class Community', in *Working Papers in Cultural Studies* 1 (University of Birmingham, CCCS, 1972); Peter Marsh, Rosser Elizabeth, and Rom Harré, 'Life on the Terraces', in *The Rules of Disorder* (London: Routledge, 1978); Wendy Fonarow, 'The Spatial Dynamics of Indie Music Gig', in Ken Gelder and Sarah Thornton (eds.), *The subcultures Reader* (London: Routledge, 1997), pp. 360-69.
16   Schulze, *Die Erlebnisgesellschaft: Kultursoziologie der Gegenwart* (Frankfurt a.M.: Campus, 1992).

Two theoretical explanations are possible: (i). the model of a chosen, self-constructed style-patchwork of 'affective alliances';[17] (ii). the model of habitus as incorporated dispositions inherited by social origin and the rules of social distribution of a society.[18]

In the first case, participation in scene practices is a temporary choice by the actor according to the life-style that s/he has developed. His/her time in the scene has only weak connections with his/her biographical past and future.

In the second case, belonging to a scene and sharing the style of the collective is determined by socialized dispositions. The life-style of a person is viewed as a socio-cultural resource. Because a scene requires the social competence to behave in accordance with certain symbolic rules, an actor is unable to participate in all scene practices but only in those to which his/her cultural resources are suited.

2. The collective assignment of scene specificities and the proto-religious dimension of its validation: salvation ways of scene practices

If we view scenes as groups of people gathered together because they are present at certain events in certain places, they also share specific styles of action and of experience. A scene, then, is a social unity loosely coupled by the 'weak tie' of a certain experience offered at scene-typical events which invite persons to participate. At the least, this depends on the individual decision of each of those present whether to stay or to leave. But although scenes reproduce and renew themselves from one event to the next, the collective assignment of a scene-specific character to events/experiences produces a symbolic structuration. The event thus counts as an offer of experience available in the scene. However, the simple emergence of the scene as a symbolic order with stable elements is not enough to induce people to take part in events. Also required is a collective assignment of relevance to the events typically associated with a scene. This means that the scene event is valued as an extraordinary mode of experience. This attribution increases the value of scene events in the perspective of the scene sympathisers.

---

17 Lawrence Grossberg, 'Another Boring Day in Paradise: Rock and Roll and the Empowerment of Everyday Life', in *Popular Music 4*, 1998, p. 22; Schulze, *Die Erlebnisgesellschaft: Kultursoziologie der Gegenwart*; Ronald Hitzler, 'Sinnbasteln', in Ingo Mörth and Gerhard Fröhlic (eds.), *Das symbolische Kapital der Lebensstile* (Frankfurt a.M.: Campus, 1994), pp. 75-92.
18 Pierre Bourdieu, *La distinction: Critique sociale du jugement* (Paris: Les Ed. de Minuit, 1979); Pierre Bourdieu, *The Logic of Practice* (Stanford: Stanford University Press, 1990).

The cultural consolidation of a scene is based on two basic requirements:

a. A shared use of meanings is needed to identify certain aspects of daily experience as modes of experience associated with the scene. A scene, therefore, is a social invention, an 'institutional fact'[19] which only exists because people believe that it exists.
b. A scene is based on 'We-Intentions',[20] because people attribute the existence of certain experiences to the emergence of certain time-spaced events which enable them henceforth to speak of 'scene-events'.
c. The scene event must be regarded as relevant. This latter aspect raises the question of how the assignment of relevance can be validated by the members of a scene.

One approach is to interpret the setting of values and/or the attribution of relevance as a proto-religious practice (although on the surface these practices are viewed as 'profane cultures',[21] a number of studies have emphasised this proto-religious feature, for example see Cohen[22] and Soeffner[23] on punk, Clarke[24] on skinhead street fights as 'remythization'). At this basic level, the extent to which this ascription of relevance is explicit or implicit is not important. One must investigate the symbolic operations by which the participants of scene events are persuaded/convinced to experience these events as extraordinary and exciting happenings.[25]

This presumes that the shared meanings of a scene include a distinction between ordinary and extraordinary events, experiences, actions, feelings, and so on. Describing something as extraordinary may be equated with taking and valuing something as 'sacred'. The sacred is extraordinary because it promises salvation, although it is seen as untouchable.[26]

It is only possible and permissible to touch the sacred when attention is paid to specific rules and procedures, in particular by being 'ritualistic'.

---

19 John R. Searle, *The Construction of Social Reality* (New York: Free Press, 1995).
20 Wilfrid Sellars, *Science and Metaphysics* (London: Routledge, 1968).
21 Willis, *Profane Culture* (London: Routledge, 1978).
22 Cohen, 'Subcultural Conflict and Working-Class Community', in *Working pagers in Cultural Studies*, 1 (University of Birmingham, CCCS, 1972).
23 Hans-Georg Soeffner, 'Punk oder die Überhöhung des Alltags', in Hans Ulrich Gumbrecht and K. Ludwig Pfeiffer (eds.), *Stil* (Frankfurt a.M.: Suhrkamp, 1986), pp. 317-41.
24 John Clarke, et al., 'Subcultures, Cultures and Classes', in Stuart Hall and Tony Jefferson (eds.), *Resistance through rituals* (London: Routledge, 1993).
25 Clifford Geertz, 'Religion as a Cultural System' in Micheal Banton (ed.), *Anthropological approaches to the study of religion* (London: Tavistock Publications, 1966), pp. 1-46.
26 Emile Durkheim, *Les formes elementaires de la vie religieuse* (Paris: Puf, 1912).

In this very basic proto-religious sense, the sacred is not necessarily associated with explicit religious belief systems. It is also visible in certain types of passion, of respect, and other forms of extreme feeling concerning this-worldly states of affairs, like love, beauty, the art of playing games, or the temptation of discovery, which are then interpreted as 'this-worldly paths of salvation by rituals'.[27]

But what precisely is meant by 'salvation in context'? Should it be thought more as a release 'from' or as salvation 'in'? If it is conceived as release 'from', then the distinction between everyday and extra-ordinary experience may be relevant. Small scene-worlds would provide extra-ordinary experience as a release from routine. Regarding this line of interpretation, however, one must ask why everyday life is seen as something from which people seek release through scene rituals, and especially how it is possible for ritualistic forms of interaction to emerge from extraordinary events. Under the other interpretation – salvation as a form of being saved or rescued – one must describe the dangers that are averted or avoided by taking part in scene rituals. Both interpretations may be justified if they are considered against the background of an increasingly rationalized modernity. Assuming the demands of a rational and a self-directed way of life, the purpose of expressive and magic rituals of scenes is the 're-enchantment' of self- and world-experience. On the one hand, these rituals liberate the individual from modern rational demands and provide salvation; on the other, they offer experiences that may be interpreted as values in themselves - as a safeguard against feeling insecure, disoriented, and rootless in a disillusioned world devoid of mystery.

2.1 The symbolic structural differentiation of validating scene practices

Doubts might also be raised concerning the thesis that the assignment of value must always be a proto-religious symbolic operation. Are there not examples of scenes which are this-worldly oriented and also motivated by formal rationality or pragmatic means-ends calculation? People might also attend scene events in order to achieve profane goals – for example, in order to regain physical fitness in gyms, or merely to make friends or find a 'lover'. It seems feasible that such profane motives may emerge after a scene has been constituted as a scene. But can they explain the constitution of the scene itself? One must ask theoretically whether a profane motive can be the core of

---

27 Max Weber, *Economy and Society: An Outline of Interpretive Sociology: Vol. 1.2.* (Berkeley: University of California Press, 1978), pp. 399, 529-38, esp. 535.

a scene event. Scenes concerned with health or physical fitness are candidates for such a description. Which shows that the motives for taking part in scene activities can be distinguished within a frame comprising an ascribed collective intention to participate (to achieve fitness, to have extraordinary experiences) and secondary motives which emerge after a scene has been constituted.

The latter motives are more general in nature and have to do with the universal characteristics of scenes as events where people come together. It is especially this 'coming together' that enables the visitors at scene events to realize intentions associated with the possibility of meeting and interacting with people at a scene.

For these reasons, the profane and sacred features of scenes cannot be strictly separated, and mediations between the two spheres are possible. Non-smoker groups are constituted by the pragmatic intent to help smokers who want to give up smoking. But as a reaction to the process of learning to reject smoking, some members of this 'scene' begin to regard their own method of giving up smoking as a general way to salvation from addiction that could be copied by all smokers. On the other hand, one could imagine examples of people who join religious groups merely to be integrated into a community and to find friends.

But analysis of scenes should draw a clear distinction between the collective intent attributed to scene events (to gain fitness in gyms; to enjoy the interplay between the musicians and the audience at open-air jazz and rock concerts) and the diverse individual motives that can be fulfilled by taking part at scene events because of the universal characteristics of collective scenes, on the one hand, and the specific frame of the events offered, on the other.

2.2 Youth scenes: local audiences of adolescents

Techno is an example of a youth scene. This aspect is relevant to the social homogeneity of a scene's audience. In the first place, age homogeneity requires that the people who meet at techno scene events are young adults aged on average between 17 and 25. This general expectation was borne out by the results of passer-by interviews conducted in Berlin techno clubs and at the Love Parade of 1997. But the more sociological issue is whether being young can be interpreted as a social characteristic. Or does membership of the same age group indicate social position?

If we presume age to be indicative of social position, we concede that the following hypotheses are correct:

a. age differention yields the social classification of age groups: to be of a certain age carries a social meaning;[28]
b. connected with this social meaning of age are certain age norms and certain opportunities;[29]
c. age norms and choice opportunities give rise to value patterns of age stages or classes;[30]
d. at a more micro-level of observation, people of the same age share features and problems typically associated with their life period.[31]

If youth scenes are age-homogeneous, one can expect their typical events and associated experiences to have certain meanings and styles in common, depending on the horizon of expectations, problems, and activities of adolescents. If techno (as well as other 'small cultures') is regarded as a youth scene, one must ask why it makes sense to frequent it if one is in the life-period of adolescence? One may expect that the core frame of events or the secondary motives of techno as a scene support actions, problems, and so on, connected with this life-period.

---

28 Norman B. Ryder, 'The Cohort as a Concept in The Study of Social Change', *American Sociological Review* 30, 1965, pp. 843-61.
29 Matilda W. Riley (ed.), *Aging from Birth to Death. Vol. 2: Sociotemporal Perspectives*, (Boulder: Westview Press, 1982); Martin Kohli, 'Social organization and subjective construction of the life course', in Aage B. Rensen (ed.), *Human development* (Hillsdale: Erlbaum, 1986), pp. 271-92.
30 Gordon W. Allport, *Pattern and Growth in Personality*, (London: Holt, 1967); Erik H. Erikson, *Identity and the Life Cycle* (New York: Norton, 1980); Erik H. Erikson, *The Life Cycle Completed: A Review*, (New York: Norton, 1982); Matilda W. Riley, Hess Beth and Bond Kathleen (eds.), *Aging in Society: Selected Reviews of Recent Research* (Hillsdale: Erlbaum, 1983); Matilda W. Riley, Robert L. Kahn and Anne Foner (eds.), *Age and Structural Lag: Society's Failure to Provide Meaningful Opportunities in Work, Family, and Leisure* (New York: Wiley, 1994).
31 Erik H. Erikson, *Identity: Youth and Crisis*, (London: Faber, 1968); Barbara M. Newman and Philip R. Newman, *An Introduction to the Psychology of Adolescence* (Homewood: Dorsey, 1979); Barbara M. Newman and Philip R. Newman, *Development through Life: A Psychosocial Approach* (Chicago: Dorsey, 1987); Erhard Olbrich and Todt Eberhard (eds.), *Probleme des Jugendalters* (Berlin: Springer, 1984).
32 Margaret M. Marini, 'The Order of Events in The Transition to Adulthood', in *Sociology of Education* 57, 1984, pp. 63-84; John W. Meyer, 'The self and the life course', in Aage B. Rensen (ed.), *Human Development* (Hillsdale: Erlbaum, 1986), pp. 199-216; Martin Kohli, 'Social Organization and Subjective Construction of The Life Course', in Aage B. Rensen (ed.), *Human Development* (Hillsdale: Erlbaum, 1986), pp. 271-92; Arne Stiksrud, *Jugend im Generationen-Kontext: sozial- und entwicklungs-psychologische Perspektiven* (Opladen: Westdeutscher Verlag, 1994).

Theories of the life-course[32] and/or the life-cycle[33] interpret youth as a period of cumulative transition. Adolescents must accomplish such objective transitions as: leaving the parental home; finishing their educations; entering their first jobs; choosing a (conjugal) mate; and, for most people, having a first child. Moreover, according to the modern value pattern of 'individualization',[34] they must solve more 'subjective' or 'identity-related' problems like selecting their central life-goals and their criteria for social and personal relations (with colleagues, friends and mates).

Scene practices can be taken to be 'rites of passage'.[35] Rites of transition are found in nearly all forms of society. The ideal type is the ritual test (which in the case of young men is often a test of courage) administered to establish whether the person is able to react as a grown-up. In modern societies, the average duration of youth or adolescence has extended,[36] and in effect there is not just one 'test' of behaviour as a grown-up. Another difference relates to the social definition of the 'test criteria', or the validation measures of transition rites. Transitions like finishing school or obtaining a job are regulated by generally valid norms like school reports, references, credentials.

Other transitions, such as mating or child-rearing, are processes regulated by highly personal expectations and preferences. Problems like defining one's self or autonomy in life are developments that cannot be directly structured by social norms or values.

Therefore, a youth scene provides transition rites whose validation criteria are set by the scene – that is, by the young people who attend. Youth scenes and their styles can thus be viewed as social spaces in which adolescents can experiment with activities to achieve validation of their

---

33 Orville G. Jr. Brim, 'Socialization Through the Life Cycle', in *Items* 1, 1964, pp. 1-5; Orville G. Jr. Brim and Carol D. Ryff, 'On the Properties of Life Events', in Paul Baltes and Orville G. Brim (eds.), *Life-Span Development and Behaviour* (New York: Academic Press, 1980), pp. 367-88; David L. Featherman and Troud Peterson, 'Markers of Aging. Modeling the Clocks that Time Us', in *Research on Aging* 8, 1986, pp. 339-65; Erik H. Erikson, *Identity and the Life Cycle* (New York: Norton, 1980); James E. Marcia, 'Identity in Adolescence', in Joseph Adelson (ed.), *Handbook of Adolescent Psychology* (New York: Wiley, 1980), pp. 159-87.
34 Talcott Parsons and Gerald M. Platt, *The American University* (Cambridge, Mass.: Harvard University Press, 1973); Talcott Parsons, 'Religion in Postindustrial America: The Problem of Secularization', in *Social Research* 41, 1974, pp. 193-225; Ulrich Beck, 'The Social Morals of an Individual Life', in Michael Dillon, Paul Heelas, and Michael J. Shapiro (eds.), *Cultural Values, Bd. 1* (Oxford: Blackwell Publishers, 1997), pp. 118-26.
35 Arnold van Gennep, *The Rites of Passage* (London: Routledge, 1960); Joseph F. Ket, *Rites of Passage: Adolescence in America; 1870 to the Present* (New York: Basic Books, 1977); Victor W. Turner, *The Ritual Process: Structure and Anti-Structure* (New York: Aldine, 1982); Victor W. Turner, *From Ritual to Theatre. The Human Seriousness of Play* (New York City: Performing Arts Journal Publications, 1982).
36 Michael Mitterauer, *Sozialgeschichte der Jugend* (Frankfurt a.M.: Suhrkamp, 1986).

collective and individual identities.[37] This leads back to the idea of the proto-religious status of scenes. In the case of the youth scene this status can be achieved through specific definition processes concerning the life-period issues of adolescents.

Youth-scene events as transition rites correspond to the proto-religious assignment of 'ways of salvation' which are 'super-revealed' solution patterns for the definition of the collective situation of a certain youth group (cohort or generation unit) and its valid coping strategies, according to a socially constructed idea of the 'real self'.[38] This seems to be one of the reasons why the youthful life-period (that 'stupid lyric age', as Milan Kundera described it in *The Art of Novel*) is so often seen as the time when specific generational experiences and therefore a generational context and generational unities emerge.[39]

2.3 Social specificities of music and dance activities

Music and dance are seen as leisure, fun, or even luxury activities. Besides the aspect of the technical reproduction of arts (in form of records, CDs, video clips), which is not central to scene analysis, music and dance share the feature of being aesthetic and artistic, at least a form of symbolic self-relatedness.

Moreover, music and dance activities as scene events share the characteristics of stage behaviour which constituts a special kind of public order. This aspect includes two asymmetrical distinctions: one between performers and audience, and the other between frontstage and backstage.[40]

Both asymmetries are of social relevance, because they effect the segmentation of action patterns or roles. But the two distinctions are not necessary features of music and dance scenes. In some – even well-known –

---

37 Talcott Parsons, 'The Kinship System of Contemporary United States', in Talcott Parsons (ed.), *Essays in Sociological Theory* (New York 1954: The Free Press, 1943), pp. 177-96; Parsons, 'Religion in Postindustrial America: The Problem of Secularization'.
38 Ralph Turner, 'The Real Self: From Institution to Impulse', *American Journal of Sociology* 81, 1976, pp. 989-1016.
39 William Pinder, *Das Problem der Generation in der Kunstgeschichte Europas* (Berlin: Frankfurter Verlagsanstalt, 1928); Karl Mannheim, 'Das Problem der Generationen' Kölner Zeitschrift für Soziologie 7, 1928, pp. 157-85, pp. 309-30; Arne Stiksrud, *Jugend im Generationen-Kontext: sozial-und entwicklungspsychologische Perspektiven* (Opladen: Westdeutscher Verlag, 1994).
40 Erving Goffman, *The Presentation of Self in Everyday Life* (New York: Doubleday, 1959); Erving Goffman, *Behaviour in Public Places: Notes on the Social Organization of Gatherings* (London: MacMillan, 1963).

cases they disappear through being mixed. In the disco scene (a precursor of techno), for instance, who is performer and who is audience is not predefined. The participants at disco events may change roles, perhaps from the dancer at the centre of a crowd to onlooker.[41]

Another important dimension of music and dance activities is their association with affection and body.[42] The base contents of music – sound and rhythm – are often interpreted as closely related to affection. Rhythm as symbolic representation of time,[43] sound as representation of mood, are inherent to the bodily expressions of dancing as 'moving pictures of the self'. Rhythm is thus the keeper of a scene-present social time order, and the bodily posture-bearing of dancing is the expression of the self experiencing the frame of the situation materialized in the sound and rhythm perceived by all those present.

The arrangement of sound and rhythm can be viewed as an important factor in the spatio-time arrangement of a music scene.[44] Similarly, the architectural structure of locations is relevant to the possibility of movement. The lay-out of the dance-floor is important for establishment of a performer-audience situation (for example, whether or not there is room for 'voyeurism' is important). The arrangement of space and time depends on the 'semiotic connection'[45] between 'sound' (what can be heard where and when) and 'vision' (what can be seen where and when) which develops into the most important backstage feature. One may therefore formulate assumptions about probable combinations of time-spatio arrangements as backstage structure with forms of expressive action in a public scene as frontstage structure.

For example, one may presume that time-spatio arrangements which include a centre (here Goffman's[46] distinction between 'centered' and 'non-centered' interaction should be developed further) of sound and space – typically a lit-up stage with a rock band – separate performers from audience, whereas diffuse patterns of sound and vision – like the 'forms of dislocation'

---

41 Richard Dyer, 'In defense of disco?', in *On Record: Rock, Pop, and Written Word* (London: Routledge, 1990), p. 141.
42 John Shepherd and Peter Wicke, *Music and Cultural Theory* (Cambridge: Polity Press, 1997), p. 125.
43 Durkheim, *Les formes elementaires de la vie religieuse*; Peter Fuchs, 'Vom Zeitzauber der Musik', in Dirk Baecker (ed.), *Theorie als Passion* (Frankfurt a.M.: Suhrkamp, 1987), pp. 214-37.
44 Keith Negus, *Popular Music in Theory. An Introduction* (Cambridge: Polity Press, 1996), p. 181.
45 Ibid., p. 88.
46 Erving Goffman, *Behaviour in Public Places: Notes on The Social Organization of Gatherings* (London: Macmillan, 1963).

in Brazilian carnival groups[47] – provide a mix between performative-productive and perceptive-consuming behaviour in each participant at a scene-event. The two alternatives support role-fixed or role-diffuse/distant self-concepts of the participating individuals.

3. Interpretive analysis of symbolic practices

3.1 Design: text analysis of described practices and their experience

3.1.1 Methodological standpoint Analysis of the practices of a social field requires methodological criteria for selection of a research design. The theoretical problem discussed above relates to the symbolic structuring of scene events, practices and experiences. The goal of the investigation is to elaborate the rules and areas of the symbolic structuring of a scene. This task requires more open and exploratory methods, such as field observations of scene activities, interviews with experts and/or insiders on their social knowledge, especially 'local knowledge',[48] or the reading of symbolic 'outcomes' of the scene like signs, flyers, magazines, and so on. Although all these types of research methods were used in the investigation described below, there was a strong emphasis on extended interviews with so-called 'techno-insiders'. The study concurred with the basic assumptions of ethnographic approaches,[49] which combine rules of fieldwork with concepts from semiotic analysis, especially 'pragmatic linguistics'.[50] Social practices take place in a sign-mediated field of actions and experiences. Talk about such 'fields' is symbolic while also being part of the field. If we assume that a field of action is structured by a more or less complex and differentiated pattern of symbolic rules, conversations with insiders must include features of these symbolic structures.

---

47   Roberto Da Matta, 'Carnival in multiple planes', in John J. MacAloon (ed.), *Rite, Drama, Festival, Spectacle* (Philadelphia: Institute for the Study of Human Issues, 1984), pp. 208-40.
48   Clifford Geertz, *Local Knowledge: Further Essays in Interpretive Anthropology* (New York: Basic Books, 1983).
49   Peter K. Manning, *Semiotics and Fieldwork. Qualitative Research Methods Series 7* (Newbury Park: Sage, 1987).
50   Charles J. Fillmore, 'Pragmatics and the Description of Discourse Organizational', in Paul Cole (ed.), *Radical pragmatics* (New York: Academic Press, 1987), pp. 143-66; John Lyons, 'Deixis as the source of reference', in Louis Keenan (ed.), *Formal Semantics of Natural Language* (Cambridge: University Press, 1975), pp. 61-83; Stephen C. Levinson, *Pragmatics* (Cambridge: University Press, 1983).

A counter-argument might be that scene practices are often constituted by forms of non-verbal communication which are not explicitly describable in conversation.[51] From the standpoint of the structural hermeneutic model of 'texts' as documents of social discourses[52] this argument breaks down because of its misplaced concreteness. Because the rules of non-verbal (and to a large extent verbal) communication are not explicit, they must be reconstructed by 'reading' the implicit or latent meaning structure of activities recorded as texts. From this point of view, video-taped non-verbal communication or recorded talks about non-verbal scene behaviour are texts which document or 'protocol' the process of attributing meanings to social practices and ordering them. It is not the physical features of gestures or of spoken words that produce meaning, but the signifiable associations made by a group which uses the same system of symbols, or in Foucault's[53] terms 'la formation du discours'. Therefore conversations about a scene as the visible practices of the scene itself are documents of the way in which the system of symbols works, or in other words, how it can be used by actors who share social (that is, local) knowledge of its use.

3.1.2 Implications for the research design A small sample of scene insiders was therefore collected. The interviewees had to fulfil certain criteria and vary along specific dimensions: (i) they should be participants of the techno scene for at least two years; (ii) there should be a more or less uniform distribution in the group interviewed of social indicators like age, sex, education, social origin, and position in the scene itself; (iii) there should be differences in the entrance onto the scene.

For these reasons, 62 persons were interviewed between 1996 and 1997. All of them lived or worked in Berlin, although more than a half of them had not been born and grown up in this city. Eight persons were not born in Germany or had lived more than five years in other countries or continents.

---

51 Laud Humphreys, 'The Sociologist as Voyeur', in Laud Humphreys, *Tearoom Trade: Impersonal Sex in Public Places* (Chicago: Aldine, 1970); Paul Willis, *Profane Culture* (London: Routledge, 1978).
52 Paul Ricoeur, 'The Model of the Text: Meaningful Action Considered as a Text', *Social Research* 38, 1971, pp. 529-62; Hans-Georg Soeffner, 'Prämissen einer sozialwissenschaftlichen Hermeneutik', in Hans-Georg Soeffner (ed.), *Auslegung des Alltags. Alltag der Auslegung* (Frankfurt a.M.: Suhrkamp, 1989), pp. 66-97; Ulrich Oevermann, 'Genetischer Strukturalismus und das sozialwissenschaftliche Problem der Erklärung der Entstehung des Neuen', in Stefan Müller-Doohm (ed.), *Jenseits der Utopie* (Frankfurt a.M.: Suhrkamp, 1991), pp. 267-336.
53 Michel Foucault, *L'archéologie du savoir* (Paris: Gallimard, 1969).

3.2 Data collection

As already mentioned, four research methods were used:

a. unstructured field observations in clubs and during street parades;
b. the reading of fanzines, flyers, internet pages, and newspaper articles on techno;
c. semi-standardized, thematically focused extended interviews (2-4 hours);
d. short passer-by interviews (5-7 minutes long, 12 questions and a list concerning personal data).

The first two methods were used for orientation on the most relevant topics, activities, events, time patterns in the scene. They were used to compile a list of themes that should be addressed in the extended interviews. The purpose of the passer-by interviews was to compare the representation of social groups at scene events with the persons interviewed in the extended interviews, who were viewed as 'experts' or 'virtuosos' of the techno scene.

The extended interviews all began with the question: 'How did you happen to get into techno?'. The respondents were encouraged to tell their own stories of how they entered the scene. Subsequently, the following information was requested and topics were identified: the meaning of music and dance in their techno activities; the importance of meeting other people at events; whether they saw techno as a certain style or way of life (the issue of drugs was now introduced if the interviewee had not yet mentioned it); how techno related to their future lives; techno and gender relations; what they thought about their future.

3.3 Data analysis

The interpretation of recorded talks offers two advantages: first, the use of symbols can be reconstructed in greater detail; second, the interaction between activity, experience and symbolization can be represented more completely. A possible drawback to the observing or videotaping of 'pure' or non-verbal behaviour is that it is only possible to collect present-sited physical operations of the body, while ones know nothing about the cognitive or mental processes simultaneous with them, and more importantly, about how these mental events are emotionally assimilated over time. This latter aspect highlights the notion of 'experience' in phenomenologist approaches[54] and raises the question of process, namely how passing mental states are shaped by the experience of ongoing psychic events. Again, these inner psychic processes are not directly observable in interviews, although they include symbolic representation of the ordering of frames of experience.

Interpretive analysis of the pragmatics of talking about a scene enables reconstruction of the natural or 'social semantics'[55] transmitted in that scene. The term 'social semantics' denotes the rules of communicating themes, of attributing meaning to aspects of the world. This view is comparable to the structural semiotic approach used to reconstruct the codes that determine how 'contents' are signified by signifiers.[56] In recent semiotic approaches,[57] 'social semantics' or 'codes' are considered to be 'fields' of the possible ways in which 'symbols' or 'signifiers' can be used.

But how can this sociolinguistic approach be applied at the more concrete level of interpretation of extended interviews, where each interview transcript runs to around 70 pages or 15,000 words?

It therefore seemed useful to distinguish among the text elements and relations that structure interviews. The basic elements were detailed descriptions provided by the interviewee of his or her knowledge and experiences of the scene. Three (formal) aspects of these descriptions were examined in greater detail. A first important feature was the opening sentence of the interviewee's description, namely how s/he started to describe an aspect of his or her scene-world. These opening sentences were interpreted as the interviewee's introduction of a horizon of meaning concerning the experiences described. The second feature was line-by-line analysis[58] of the exposition and closure of the opened horizon of meaning.

---

54 Alfred Schutz, *Der sinnhafte Aufbau der sozialen Welt: eine Einleitung in die verstehende Soziologie* (Frankfurt a.M.: Suhrkamp, 1974).
55 Niklas Luhmann, 'Gesellschaftliche Struktur und semantische Tradition' in Niklas Luhmann, *Gesellschaftsstruktur und Semantik.* Band 1 (Frankfurt a.M.: Suhrkamp, 1980), pp. 9-71.
56 Ferdinand De Saussure, *Course in General Linguistics* (New York: McGraw-Hill, 1966).
57 Umberto Eco, *A Theory of Semiotics* (Bloomington: University of Indiana Press, 1979); Umberto Eco, *Semiotics and the Philosophy of Language* (London: Macmillan, 1984); Peter K. Manning, *Semiotics and Fieldwork. Qualitative Research Methods series 7* (Newbury Park: Sage, 1987).
58 Oevermann, 'Genetischer Srukturalismus und das sozialwissenschaftliche Problem der Erklärung der Entstehung des Neuen'; Anselm Strauss and Juliet Corb, *Basics of Qualitative Research* (Newbury Park: Sage, 1990).

Ecstasy as 'this-worldly path to salvation' 107

The third feature was the grouping of themes and their expositions in the interviews with the scene-insiders. This last feature was divided into four sub-analyses:

a. clarification of the central themes emphasised and elaborated by the interviewees;
b. the possibly diversified set of meanings that the interviewees associated with the central themes;
c. the social contexts related to the themes;
d. the rules presumed relevant to the reference social contexts.

The overall intention was to reconstruct a finite 'archive' of the meanings attributed to scene practices. Various concepts of communication analysis appear to match this intention to reconstruct the 'said' (*das Gesagte*) of the text[59] or the 'passing theories'[60] of 'finite vocabularies'[61] stored in 'the archive of discursive formations'.[62]

In sociological theories or in social philosophy, 'passing theories' have also been termed 'frames of relevance'[63] or 'background capacities'.[64] All these expressions are part of an endeavour to conceptualize a set of assumptions shared by sign users or participants in discourse so that they can contribute to the process of symbolic activity mediated in a social context.

4. Results

4.1 Symbolic structuring of scene events

Although numerous differences emerged in how the interviewees had entered the techno scene, and how they felt involved in it, they all talked about

---

59 Paul Ricoeur, 'The Model of the Text: Meaningful Action Considered as a tex', *Social Research* 38, 1971, pp. 529-62.
60 Donald Davidson, 'A Nice Derangement of Epitaphs', in *Truth and Interpretation. Perspectives on the Philosophy of Donald Davidson* (Oxford: Blackwell, 1986), pp. 433-46.
61 Richard Rorty, 'Pragmatism, Davidson and Truth', in Ernst LePore (ed.), *Truth and Interpretation. Perspectives on the Philosophy of Donald Davidson*, pp. 333-55; Richard Rorty, *Contingency, Irony, and Solidarity* (Cambridge: University Press, 1989).
62 Foucault, *L'archéologie du savoir* (Paris: Gallimard, 1969).
63 Schutz, *Der sinnhafte Aufbau der sozialen Welt: eine Einleitung in die verstehende Soziologie*; Erving Goffman, *Frame Analysis: An Essay on the Organization of Experience* (Cambridge, Mass.: Harvard University Press, 1974).
64 John R. Searle, *The Construction of Social Reality* (New York: Free Press, 1995).

specific experiences of ecstasy through dancing, which they often expressed with metaphors of 'flying', 'taking off' or 'the feeling of being in another world'. A typical description follows:

> So I went to Tresor later somehow and asked myself over and over again, 'What's going on here actually?' People are meeting in the middle of the night in a cellar, now in Tresor, to shake somehow to strobes, flashing lights and eeuh eeuh sounds and somehow to, well, I was ... I hated to dance too, but ... //I: Earlier?//Earlier. Always. I never danced. And I thought to myself, 'What are they doing here actually? At three o'clock in the morning they meet in a cellar in order to somehow move around somehow to ... and flashing lights. What they can do you can do too.' So then I started dancing. And then I danced for the first time and simply kept on dancing a long time, abandoned myself there to what I never wanted to end... I don't know. It was simply fantastic. It was an experience.
>
> ...
>
> but I simply had somehow, um, this feeling, that you don't have with Techno when you only go in and listen. You don't get it then. No, you really have to go in, close your eyes and follow the bass over a long period of time in order to fall into a trance somehow. I experienced that, dancing for 28 hours, 48 hours, going at it 48 hours and somehow overcoming sleep and somehow the, this beat, so that you simply forget about the time because it's infinite. It endlessly goes 'bum, bum, bum, bum,' and you have the feeling of being in another world. You are really in another world. And when you come out of the club, yeah, then it's simply like you suddenly have all your commitments again and you have to do everything again (Yves).

A line-by-line analysis of this interview extract would be beyond the scope of this article. I shall therefore move to reconstruction of the 'passing theories' that clarify how the speaker uses the signs stored in the 'symbolic archive' of the scene. By interpreting how the speaker makes sense of his or her scene activities, one can collect the ways of appropriating worlds valid in the local context of the scene. Examination of the extract in this way yields 'passing theories' which make sense of the selected (used) signs on two levels.

Using the first perspective, we can develop the speaker's (Yves) individual history from someone who 'never dances' to someone who 'dances 48 hours', 'endlessly' and who 'forgets time', who 'overcomes sleep'. The individual history perspective reveals the dramatic pattern of conversion.

On the second level, the speaker uses vocabulary expressing a certain kind of 'extraordinary experience' which includes the following mental states: excitement, eccentricity, extremism, excess, extra-ordinariness, endlessness, ecstasy.

If we look for a pattern or 'leitmotif' connecting the ideas and meanings traversing the above description, we find that it consists of a (finite) vocabulary of transgression arranged along two axes: (i) knowledge of, and (ii) the time of, the (rave) practice. Along the knowledge axis, disorientation and the breakdown of (situational) frames and background capacities to cope with present situations are emphasised. Along the time axis, the deregulation of schedules and disregard for (physical, bodily) time boundaries are mentioned. The use of a vocabulary of transgression highlights the following process: an infinitely continuing stream of ongoing (bodily) activities not describable with a common or a shared vocabulary, which resists any attempt at interpretation and which can only be described as basically idiosyncratic forms of behaviour.

At a rave, the participants construct a double exposure of a public-private order. Outwardly, the event – a rave as a dance party – is public. The people who take part meet as anonymous individuals. One can attend a party of this kind without being known to anyone present. In this respect, techno constitutes a public sphere.

Regarding the collectively-constructed activity – taking part as basically idiosyncratic eccentric behaviour – this public order generates a social desire to communicate out of character,[65] which is usually taboo in public life because it belongs to backstage processes or intimate privacy.

Therefore, raves deconstruct themselves as public orders involving ritual dancing in order to transgress, to symbolize individuality by communicating out of character, by moving to pulsating rhythms.

A first result is that interpretation of the above description reveals a symbolic pattern found in nearly all the other interviews: the use of a finite vocabulary which expresses 'collective transgression' as the purpose of experiences and/or activities in the techno scene. This bears out the thesis that rave events are symbolized as proto-religious phenomena comparable with 'salvation paths by rituals'.[66] To transgress is first to cross the boundaries of everyday experience, and second to obtain release from the demands of self-control expressed in the metaphors of 'flying' or 'letting oneself go'. The latter metaphor in particular assumes a background of self-control constraints which prevent the self from 'going' or more generally from moving. This is accompanied by an inversion of values. The expressive forms of 'crossing over' manifest in the scene context would be viewed as taboo – transgression

---

65 Goffman, *The Presentation of Self in Everyday Life*.
66 Weber, *Economy and Society: An Outline of Interpretive Sociology*.

in the sense of misconduct or sinfulness – in the public sphere. For these reasons, the techno scene stage-manages itself as a deviant culture, as evidenced by the slogan of street parades: 'We are different'.

4.2 The spatial arrangement

The mixture between private affections like transgressions collectively shared in the public order of techno events raises the question as to how it is possible for people to lose their self-control and keep dancing to the music. I shall accordingly analyse two descriptions of the spatial arrangement of techno parties. The first extract is from an interview with two female disc jockeys; the second is from a conversation with a party organizer. The task of interpretation is to work out the correspondence between the passing theories which guide the desciptions compared.

> Cora: Well, there was, for example in [name of club], that was, hum, four years ago or when, well, when the club really existed, well, it was one of the few clubs anywhere in the world that, hum, absolutely anywhere, had a name, and, hum, it, when you went in it was like ... Were you ever there?
> I: No, no.
> Cora: You don't have to go there any more because it doesn't have anything else at all to do with that. It is really, well, you can just as well go to a corner pub. Really, it is, hum, definitely over. Nothing's going to change that. In any case, hum, it was like that when you went in, hum, there was a door where, hum, somehow it was clear from the start that something was happening there, right? Well, I don't think you really even noticed the music. There was a dance floor above that was relatively moderate at first. Maybe it even played Hip-Hop or Hip-Hop to House and, hum, was more there for students and, hum, well, it was really pleasant up there, also easy to talk and so on, and there was even a DJ ...
> (Interview Cora and Steffi).

Cora tries to explain to the interviewer the atmosphere of a 'real' techno club. She begins by stating that the club used to be one of the leading clubs in the world. But today it has lost this atmosphere and is comparable to an ordinary pub. Hence, we again find the distinction between the ordinary and the extra-ordinary, here attributed to the past and the present of the club. The second aspect emphasised by the speaker is the extra-ordinariness felt as atmosphere when entering the context of the club event. The situation of entering is clearly pointed out by mentioning 'a door' from where 'it was clear from the start that something was happening there'. If we try to imagine a background which would fulfil the presupposed quality 'that something was happening there' we find an implicit difference between something versus nothing happening. This means that a distinctive quality and thereby a certain relevance is attributed to the sequence of events ocurring in the club. This distinctive quality is described in more detail in the continuation of the narrative.

> About then there was this corridor, hum, and when you came in you simply noticed somehow, hum, it's pretty extreme here, because there was a fog in this doorway and then there was a stairway going down completely enveloped in a fog. You couldn't see a thing, you couldn't see where you were going, and you didn't know how long the stairway was, whether it went anywhere at all, hum, whether you would run into the wall anywhere at the end, or, and the only thing that led you on were the basses that got louder and louder pretty fast. Well, they were enormous. Really it was like being almost battered by them.
> I: I imagine it to be like...
> Steffi: Yeah, the loudness.
> Cora: From the loudness. Well, the closer you came, right?
> I: Hm, yeah, sure.
> Cora: You really went through a, well, if you saw it now, it's so pitiful, well, if you saw it now...
> Steffi: It's hard to imagine (Cora and Steffi).

Describing the scene, Cora again states that any visitor to the club would have felt ('simply noticed somehow') the special aura near the door leading to the dance floor in the cellar, thereby emphasising the evidence of the scene atmosphere. The first adverbial expression 'pretty extreme' indicates an ambivalent or possibly inverted assessment of the atmosphere. 'Extreme' refers to the feeling of being confronted with, or even being assailed by, distorting, irritating, aggressive, destructive surroundings. The term 'pretty' is attached to the feeling of fascination that induced her to more closely approach the 'extreme'.

Cora explicitly expresses the disorientation caused by the restricted opportunities of perception:

> You couldn't see where you were going and you didn't know how long the stairway was, whether it went anywhere at all, hum, whether you would run into the wall anywhere at the end.

She then states the element that became a guiding factor in this disorientation:

> The only thing that led you on were the basses, which got stronger and stronger pretty fast. Well, they became enormous. Really it was like being battered by them.

Again the description reflects the ambivalence of a situation which, on the one hand, attracted the girl as she entered the club and, on the other, produced a feeling of irritation, perhaps of fear. At any rate, she entered the context, which apparently imposed the enormous and perhaps unreasonable demand of reacting under conditions of radically changed perception and limited self-control, and of being confronted by a style of music felt to be physically irksome.

> Cora: Yeah, in any case a manic mind, I'd say. It couldn't be a person somehow who, hum, who sat in a meadow a while and read a book. I can't imagine that somehow. It really had to come about in extreme circumstances, the idea. Come on, we'll make lots of fog and then we'll turn on the strobe light. Because that's, you are at that moment simply in another space, right? And, hum, you no longer perceive your own movements and, hum, you're also surrounded by extremely loud music and hum, because the fog has a smell, kind of a like a sauna, well, hum ... It's simply that you don't have any more control, right? And it was just that, hum, I mean, why I said before that I didn't experience it like that, simply, hum, in [name of club] you really got battered, well, there was no place, there was, hum, the House DJs were [name] and [name]. [Name] was a compulsive gabbler, Hardcore fan, okay, well, the only one, the hardest...
> Steffi: Fast rhythms, like they assaulted you.
> Cora: ...DJ in Germany and, hum, a real muscle man, tattooed and he likes little juicy boys somehow, and he gave it to them, right? [Steffi laughs softly] And he gave it to me too. Well, hum, that was simply really extreme. It was like, hum, the Blade Runner or something, right? (Cora and Steffi).

I note in passing the masochistic connotation of the narrative implied in the concluding comment on the homosexuality of the disc jockey and his tendency to 'give it' to the 'little juicy boys', and the additional remark that he likewise 'gave it' to her. The decisive point is that the interviewee is attracted by the spatial arrangement of the club, which has deconstructed the usual forms of reality control. This dispersal of the reality controllable by one's perceptions – accompanied by the impression that one's body is being attacked by the music – is evidenced by the statement that only a 'sick, in any case manic brain' could have invented it.

The vocabulary used to described the distorted reality and the feeling that one is losing self-control is again one of transgression. Here it is coupled with the symbolization of entering a strange and hostile spatial arrangement which exerted an ambivalent but exciting attraction.

The second extract comprises statements made by the party organizer, Robin, who use similar meanings and metaphors to describe his vision of the concept of his parties.

Ecstasy as 'this-worldly path to salvation' 113

Robin: Because, hum, well, I mean the comparison fits somehow between that and how such a [...] looked and something else that you already know. This scene is from Schwarzenegger, from Terminator 1, where machines, hum, go after people.
I: Um, uh huh.
Robin: Smoke, lightning, thunder, noise and, hum, laser beams somehow, and they simply shoot at people, and, hum, the machines, hum, they mercilessly impose their power on the people somewhere and force them somehow to do what it is. And this, hum, this, let's say, hum, something, hum, negative or destructive thinking, this should turn itself exactly into positive energy. Somewhere, this is like a prediction somewhere, something that (one) could expect, so it was only a vision. That is, hum, in a certain sense a science-fiction vision, that the machines aren't at war, the people aren't at war, but rather they bring things, that is, they begin to move when they hear the rhythm and the bass sounds, hum, that is, they subordinate themselves totally to the machine somewhere, but that, hum, again with a positive element, namely creative self-identification, that is, in the group, hum, that this had to lead to positive energy (Robin).

The first element in this explanation is Robin's remark about destructive elements taken from the film *Terminator 1*. This vision of destructive elements corresponds to Cora's view of being physically attacked by the music and the surrounding atmosphere. The second element in Robin's explanation is his distinction between his kind of party and conventional ones. This also corresponds to Cora's distinction between the extraordinary club that it used to be and the ordinary pub it has now become. A third shared element is the coupling of constructive (positive, attractive) and destructive (negative, aversive) associations with the spatial atmosphere.

So that happened now, hum, perhaps very carefully, but this fundamental concept of [name of club] earlier, this actually, hum, appeared when a positive general consciousness arose through excessive dancing, that is, through free dancing in, inside the group of people. Because when someone notices that he, that is, notices while he is dancing, that he, hum, that it doesn't matter whether he is somehow making a fool of himself or whether he is being vain or cool or uncool, that it is really only important that he has fun doing it and imparts this fun to other people, hum, then this must actually carry over to the whole, the whole party and then, again, hum, it must also retain something from everday life, that is, in other words: discotheques are always characterized by aggressiveness, hum, there is always a certain underlying aggressiveness stored up there because of, hum, vanity, because of, hum, people's personal craziness, that is, because of this rooster game the people are always paying attention to not losing face, to always looking out for, that nobody's at their throats and somehow, hum, and no, at the slightest movement, that is, the thing is all so played up, and everybody simply plays their role, but it isn't actually himself, but rather he is playing a role (Robin).

Whereas the conventional milieu of discotheques gives rise to a narcissistic 'rooster game', the intention of Robin's concept and arrangement of parties was to encourage excessive dancing, liberated dancing, becoming open-minded. His description is guided by a logic of inversion. The spatial atmosphere of discotheques, outwardly controlled and well-formed, produces aggressive emotions in the dimension of inner processes and dispositions. Conversely, the techno atmosphere is symbolized as outwardly aggressive and destructive, but as liberating in the dimension of inner developments and dispositions.

The extract quoted contains explications of the organizer's 'socio-technical' knowledge of the relationship between the spatial arrangements of the event and the atmosphere thus created: the special effects produced by the stroboscope and fog, the reduction of sounds by concentrating on rhythm and the bass line, and the consequent separation between dance floor and the 'chill-out area'. This was intended to create an atmosphere where the people present were only affected by music and only able to dance. Hence the presence of people who just watched and 'consumed' the dancing bodies would be prevented. The function of the extreme atmosphere of techno clubs was to produce a radical disjunction in the feelings of visitors to techno parties, forcing them to choose between being totally attracted or totally disgusted. This disjunction should select the visitors, so that the open-minded ones stayed at the party and the conventional narcissistic ones left.

The elements of the spatial arrangement can be analysed as an attempt to control the social atmosphere of the techno club.

> Robin: that he breaks people's habits to such an extent that they really can begin, really must begin to open up ... So it's exactly strobe lights that are good, that is, you use lots of strobe lights, fog is good because the people can't be seen, so you make lots of fog, hum, sound is good and sound is important, so you produce lots of sound, and the bass is particularly important, so you produce lots and lots of bass, hum, rhythm is important for dancing, so you produce lots and lots of rhythm, singing isn't so important, so you don't sing much. Hum, just like that. So sitting is only conditionally necessary, because people are supposed to move, and when people sit down, they should do it where you can't dance, which is to say not necessarily dancing around the edges, but rather the people who want to sit should do it separate from those, from those people who simply want to dance, so that people don't, so that people simply can't sit down and spread or cross their legs and look around at how the people there on the dance floor jump around, rather a kind of separation should simply somehow happen. And I think this, this experience, that is, this thing was in fact able to be realized, that is, it was then, hum, really achieved, everyone could come to this, in this party, that is, through very, hum, let's say very suggestive advertising they came to the party

because we were a little open-minded or we were a little interested in, in new things and ...we could more or less decide, you had to decide: 'Do I find this thing totally good?' or 'Do I find this thing totally shitty?' At that moment, hum, that's also a principle that I actually say, everything else that's happened in the meantime is cold coffee, spare me, it's useless, it's a habit and it's ... and habits don't bring anything forward. So either you confront them so they're enthusiastic, hum, or so they reject it. And it was the case that there were already people who went in or, on the other hand, couldn't go in because they couldn't handle it or they were afraid of what was going on inside because there was more bass than normal, that is, the main thing was the bass and more than the normal amount, that is, abnormal, hum, weird. The people acted like they were on another planet and it simply looked really horrible in a certain sense. And only when people got their bearings and looked at what was actually going on, then they saw laughing faces and, hum the fun that the people were having and their enthusiasm. And this enthusiasm transmitted itself somehow, and somebody who really stood there a while was incapable at some point of doing anything else but this movement, that is, this rhythm suggested to him by light, by music, by the bass, by vibration and by looking at other people, that is, he was able to submit really slowly to this rhythm, and at the moment when he began to move his head he was already lost, he was actually already, it was already clear that in twenty minutes he would belong to the convulsing people somewhere. And that, hum, existed in Berlin an Urknall, that is, there was really this, hm, the, really this insanity here that the people really, well, the word got around. Well, everyone wanted to see it sometime, experience it somewhere. People reported that it was really like aliens had landed and brought something here that had never existed in this form. It was unbelievable.

The limited opportunity to watch the people in the situation, like the limited opportunity to talk to them, optimized or created a condition in which the only option was to dance. Furthermore, because those present were seemingly compelled to dance, they forgot about their self-presenting strategies. They had the impression that others were unable to observe them in the usual way, that they could not talk to them on the dance floor, and that in these circumstances they could only stay and dance with them. Consequently, this strange atmosphere gave rise to a homogeneous experience of the social situation and to the curious experience that dancing in that atmosphere produced 'fun'. Thus, reducing the elements of everyday perception and activity increased the special elements relative to dancing:

> This can only work through reduction, that is, through reducing from, from the, from the things simply that happen, and on the other hand again by increasing the power of things that are simply necessary, so that they really dance (Robin).

This combination of reducing and increasing the elements of the situation has been analysed by Michel Foucault as the nucleus of modern power structures. It consists in exerting control over a situation by reducing its elements in order to multiply highly specific characteristics. A central aspect of this strategy is controlling what is present in the situation, or in other words, controlling which elements are present and which are absent, the people who are present and those who are absent. This process of control needs constant attention and systematically concentrated socio-technical knowledge. The knowledge of techno events is concentrated in the competence of the party organizers, since these know about the interrelations between spatial equipment, musical characteristics, and the reactions of human bodies in this visual/acoustic arrangement. If this knowledge is put into practice, extraordinary emotions, ecstatic states can be produced and experienced. 'Incessant spirals of power and desire'[67] arise to produce a special way of experiencing one's own self or, as Robin puts it, 'creative self-identification'. But the specific self constituted in the atmosphere of techno parties is not a self that feels individualized. It is not a self which seeks to control presentation in everyday life in order to maintain a certain identity. The atmosphere of the rave enables the person to lose control, to dissolve the barrier between body and self.

Combining the interpreted elements reveals how the organizer's socio-technical knowledge of the 'mechanics of gatherings' and the 'aligned symbolic order of club atmospheres' is again expressed using a vocabulary of transgression augmented with meanings that refer to the time-spatial structure of scene events.

4.3 Non-verbal rules of validating symbolized identity

4.3.1 Non-verbal constitution of interpersonal encounter Thus far I have reconstructed the general frame of transgression and a symbolically coherently aligned view of a spatial arrangement of scene localities. One might at this point enquire about the interactions that take place in this order of collective transgression, or else enquire whether interpersonal encounter or micro-level communication break down in rituals of this kind. Further exemplary descriptions follow:

> At the beginning you always looked around a lot, 'Is this possible?' 'What are you listening to exactly?' 'It's really unbelievable what I'm hearing.' People looked at each other, so unbelieving, they laughed, they grinned, 'True, isn't it?' (Yves).

---

67 Foucault, *L'archéologie du savoir*.

> And I had contact somehow first with the people who for instance danced in the same corner as I did. Fairly quickly you find your place where you feel good. Everyone does it differently. There is also hardly ... with B. for instance I hardly ever dance in the same corner. We dance past each other now and again, but we also split up again fast because we feel better with other people. And when you see them again and again and then somehow, I don't know, then he looks at you for the tenth time, or you ... for the tenth time you turn around somehow and look him accidentally in the eyes, when you open your eyes or whatever, and then there's a little laughter here or, I don't know, during the same song someone begins to scream and you notice, ah, something's happening, somehow like that, he has the same waves of emotion or something, somehow like that, or much more. Or that someone's eyes begin to shine because ... in certain kinds of light that someone ... (Ariane).

Both descriptions emphasise the accidental mode of meeting someone. The background generating these coincidences is one in which everyone is confronted with, and confused by, the strange atmosphere. The main activity is being preoccupied with one's own idiosyncratic dancing activities – listening to the rhythm and constantly trying to find new moves and new gestures. But for a small instance of time one strays, looks around and notices that someone else shows the same emotional reaction at the same moment ('look him accidentally in the eyes when you open your eyes', 'a little laughter', 'during the same song someone begins to scream', 'he has the same waves of emotion').

Karl Mannheim has called this process the 'conjunctive experience of community'. People assembled in the same place notice that they all regard the scenery in the same emotional manner, so that they feel that they belong to each other. My interpretation so far yields the thesis that techno parties, or raves, generate a 'metaphysics of symbiosis'. Now, however, I shall quote statements which contradict this thesis. Yves, who was quoted earlier, mentioned:

> One had at least the feeling that the other thought in the same way. But obviously everyone thinks for themselves, and usually one made conversation after a visual contact and noticed the other had got a really different attitude ... (Yves).

Hence, in some manner, Yves conveys the idea of two different processes – one emphasised and the other set in brackets – or to use different teminology, processes presented frontstage and processes performed backstage. On frontstage you feel, and everyone else feels like you do. On backstage you know that 'everyone thinks for themselves'. Seen in this light, rave participants seem able ironically to deconstruct their own collective activities.

4.3.2 Erotic playfulness of dancing bodies This aspect is highlighted by descriptions of the erotic dimension of raves. Let me again analyse a quotation:

> And you could also look around, and it was great and somehow, it was also ... sex plays a big role, definitely, but not, not as an attack on, on me or something like that. What I mean is I can be more choosy. And it was more this openness or something, I don't know, this whole, this prickly feeling that was hovering there in the air, somehow like that. You look around somewhere and all over something is happening. And, wap, now you're looking here and now there and somehow I, and uh, what's actually happening to me and the like. How do I even look today? (Ariane).

The central term in this passage is 'openness'. It symbolizes the open range of erotic happenings that could be chosen by the actress. On the one hand, this description derives its specific sense from the background assumption that sex is sexist, a potential 'attack' on women seen as passive. But this image is dispelled by the statement that she could 'be choosy'. On the other hand, the atmosphere produced by the impression of a wide variety of erotic happenings 'here and now there' seems to be more important than the actual choice of one of them. This aspect is expressed more clearly in a dialogue between Ariane and Anja:

> Ariane: It wasn't simply like being stuck in a rut, I belong to him and he belongs to me, but somehow what I also meant before, simply, complete strangers do these most erotic dances with each other and somehow all these bodies rub up against each other somehow, eeee, I'm with a strange man on the dance floor somehow, I'm standing there, and I don't know, we grab each other and somehow, there are simply no inhibitions any more, right? That never happened to me before. For God's sake. If somebody had grabbed me before I would have punched him in the face or something, I don't know what. But this was ...
> Anja: Yeah, but despite that, this somehow didn't have to do with, well, it was, that was there on the dance floor and actually had little ...
> Ariane: That had nothing to do with the outside world.
> Anja: Yeah, that meant nothing anymore somehow. You went down there, let's say you talked to the guy totally normally and that was simply somehow, it happened because the music at that moment was somehow, it animated you somehow, but that didn't mean that you had to leave with him and go to bed or some such thing. That was simply a form of expression ...
> Ariane: Exactly (Ariane and Anja).

The starting point is again the idea of 'openness', here expressed by the reverse image of 'being stuck in a rut' as a certain form of belonging to each other. By contrast, an erotic encounter between strangers is visualized and interpreted as a total lack of inhibition in the statement 'simply no inhibitions any more'. Ariane's interpretation again rests on the assumption that her former sexual experiences were associated with the feeling of being attacked, here instantiated by the 'punch in the face' after being 'grabbed' by somebody.

One must therefore ask what made it possible for Ariane to be 'with a strange man on the dance floor somehow', each of them 'grabbing' the other without inhibitions? The answer is given by Anja's intervention: 'that was there on the dance floor' and Ariane's completion: 'that had nothing to do with the outside world'. The two girls assume that dancing in this way can not be taken as a commitment or as a promise of sexual intercourse. The manifold erotic happenings are only regarded as imagined possibilities while on the dance floor; they had no meaning after the stage is left: 'that meant nothing anymore somehow ...'

This rule makes it possible for everyone to become everyone else's sexual fantasy on the dance floor, but only there. I shall call this 'erotic playfulness' because it generates the image of a situation in which erotic encounters are possible for everyone. But conversely it means that everything is possible only because every concrete realization is impossible. Do we therefore have to conclude that it 'was simply (or even 'exactly!': Ariane) only a form of expression', as Anja declares?

Again, this is to miss the point, especially as regards the sort of motivational energy catalysed by erotic playfulness. Ariane herself rejects the possibility that it could have been 'only expressing':

> It's also totally going all the way (*totales Ausleben*). Not only expressing, but that you can go all the way somehow and jump through the place completely free and uninhibited and stuff like that. I mean, the people there were half naked, it didn't matter. I mean, hardly anyone does that today because in the meantime there are so many people who stand in the corners and stare around stupidly or try to pick you up and wild proles who, well, don't make any effort, who only consume from other people who are making an effort. It simply wasn't like that, well, maybe that it was like that before. Everybody brought his party, his little piece of a party, and it all got mixed together and out of that came totally extreme parties because everybody brought his only little piece of extremism with him (Ariane).

Ariane's comment divides into two parts. In the first, she explains that erotic dancing was not only expression for her. Here she uses the substantive form of the verb *ausleben* as *totales Ausleben*, an expression difficult to translate literally into English. On the one hand, it again emphasises freedom from inhibitions; on the other, it expresses the acting out of impulses to the limit. The term *ausleben* connotes the impulses felt as the emotional energy that drives the self. On such a view, raving is being one's self, letting go of one's self without running the risk of making a concrete choice. This reintroduces the 'time order' which I reconstructed when interpreting the phrase 'abandoned myself there to what never wanted to end'. This odd time perspective is constructed by a corresponding rule: making a concrete choice would be the beginning of the end. Hence the will to take part in an infinitely ongoing activity is backed by resistance against concrete choice or realization.

The same idea is expressed in the following statement by Hendrik, who visualizes raves as 'sex with the masses'. In his view, the infinite delay of individual gratification provides 'optimal lust of the big body', by which is meant the raving crowd as a body.

> ...to get back to yourself, uhm, uhm, hum, optimal lust, feeling in your body, optimal lust in the big body but correspondingly also as a part in one's own body. Sex with the masses. The DJ will say that when he's standing at his sound board and his beats are thundering down, the audience, that's pure sex to see the masses twitching. Yes, there's lust in the masses, namely this permanent vibration hovering there in the air. The, this permanent eroticism. I mean the promise never to be kept, you know, the big tickle. It doesn't come to the final lay, to the final fuck. Always to be aroused at the highest level! It's really crazy. To always be just on the verge of an orgasm (Hendrik).

Here all the elements combine: the erotic arousal of the dancing crowd, the importance of the beats of the rhythm, the individual and the collective as imagined bodies and as selves acting out their physically felt impulses (rejecting final and/or definite goals), and the time perspective of an infinitely ongoing process.

Conclusion

Three main results have been yielded by interpretation of segments of typical interviews with young people who participate in rave (techno scene) events.

The first was the specific pattern of collectively felt or experienced transgressions displayed by techno events, which are comparable with proto-religious salvation paths through rituals, especially ritual dancing.[68] This pattern forms the boundaries of the general symbolic frame of the Technoscene. It depicts the intersubjectively shared horizon of scene practices.

---

68 Durkheim, *Les formes elementaires de la vie religieuse*; Weber, *Economy and Society: An Outline of Interpretive Sociology*.

The second result relates to the time-space arrangement that generates the scene-typical local atmosphere, the felt meaning of the place. Here we may cite the theories of Foucault and Goffman. Evidence was found for Foucault's assumption of certain strategies of controlling the spatial arrangement of places in order to affect modes of the self. The spatial arrangement of techno events – consisting of a restriction of opportunities for mutual perception and of resonance on auditory, visual, and tactile channels – produces certain modes of encounter between forms of being oneself in public. It increases the possibility of processes experienced as individual conversion and as collective transgression.

The third result applies to the social rules or the code regulating the encounters possible in techno scene. Two features were emphasised by the interpretative reconstruction of techno insider descriptions:

a. The codings that evidence the scope of bodily interactions possible at techno events. These provide the normative background on which extraordinary activity and experience can take place.
b. The regulative scheme of a positive valued virtuality – erotic playfulness – that grounds the vision of infiniteness, especially of infinite excitement.

These results bear out the three main theses formulated in section 2.

a. In the case of the techno youth culture, the emergence of a extraordinary scene practice is coupled with processes symbolized as proto-religious experiences by the insiders.
b. The time-spatio arrangement of the places of the techno scene are of great importance in the creation of scene boundaries and in regulating the inclusion/exclusion problem.
c. Bodily interaction codes fit the horizon of youth as a life phase. This is visible in the experimental or virtual character of the norms regulating 'erotic playfulness'.

However, these general results are also somewhat unsatisfactory, given that they could have been expected in light of other studies which have shown similar processes and forms of symbolic structuring in distinctive youth, music and dance cultures. As mentioned in section 2, a series of investigations have identified strategies of territorial delimitation in order to establish the scene's hegemony on places: most notably Whyte's classic *Street Corner Society*,[69] but also recent studies on youth cultures, for example

---

69 William Foote Whyte, 'The Problem of Cornerville' in *Street Corner Society* (Chicago: University of Chicago Press, 1943).

'hooliganism',[70] the British music club scene,[71] or the 'Indie Music Gig'.[72] Moreover, the articulation of ecstatic affection has been analysed in the case of various popular music and/or dance scenes: jazz musicians,[73] juvenile rock bands,[74] even the classical *'Wagner-Szene'*.[75]

One must therefore enquire as to the specificity of techno as a contemporary youth and dance scene, especially with regard to its impact on social and cultural change. Combining the youth aspect with the topic of generational contexts and units yields more socio-analytical precision. The collective practice and experience of transgression should be interpreted as a 'rite of passage' initiated and established in and by the participants of the techno youth scene. Again from the general point of view, this could be expected in modern youth cultures.

When reconstructing techno youth as a generational unit in Karl Mannheim's sense,[76] two aspects must be explained: the distinction between techno and the youth cultures of former generations, and its difference from other contemporary styles of adolescent scenes.

The discussion conducted in the last section emphasised that the symbolic specificities of the techno scene analysed should be interpreted as a general unity. However, these reflections on the results of the interviews with scene-insiders should be supplemented by further research, especially as regards the two dimensions that delimit techno youth as a generational unit. Three lines of differentation and delimitation should be examined with greater precision:

a. marking out the techno scene from distinctive youth scenes and movements, from a historical as well as contemporary perspective. Investigation of simultaneously existing scenes appears to be less methodologically problematic, because for the older generations it is

---

70 Bohnsack, Ralf, et al., *Die Suche nach Gemeinschaft und die Gewalt der Gruppe* (Opladen: Leske & Budrich, 1996).
71 Sarah Thornton, *Club Cultures. Music, Media and Subcultural Capital* (Cambridge: Polity Press, 1995).
72 Wendy Fonarow, 'The Spatial Dynamics of Indie Music Gig' in Ken Gelder and Sarah Thornton (eds.), *The Subcultures Reader* (London: Routledge, 1997), pp. 360-69.
73 Howard Becker, 'The Culture of A Deviant Group: The Dance Musician' in *Outsiders* (Chicago: The Free Press, 1963).
74 Winfried Gebhardt, 'Techno-Kult und Wagner-Szene' in Hermann von Artmaier, Ronald Hitzler, Franz Huber, and Michaela Pfadenhauer (eds.), *Techno zwischen Lokalkolorit und Universalstruktur* (München: Stadtjugendamt, 1997), pp. 17-22.
75 Burkard Schäffer, *Die Band* (Opladen: Leske & Budrich, 1996).
76 Karl Mannheim, 'Das Problem der Generationen', *Kölner Zeitschrift für Soziologie 7*, 1928, pp. 157-85, 309-30.

difficult to augment data directly comparable concerning the specific age phase. Moreover, when analysing the techno scene as a generational unit, one must more precisely measure differentiation in age, strata, educational level, and social milieu of origin by means of statistically representative samples.
b. the life-courses of techno participants must be analysed in more detail, because we expect the person to be only temporarily included in the scene. One must therefore ask about the 'stations' before and after joining the scene, as well as the timing of the scene-entry within the life-cycle. For this purpose re-interviews would be useful.
c. In the same way, the scene may change in the composition of its personnel during its history: the aging of the scene, so to speak. This may modify the specific style of techno as well as leading to the emergence of scene sub-differentiations.

Besides the suggestions for further research, the results set out here can be taken as a first exploration of the validation criteria used in the Techno scene to symbolize collective and individual identities by the scene-specific practices.

Having made this claim, I conclude that the vocabulary used by the participants to describe their activities is governed by a coherent set of rules on using symbols which validate the rave as a meaningful and extraordinary practice. The forces driving this stream of collective activities were described earlier:

(i) the ideal of transgression; (ii) the imagination of an infinitely ongoing activity; (iii) erotically experienced and/or felt playfulness, and (iv) avoidance of concrete goal attainment, which amounts to rejection of the definition of an end. Hence the corresponding rule would be the pleasure of exciting games-playing and the mounting desire to continue endlessly, but this can only be achieved by abjuring the attainment of concrete goals. The crucial point is that this practice consists of a process of self-referential and self-satisfying symbolization: in short, successful expressivity. The leitmotif of the techno scene is the idea(l) of a process of bodily expressions of the collective and individual identities of rave participants as a form of ritual dancing. The reproduction of moments of successful self-expression (in both dimensions) is all that matters: being attracted by the successful self-expression of others, willingness to be persuaded by one's own successful self-expression, and being persuaded by the atmosphere of 'this whole, this prickly feeling that was hovering there' (from the interview with

Ariane). But this form of symbolic practice is more than merely the fun-orientation of a non-politically apparent generational unit. We can interpret it as a neo-sceptical habitus of youth for which the universal claims of discursive explicitness, of reflective argumentation, and definite goals of individual and collective developments have been suspended. That what counts should be controllable; especially, it should be perceptible from the standpoint of participation in the process of expression, and of experiencing the expressions of others, and of the process itself.

7 New religious phenomena in Eastern Europe

TADEUSZ DOKTÓR

Introduction

Since the end of the 1980s the countries of Eastern Europe have been confronted by a new phenomenon: the appearance and growth of new religious and para-religious movements (NRMs). With the fall of the communist regime and its official atheist ideology, a promising new market has opened up in Eastern Europe for the missionary activity of religious groups seeking to fill the ideological gap left by communism. When the restrictions on religious activity were removed in a situation where large segments of the population remained unchurched, new religious movements began to compete with traditional churches. Some of these movements had already been present before the fall of the Berlin Wall, but they were usually subject to various forms of restriction, ranging from a refusal to legalize their activities (in most of the Eastern European countries) to imprisonment of their members (as in former USSR).

Although the traditional churches were affected to various degrees by this repression, they now occupy a better strategic position in the 'battle' for souls: they are more deeply rooted in the culture of the Eastern European nations, sometimes even in the sense of national identity; they possess greater human, material and institutional resources for their operations; and they are closer to the sources of political power. Their attempts to regain their former positions and the property confiscated by the communist state, as well as to influence the course of education, are usually more successful than those of their non-traditional rivals.

Partly for these reasons, the traditional churches are often perceived as too closely involved in politics, and as engaged in more secular than spiritual pursuits. Their influential new position is sometimes interpreted as a replacement of the old communist ideology with the new Christian one, likewise supported by the state. As a result, instead of the expected growth in the indicators of traditional church religiosity, we find that they continue to decline.

Theories explaining religious change and the growth of NRMs are formulated and tested mainly on empirical evidence from Western and Third World countries, with almost no reference to Eastern Europe. This is also true the theory proposed by Stark and Bainbridge,[1] which is often cited as an example of an emerging economic paradigm in the study of religion. Stark and Bainbridge's main thesis – that new religious movements in the form of sects and cults grow from the ruins of the traditional churches – has been tested with positive results on a wide range of data, mainly from the USA and Western Europe.[2] But the real challenge against the thesis is raised by Eastern Europe, which is undergoing radical socio-cultural transformation (which is one of the factors that contribute to the growth of NRMs, according to Stark and Bainbridge) while generally displaying low levels of religious participation (with the exception of Poland). The combination of these various factors should instead lead to the dynamic growth of NRMs. At the present moment, attempts to test this theory on the materials from the region would be premature, but we may look at the available data in the light of this theory, as a preliminary step towards more rigorous empirical tests in the future.

However, account should be taken of the fact that the secularization of Eastern Europe was not a 'natural' process brought about by the structural differentiation of the socio-cultural system. At least in part it was caused by the deliberate attempts of the communist state to restrict religious activities of all kinds. After atheism was renounced as the official ideology (in all the Eastern European countries), and after the state withdrew from regulation of religious market (to different degrees in different countries), possibilities for growth opened up for all kinds of religious organizations, but also for the growth of irreligiosity.

Because of this different pattern of religious evolution, its further course may also differ from that observed in other countries. It is difficult to predict at this stage what will fill the gap created by the disappearance of communist ideology: traditional or alternative forms of religiosity, or perhaps irreligion. On the basis of Stark and Bainbridge's theory, we can expect that future developments will be related to existing level of church religiosity and to the degree of state control of the religious market. From their thesis that sects and cults are reactions to a different degree of erosion of traditional churches, we

---

1   Rodney Stark, and William S. Bainbridge, *A Theory of Religion* (New York and Bern: Lang, 1987).
2   Rodney Stark, 'Europe's Receptivity to New Religious Movements: Round Two', *Journal for the Scientific Study of Religion 32 (4)*, 1993, pp. 389-97.

can conclude that in countries with similarly low levels of religious participation but with a high level of state control of the religious market (as in former East Germany and the Czech Republic), there will be a further decline in church religiosity accompanied by the growth of cults or cult-like phenomena (New Age-type beliefs and practices). In countries with less state control of the religious market (as in Russia at present) we may expect religiosity of the church, sect and cult type to grow. In countries with a high level of church religiosity and no state regulation of the religious market, we can expect a slight decline in church religiosity and the growth of sects and sect-like movements within the dominant religious tradition.

These changes manifest themselves differently in different segments of the population. The growth of alternative forms of religiosity are more visible among those who are the most sensitive to religious change. Younger, better educated and urban segments of the population are among those most receptive to both secularization and religious renewal, especially in its alternative forms.

1. Church religiosity

On average, church membership in the Western world is higher than in Eastern Europe (with the exception of Poland). In the countries covered by the European Values Survey in 1990 (Czechia, Bulgaria, East Germany, Hungary and Slovakia), the proportion of the unchurched population was 24.1 percent, compared to the 32.8 percent of the Western countries examined by the same study). Eastern Europe is, however, highly differentiated in this respect. The percentage of the unchurched population varies from 3.7 in Poland to over 60 in East Germany, the Czech Republic and Bulgaria.[3] According to census data (in those countries where questions were asked about religious participation), the percentages of the unchurched were usually lower, but still relatively high. In the Czech Republic, for example, the census of 1991 revealed that 40 percent of respondents did not belong to a church, while 16.2 percent did not answer the question.

Other religious indicators, like belief in God and church attendance, are usually lower. But these too are significantly differentiated among the Eastern European countries.

---

3   Peter Ester, Loek Halman and Ruud De Moor (eds), *The Individualizing Society* (Tilburg: Tilburg University Press, 1994).

Table 7.1: Belief in God and weekly church attendance in Eastern and Western countries

Country	Believes in God	Attends church every week
	%	%
Czechia	31.4	8.9
East Germany	32.2	8.8
Hungary	57.6	13.7
Latvia	20.3	4.6
Lithuania	50.1	15.7
Poland	94.5	65.3
Slovakia	63.7	32.7
Slovenia	55.0	22.8
Average	**50.6**	**21.6**
Austria	76.9	24.7
Belgium	63.3	22.9
France	57.1	10.2
Great Britain	70.9	13.0
West Germany	63.5	18.6
Netherlands	60.9	20.7
Ireland	96.0	80.8
Usa	92.9	43.4
Average	**72.7**	**29.3**

Source: Paul M. Zulehner and Hans Denz, *Wie Europa lebt und glaubt. Europeische Wertstudie* (Dusseldorf: Patmos Verlag, 1993).

These data, however, include only the more western part of Eastern Europe – often called 'Central-Eastern' – which is socially and culturally different from Russia, Belarus and Ukraine. As can be seen from the results of the New Democracies Barometer survey conducted at the end of 1992 and the beginning of 1993, the level of church religiosity in these countries is even lower.

Table 7.2: Church attendance in Eastern Europe (answers to the question 'How often do you attend church?')

Country	Once a week	Once a month	Several times a year	Less than several	Never
Poland	54	18	12	12	4
Slovakia	35	12	12	26	15
Romania	16	14	24	36	10
Croatia	15	12	26	25	21
Slovenia	13	15	25	18	29
Czech R.	12	8	13	31	37
Hungary	11	7	17	31	35
Ukraine	5	10	24	34	26
Bulgaria	5	6	23	29	37
Bielarus	3	7	19	36	35

Source: Richard Rose and Charles Haerpfer, *Adapting to Transformation in Eastern Europe: New Democracies Barometer-II* (Centre for the Study of Public Policy, University of Strathclyde, 1993).

Significant differences between the East and West have also been revealed by another comparative study (ISSP91), which covered five Eastern European countries: East Germany, Hungary, Poland, Russia and Slovenia.

Table 7.3: Beliefs in God in Eastern Europe and in the Western world among younger and older segments of the population

	East		West	
Age	18-29	30<	18-29	30<
I don't believe in God now and I never have	42.2	32.8	16.5	9.3
I don't believe in God now, but I used to	8.1	11.7	13.5	12.6
I believe now, but I didn't use to	14.3	8.3	7.6	5.9
I believe in God and I always have	35.4	47.2	62.4	72.2
N	1725	5518	3195	10875

Source: Cumulative data set, *Zentralarchiv für Empirische Sozialforschung an der Universität zu Köln*, ISSP 1991.

The results of this study, which confirm the low level of religiosity in Eastern Europe, highlight another significant phenomenon: the greater proportion of people who are more religious at present than they were in the past. It seems that the secularization trend is beginning to change direction, especially among young people, in which category 14.3 percent of respondents stated that they now believed in God but did not in the past. This trend is most evident among young Russians, 29.3 percent of whom affirmed this position compared with the 3.4 percent of those who had lost their faith in God. This phenomenon does not emerge in the other Eastern European countries, where the proportion is more or less similar, or even reversed. For example, in former East Germany the proportion was 5 percent of new believers to 13.4 percent of those who had lost their former faith, which indicates that the process of enforced secularization distinctive of former decades persists in the new circumstances as a more 'natural' phenomenon.

2. Alternative religiosity

The largest proportion of young Russians who believe in God but did not do so in the past are now members of the Orthodox Church (58.3 percent), although 39.4 percent are not affiliated to any church. These subjects belong to the area of non-institutional and diffused religiosity indicated by the percentage of Russians describing themselves as 'Christians in general' who are neither Russian Orthodox nor belong to any other confession. Their numbers have grown significantly in recent years: 22 percent in 1990; 47 percent in 1991; and 55 percent in 1992.[4]

This disaffection with the dominant church may be due to conservatism in political matters and the information published in December 1991 on the extent of the collaboration between the Orthodox clergy and the KGB. Between 1990 and 1992, the initially high social support for the idea that the Orthodox Church helped to promote the cause of democracy and human rights fell from 65 percent to 25 percent.[5] Therefore, although the percentage of the Orthodox Church's membership is increasing, minority religious groups like the Roman Catholics or Pentecostals are growing at a significantly more rapid rate.

Another reason for the popularity of non-church invisible religion are its links with science or para-science. Seven decades of domination by the so-

---

4 Sergei Filatov, *On Paradoxes of the Post-Communist Russian Orthodox Church. Religions sans Frontiers?* Atti della Conferenza internazionale promossa dall'Università degli Studi di Roma 'La Sapienza 12-16 luglio 1993', 1994, pp. 117-25.
5 Ibid.

called 'scientific world-view' and attacks on religion have resulted in a significant strengthening of the social respectability of scientific (or para-scientific) ideologies in all the post-communist countries. However, the phenomenon is perhaps most pronounced in Russia.

At the beginning of the 1990s (in 1990 and 1992), acceptance of para-scientific or para-religious beliefs was generally higher than the acceptance of belief in God, and growing. The percentage of Russians who believed in telepathy had grown from 58 percent to 66 percent; in UFOs from 39 percent to 46 percent; in astrology from 49 percent to 56 percent; in reincarnation from 8 percent to 11 percent; in God from 29 percent to 40 percent.[6] The socio-demographic correlates of both types of belief were, however, quite different.

Para-scientific beliefs were more frequently expressed by the better-educated (for example, 39 percent of respondents with primary educations believed in telepathy, compared with 74 percent of those with higher educations) and younger subjects (67 percent of those aged under 30 believed in telepathy, compared with 44 percent aged over 60). The socio-demographic characteristics of those who believed in God displayed the reverse pattern (61 percent with primary educations and 20 percent with higher educations; 20 percent of males and 25 percent of females aged under 30, and 30 percent of males and 68 percent of females aged over 60).[7]

Not surprisingly, therefore, movements which stress the para-scientific character of their doctrines (like theosophy and its offshoots and other para-scientific and para-religious movements) are relatively strong. They have grown not only from the ruins of the churches but also from those of the para-scientific doctrines of marxism and leninism. Some of their critics, notably Sergei Kapica, consider the growing popularity of para-scientific and occult beliefs as resulting from a pseudo-scientific metamorphosis of the reasoning inherent in communist doctrine, and they stress the ideological, institutional and sometimes personal elements in their continuity.

Para-religious and para-scientific beliefs are relatively widespread in the other post-communist countries as well. Polish university students surveyed at the end of the 1980s out-distanced their Western counterparts in their acceptance of occult and para-scientific beliefs, and this tendency seem to have continued into the 1990s, while the indicators of traditional religiosity

---

6   Ludmila Vorontsova, Sergei Filatov, 'The Changing Pattern of Religious Belief: Perestroika and Beyond', *Religion, State and Society* 22(1), 1994, pp. 89-96.
7   Leonid Byzow, Sergei Filatov, 'Religija i politika w obszczestwiennom soznanii sowietskowo sojuza', Sergei Filatov, Dimitri Furman (eds.), *Religija i demokracja*, (Moskwa: Kultura, 1993).

have slightly declined.[8] Among Hungarians aged between 17 and 18 years old, 35.5 percent believe in reincarnation, 49.6 percent in telepathy, 43.8 percent in UFOs, and 45 percent in God.[9]

Comparative data from ISSP91 permit comparisons only among those countries in which the questions concerning parallel beliefs have been asked (in the case of Eastern European countries, only East Germany and Slovenia).

Table 7.4: Percentage of acceptance (definitely true and probably true) of statements concerning parallel beliefs in Eastern and Western countries among younger and older segments of the population

	East		West	
Age	18-29	30<	18-29	30<
Fortune tellers can foresee the future	53.6	38.3	38.8	28.8
Good luck charms do bring good luck	46.6	31.4	36.3	23.1
Horoscopes affect the course of the future	39.8	31.8	32.2	27.9
N	675	2365	1556	4656

Source: Cumulative data set, *Zentralarchiv für Empirische Sozialforschung an der Universität zu Köln*, ISSP 1991.

The results of these comparisons indicate that parallel beliefs may be more popular in Eastern European countries than in the West. The differences seem to be even more significant among young people. Although these data are not definitive, they suggest that the eastern part of Europe may be fertile ground for new religious movements, which often draw on a broad spectrum of beliefs of this kind.

The data concerning NRMs in this part of Europe are, however, even more scarce than those from the survey quoted earlier. In particular, the memberships of NRMs are difficult to estimate because of the lack of relevant statistical data (for example from censuses). As a consequence, the existing

---

8   Tadeus Doktór, 'Mysticism, World View and Personality among Students in Poland in 1987 and 1992', in Georg Holm, Karl Bjorkwist (eds.), *World Views in Modern Society: Empirical Studies on the Relationship between World View, Culture, Personality and Upringing* (Turku: Abo Akademi University, 1996), pp. 47-57.
9   Miklos Tomka, 'Religionsverlust bei der Jugend in Ungarn - Langzeitwirkungen des Kommunismus', in Ulrich Nembach (ed.), *Jugend - 2000 Jahre nach Jesus. Jugend und Religion in Europa II*: Bericht vom 2. internationalen Gottinger religionssoziologischen Symposion (Frankfurt a.M.: Peter Lang, 1996), pp. 261-74.

literature on the subject rarely takes this phenomenon into consideration, given the lack of data and of systematically conducted research in the Eastern European countries, where the social sciences of religion have been little present in the universities until the present moment.

Relatively precise quantitative data on sects (within the dominant religious tradition) and cults (outside the dominant religious tradition) are available only in some cases, but they are usually provided by the movements themselves and should consequently be treated with caution. For example, despite its high visibility in the media, the widely publicized group known as 'The Family' reports that it has only around 115 full-time adult members in the region. The mail ministry of the movement (personally answered letters) is in regular contact with 5,500 persons in Russia, 400 in Poland, 400 in Romania, 150 in Bulgaria, 100 in the Czech Republic, 25 in Hungary, 20 in Yugoslavia, and 10 in Albania. These figures are not directly related to the amount of translated literature, which in comparison to the above numbers may be more indicative of the effectiveness of the movement's missionary efforts. Some 515 different (but usually short) pieces of literature have been translated into Polish, 242 into Serbo-Croatian, 165 into Russian, 126 into Czech, with lesser amounts into other Eastern European languages.[10]

The data on the amount of translated literature seemingly reflect the history of this movement in Eastern Europe, with its beginnings in Poland in the early 1980s, while the number of mail-ministry contacts reflects the more current priorities of the movement.

Certainly, Russia as a great and supposedly empty market has become the main target-country for proselytization – the 'promised land' for a wide variety of religious organizations, including established churches, sects, cults and New Age groups. In the other Eastern European countries, these organizations have usually appeared earlier (some of them already in the 1970s), although their rates of growth have diminished, and many internationally-operating movements have shifted their human and material resources to Russia, where the possibilities for growth are much greater. In Poland, one of the major factors contributing to the growth of non-traditional religious groups has been the relative openness of its borders to ideas and people connected with non-traditional forms of religion. Indeed, Poland was perhaps the most open country in the Eastern bloc, and these movements have have the longest tradition in that country, with the possible exception of

---

10 J. Gordon Melton, 'The emergence of New Religions in Eastern Europe since 1989', paper presented at the RENNORD 94 Conference on New Religions and New Religiosity held at the University of Copenhagen August 22-5, 1994.

Buddhism in Hungary. Numerous Polish members of international NRMs are currently engaged in missionary activity in Russia, while the growth of their movements in Poland has now reached the plateau phase; or, as in the case of 'The Family', they have significantly declined, partly as a result of their failure to obtain official recognition. Another significant reason may be the proximity of the larger and less crowded religious market in Russia, which seems more attractive. Other movements also report that they have larger numbers of members in Russia. One of them is ISKCON, which also registers the largest membership in Russia, although it is still relatively stronger in Poland than in many Western countries.

Table 7.5: Members of ISKCON in Eastern Europe and the former Soviet Union in 1995

Country	Members living	
	in ashrams	outside ashrams
Armenia	20	•
Azerbaijan	30	150-200
Belarus	100	250
Bosnia	10	100
Bulgaria	40	100
Croatia	165	150-200
Czech Republic	100	300
Estonia	11	60
Georgia	25	50-100
Hungary	150	700
Latvia	50	300
Lithuania	100	500
Macedonia	12	50
Moldova	15-20	50
Poland	300	1000-5000
Romania	11	30
Russia	1500	10000-40000
Serbia	100	500-1000
Slovakia	3	10
Slovenia	60	400
Ukraine	350	700
Uzbekistan	30	30

Source: Paul Claesson (1995), 'ISKCON in the Eastern Europe and FSU', paper presented at the conference *New Religious Phenomena*, Kraków Instytut Religioznawstwa UJ, 16-18 XII, 1995.

The ratios of ashram ISKCON members to the total population differ among countries (about ten ISKCON members per one million population on average) but in a way which neither confirms nor falsifies the predictions of Stark and Bainbridge's theory. They are lower in Bulgaria, Romania, Slovakia, and higher in Croatia and Hungary, a finding which seems to reflect factors other than the level of traditional religiosity and the degree of state regulation of religious market. The most detailed data, which also include annual rates of growth, are published annually by the Jehovah's Witnesses in the first issues of their journal *The Watchtower*. Their reports on membership are rather conservative and include only the most devout members. Consequently, the proportions are usually lower than the data from censuses.[11] The Jehovah's Witnesses have been active in Eastern Europe for several decades, but it is only in the last ten years that their numbers have significantly grown in the region. Although the data for the years 1993 and 1996 show high rates of growth in percentages (greater than in Western Europe, where they never exceed 5 per cent), the absolute numbers of committed followers are usually much smaller than in Western Europe.

Table 7.6: Number of Jehovah's Witnessess in 1993 and in 1996 and the percentage growth in comparison with the previous year

Country	Number of Jehovah's Witnessess		Percentage growth	
	1993	1996	1993	1996
Albania	164	759	244	52
Bulgaria	413	710	61	19
Czech R.	15713	16209	6	0
Estonia		2947		18
Hungary	14347	17342	11	9
Moldova		12565		23
Latvia		1157		32
Lithuania	804	1770	•	29
Poland	113551	122982	5	2
Romania	28285	34368	15	6
Russia		61843		31
Slovakia	11100	12231	4	3
Slovenia	1599	1740	4	3
Other countries of the former Soviet Union		86973		29

Source: *The Watchtower* (1994, 1997).

---

11   Rodney Stark, Laurence R. Iannaccone, 'Why the Jehovah's Witnesses Grow so Rapidly: A Theoretical Application', *Journal of Contemporary Religion* 2, 1997, pp. 133-57.

After the initial high rates of growth at the beginning of the 1990s, one notes a slowdown in the second half of the decade, especially in the countries with the highest proportion of citizens to Witnesses. In Poland in 1995, there were 311 citizens for each Witness (the highest proportion in the region), whereas in Russia there were 2217 (one of the lowest). Again, this does not provide decisive confirmation of Stark and Bainbridge's theory, but the data on the percentages of growth seem to match its predictions more closely: they are usually higher in countries with higher percentages of the unchurched or less church-attending population.

The data on the majority of non-traditional religious groups in Eastern Europe would probably be similar: high percentage rates of growth not always reflected in absolute numbers. These groups are growing substantially, but many of them are doing so from zero or nearly zero. This feature is most evident in Russia, where the figures are most impressive. Some of the imported movements, moreover, have been present only in Russia and not in other Eastern European countries. Sometimes the number of followers is higher than in the mother country, this being the case of Aum Shinrikyo, for instance, whose followers have been estimated at 54,000 compared with around 30,000 in Japan.[12]

Although NRMs start their activity from the more difficult position resulting from their lack of an institutional structure in the Eastern European countries, some of them can count on support from their international organizations. The operations of the latter can be compared to those of the multinational companies now entering the region's promising market with their material and human resources. This, however, applies only to imported movements which operate internationally.

The indigenous movements find themselves in a more difficult situation because they are usually only able to rely on their own resources, although they can exploit their better knowledge of demand in the local market. One of their resources may be the existing ideological tradition, on which they can base their own unique product. This feature is perhaps most pronounced in neo-pagan movements which stress their roots in pre-Christian religions reconstructed from scattered remnants in historical and ethnographic materials. Usually, however, this consists more in creation than reconstruction, given the scarcity of sources on the old Slavic religions. Beliefs and rituals connected with the ancient Slavonic and Baltic deities are interpreted as the nation's only true religion, extinguished in the past by

---

12 Goulnara Baltanova, 'Totalitarian Sects and Youth in Modern Russia', in Nembach (ed.), *Jugend - 2000 Jahre nach Jesus. Jugend und Religon in Europa II*, pp. 221-6.

enforced Christianization, a foreign element not suited to the national character. One may cite the Ukrainian Runvira, Ladovira, the Order of the Sun God and the cult of Yahna,[13] Lituanian Romuva and Latvian Dievturiba[14] as the most evident examples of movements of this kind, which seem to develop in countries in which the question of national identity is perceived as important, and as threatened by neighbouring countries. In these countries traditional religion, for different reasons, is not as closely related to national identity as it is in Poland and Russia.

The national element is also evident in movements which emphasise the very special and universal mission of a particular nation, group of nations or a race, the latter not usually understood in the biological sense. Often drawing their inspiration from theosophical and post-theosophical sources, these movements are perhaps most common in Russia. They comprise elements of nineteenth-century Russian messianism and a variety of post-theosophical beliefs, including the anthroposophical assertion of Russia's special cultural mission in the future. In other post-Soviet republics, movements based on different forms of this tradition are also relatively popular, although not to the same extent as in Russia itself. Russia, indeed, is the mother country of Helena Blavatsky, the founder of the theosophical movement, and of Nikolai and Helena Roerich, the founders of the post-theosophical Agni Yoga movement. One of the recently-founded movements which also draws on the theosophical tradition is the White Brotherhood, which originated in Ukraine but also operates in Russia and Bielorussia.[15] Other movements bearing the same name (related to the theosophical tradition) were founded in Bulgaria in the 1920s. Some theosophical ideas are embraced by Antrovis, a movement of Polish origin which combines elements of national messianism with beliefs in UFOs. The theosophical movement also seems to be reviving in Russia, while the anthroposophical movement is active in all the other countries in the region (the former president of Georgia, Zviad Gamsahurdia, was a member).

In countries with significant percentages of Roman Catholics – Poland especially – the largest proportion of NRMs consists of renewal movements within the church. One of the most dynamically growing new Catholic religious movements is the Charismatic Renewal Movement, which appeared

---

13 Sergei Kapranov, 'The Native Ukrainian Religions in the Context of Worldwide Pagan Revival Movements', paper presented at the conference 'National And Religious Self Identification', Instytut Europy Srodkowo-Wschodniej, Lublin 19-21.10, 1993.
14 Michael York, 'Pan-Baltic Identity and Religio-Cultural Expression in Contemporary Lithuania', paper presented at the conference 'New Religions And The New Europe', London 25-28 March, 1993.
15 Anatolyi Skachov, *The Great White Brotherhood. Update and Dialog 1*, 1993, pp. 16-7.

in Poland in the late 1970s: although its permanent members are estimated at around 30,000, far more participants gather at its congresses: 15,000 in 1986, 100,000 in 1993, 150,000 in 1995, 200,000 in 1996.

The development of intra-church Catholic movements has been one of the most significant factors responsible for the change in the Polish religious scenery during recent years. Some spectacular conversions of popular journalists and rock musicians have gain much publicity in the media. The growing number of movements and their members (now amounting to more than one million) therefore constitutes, both quantitatively and qualitatively, perhaps the most effective alternative to the secularization trend mentioned earlier. These 'small churches' within 'the big church' create the possibility of pluralism within the Catholic Church; pluralism which, according to the market theory of religion, may be conducive to better fulfilment of individual religious needs and to stronger commitment by its members. They are not negatively stigmatized like some sects and cults; instead, they are to some extent their endogenous equivalent, which contributes to better resources allocation within the Church. According to some estimates, a large proportion (about 60 percent) of priestly vocations arise from these movements. They have been supported by Pope John Paul II, who, in a letter to the participants of the Congress of the Catholic Movements in 1994, stressed their significant role in religious renewal, comparing them to a 'spring in the Church'. This may have changed the reservations of some bishops as regards these movements.

Some of the Catholic communities, however, have grown too radical to remain within the Roman Catholic Church, as a result either of their own decisions or those of the local bishop. After severing their ties with the institutional church, these communities often register as separate religious bodies and define themselves within the Protestant tradition.

3. Characteristics of members

One usually finds an over-representation of younger, urban, better educated males, and persons from non-religious or less religious family backgrounds, in the memberships of NRMs. This is also typical of Eastern Europe.

These various features may be viewed as a prerequisite for religious experimentation, although to different degrees in different kinds of movement.

In the light of Stark and Bainbridge's economic theory of religion, the over-representation of young people in NRMs can be interpreted as a greater propensity to religious experimentation in this specific life-period, during which some forms of social control in the religious sphere are significantly weakened. Youth is a transitory phase in which social bonds with the primary family slacken and new family ties have not yet been formed (looser 'attachments' in terms of Stark and Bainbridge theory). Forms of social control related to age and family status therefore significantly diminish in this period of life (especially in the case of young men), thereby creating more space for experimentation with alternative lifestyles in new religious movements. The proportion of youth is the highest among oriental NRMs, especially in ISKCON, but it is also significant in other movements. Participants are usually in their twenties and thirties, and sometimes, as in the Catholic 'Oases' of Poland, the majority of members are in their teens. To a lesser extent the feature is also present in mainstream and marginal Protestant groups. Some movements founded before the Second World War (as neo-pagan and theosophical movements), and now re-starting their activities after a long period of suspension, have larger proportions of two age categories – older members (about sixty) and younger (in their twenties or thirties) – with almost no middle-aged members.

Although this over-recruitment of youth may bring spectacular successes in the short run, it is one of the most controversial issues of public debate, especially as regards those movements in which young recruits radically change their lifestyles, breaking contacts with their families and interrupting their educational careers. The most negative social – and sometimes also governmental – reaction is therefore usually directed against these particular movements.

The other precondition for participation is an ability to understand and evaluate the substantial amount of new culture present in non-traditional NRMs. As in the case of the other forms of cultural innovation, the better-educated are more receptive to new religious ideas and practices: for instance, more than half the members of Zen groups in Poland have academic educations. The opposite pattern is displayed by movements which do not make a radical break with the dominant religious tradition and whose doctrines are therefore easier to comprehend, especially when they are presented in simple and standardized terms, a case in point being the Jehovah's Witnesses, only 2 percent of whose members have academic educations (compared to 8 percent of the general population).

Some movements also have greater proportions of male members. In the case of oriental movements in Moscow, for example, the proportions are between 2:3 and 3:4.[16] Some over-representation of the male gender can also be observed in Poland, but only in the case of movements which demand higher levels of commitment.

We may expect movements outside the dominant religious tradition to be also more appealing to individuals who have not found satisfactory answers in traditional beliefs. A large proportion of the members of oriental NRMs have non-religious family backgrounds, which confirms Stark and Bainbridge's[17] thesis that NRMs recruit mostly non-religious or only nominally religious individuals, and therefore that the activity of these movements to some extent restricts the secularization process.

Another significant feature connected with family background is the relatively high rate of paternal absence among members of NRMs, especially those with male leaderships. The average number of years of the father's absence in the first twenty years of life was 3.0 among members of Oases, 1.5 among members of Charismatic Renewal, 2.9 among members of Zen Chogye, 1.5 among Brahma Kumaris, 2.5 among practitioners of Rebirthing, and 3.4 among advanced TM meditators, compared with 1.5 in the control group.[18] Paternal absence seems to be a factor which predisposes people to seek a father-figure in the male spiritual leader of the movement (in the case of movements with female leaders, like the Brahma Kumaris, this factor does not seem to be influential).

The psychological profile of NRM participants does not justify the popular opinion that the members of these movements are characterized by worse mental health indicators than their peers. On the contrary, the results of personality tests are more positive in the case of members of NRMs than among subjects in the control group (the most pronounced differences are usually observed in the meaning of life).[19]

4. Reactions to NRMs

At the begining of the 1990s the NRMs in Eastern Europe began to be perceived as a 'sect problem'. Some harmful consequences of the activities of

---

16   Alexander Agadjanian, 'Les cultes orientaux et la nouvelle religiosite en Russie', *Revue d'etudes comparatives Est-Ouest 3-4*, 1993, pp. 155-71.
17   Stark and Bainbridge, *A Theory of Religion*.
18   Tadeus Doktór, 'New Religious Movements in Poland and Stark and Bainbridge's Theory of religion', *Temenos 29*, 1993, pp. 37-45.
19   Tadeus Doktór, 'Psychological Characteristics of Members of New Religious and Parareligious Movements', *Archiv fur Religionspsychologie*, Bd. XXI, 1994, pp. 232-8.

certain religious groups – like the recruitment of persons under the age of eighteen, who sometimes severed their family ties and terminated their educational careers – were generalized and given a great deal of publicity in the media. All the NRMs (including some mainstream and marginal Protestant groups) were lumped together in a single category of 'dangerous sects'. As a consequence, an emotionally laden and cognitively simplistic stereotype emerged which came to dominate media coverage of this phenomenon.

Additional support for construction of this negative stereotype has been provided by the activity of certain organizations which feel threatened by the activities of the NRMs. In Poland, as in other countries, two forms of organized opposition to NRMs can be distinguished: 'organicist' and 'individualistic'.[20] The former reaction is dominated by a concern to protect a unitary religious culture, which is often connected with the sense of national identity, while the latter emphasises a threat to individual freedom.

The 'organicist' reaction apparently predominates in Eastern Europe, and it is supported by the traditional churches and by political organizations for which a blend of national and religious elements is central to their ideologies, especially in mono-religious countries. Among the other Eastern European countries, Poland and Russia share several common characteristics as far as NRMs are concerned.

The traditional churches react to the presence of competing religious groups in similar ways. In both Poland and Russia religious homogeneity is relatively high, and religious and national identities are closely mixed together – although this situation has a longer tradition in Russia than in Poland, where it has existed only for some decades. The same applies to the degree of structural differentiation between Church and State. In Russia, the tradition of the Orthodox Church as the state religion is longer and more pronounced, and the Church is more effectively able to influence legislation on religion. In both countries, however, NRMs are often perceived as a threat to this organic religious and national unity, whereas in other Eastern European countries, especially those with higher levels of religious pluralism, it is usually the threat to individual freedom, rather than to the integrity of the nation, which is emphasised. Symptomatic in this regard are public statements by church leaders: Metropolitan John[21] declared that '"Patriots"

---

20   James A. Beckford, 'The "Cult Prob" in Five Countries: The Social Construction of Religious Controversy', in Eileen Barker (ed.), *New Religious Movements: A Perspective for Understanding Society* (New York: Edwin Mellen, 1984).
21   John Metropolitan, 'The Building of Statehood', *The Journal of Moscow Patriarchate*, 2, 1993, pp. 28-30.

who swear love for Mother Russia while rejecting orthodoxy love some other country they have invented for themselves. The "patriotic" press calling for Russian revival while advertising on its pages extrasensory and other "healers", astrologers, and sorcerers seemingly lack an elementary national instinct',[22] while John Paul II,[23] in his Westerplatte Sermon to Youth, compared the 'sects and other unions so alien to the culture, tradition and spirit of our nation' to alcoholism and drug addiction.

The most significant allies of the dominant churches in their campaign against non-traditional religions are the nationalistic political groups. In Russia this campaign sometimes takes the form of physical aggression, as in the case of the attack launched by nationalist extremists from 'Black Hundred' (*Chernaya Sotnya*) and Orthodox believers against the Protestant mission in Moscow in July 1994.[24] In Poland, it takes the more benign form of anti-cult activity by the Bureau for Information and Documentation for New Religious Movements organized by *Civitas Christiana* (formerly *Pax*), a nationalistic religious association which collaborated closely with the communist regime prior to 1989.

Political configurations, in particular when they wield greater political power, are able to influence the activities of the state agencies. In autumn 1995, the Polish Bureau for National Security, headed by a member of the Christian-National Union party, issued a report (based largely on 'church sources of information') which pointed to an invasion by sects as one of the greatest threats to national security. The report was positively received by representatives of the Church hierarchy, although later the Bureau, in a different political configuration, distanced itself from the document's findings, judging them too exaggerated. Similar reports containing questionable information have been issued by the Russian Ministry of Internal Affairs.[25]

The 'self-help' response to non-traditional religious groups stresses the harmful individual consequences of participation. These movements are interpreted as threatening the freedom and psychological well-being of the individual, while their members are described as brainwashed, hypnotized and manipulated by totalitarian groups whose primary aim is to identify and exacerbate latent psychopathology for the purpose of recruitment. The main

---

22   Ibid.
23   John Paul II, 'Westerplatte', *Tygodnik Powszechny,* 25, 1987, p. 11.
24   Vladimir Solodnikov, 'In Whose Name?', *Frontier* 2, 1995, pp. 12-4.
25   Anatolyi Kulikov, 'Inquiry of the Activities of Certain Foreign Religious Organizations Gathered from Materials of the MVD, FSB Ministry of Health, Ministry of Welfare and General Attorney's Office', Ministry of Internal Affairs of the Russian Federation, 1996.

social vehicles for this type of response are voluntary associations of 'victims' (ex-members and 'concerned parents'), often supported by psychiatrists and clinical psychologists. These associations frequently emerge in reaction to a particular crisis situation, as in the case of the White Brotherhood in Ukraine when the Poratunok organization was formed. Their development is, however, dependent on an adequate level of social self-organization. The tradition of voluntary associations has been largely eroded in post-communist societies, with the consequence that this particular form of response is not as strong as it is in the United States, for example, where it is the primary response. In Eastern Europe the voluntary associations usually cooperate more closely with the traditional churches, and they depend on anti-cult organizations in the West for their materials, personnel training and publications. They sometimes even mirror the names and activities of these Western organizations, as in the case of the Polish equivalent of the French *Les Associations de Defense de la Famille et de l'Individu* (which takes the same name in Polish).

In generally, however, the various forms taken by the 'psychologization' of the 'cult problem' in Eastern Europe are not as pronounced as they are in the West (particularly in the USA, where psychiatrists and clinical psychologists are more actively involved in anti-cult movements). Memories of the use of psychiatry as a tool of political repression in some Eastern European countries are probably still too vivid. In some cases, however, psychiatric (and parapsychological) interpretations are used in the 'organicist' frame of reference, as in the case of the White Brotherhood, which was depicted in the Ukrainian press as resulting from the psychological and parapsychological techniques used by Russian secret service agents to destabilize the situation in Ukraine. Because both types of response often appear together, 'psychopathological' arguments against sects are frequently used by the churches or their specialized agencies. They usually repeat interpretations from the Western popular anti-cult literature without reference to academic studies, which are almost entirely lacking in Eastern Europe. These interpretations often obscure the underlying sources of conflict, and they are functional to building a coalition against groups targeted in broader segments of society. Formulations using paramedical metaphors are most frequently used by the media and the representatives of the church, which makes conflicts more difficult to resolve.

The negative attitude of the traditional churches towards opening up 'the religious market' and the activity of secular anti-cult organizations often focuses on changing the legislation on religious minorities. The legal status of

NRMs in the Eastern European countries is now undergoing significant change. In all the countries of the former Soviet bloc, restrictions were imposed on the activities of religious organizations. A special governmental agency, the Ministry for Religious Affairs, modelled on the Soviet Union, controlled everything connected with religion, including NRMs. The strategies of control, however, differed from country to country. The most hostile attitudes towards alternative religion were evident in the Soviet Union: members of ISKCON, pentecostal groups and Jehovah's Witnesses were arrested and sentenced to long terms of imprisonment; their houses were searched and their property confiscated. In Poland or Czechoslovakia, by contrast, despite their lack of official registration, they were relatively free to conduct their activities (publishing, distributing their literature, and organizing public meetings).

At the end of the 1980s and the beginning of the 1990s, the law was liberalized in the majority of these countries (Czechoslovakia was the only exception). New legislation was introduced which more closely resembled America's than Western Europe's in respect to the degree to which the religious market was regulated. However, this new religious freedom did not last very long, partly because of the attitude of traditional churches, which grew anxious about the wave of new religious movements flooding into Eastern Europe. With the overthrow of a government formerly identified with atheistic communism and its repressive and restrictive measures against religion, the traditional churches have often attempted to fill the void by restoring their former positions of power and prestige. The new religions that have arisen from political and social transformation have often been seen as a threat to these aspirations.

The most visible form of this reaction are attempts to amend the liberal regulations of 1990 by the Russian Parliament backed by the Russian Orthodox Church. New regulations issued in April 1993 significantly restricted the activities of religious organizations with headquarters abroad (including the Roman Catholic Church). After much protest by religious groups, as well as by some politicians (including presidents Kohl and Clinton), this new law was suspended by Yeltsin in September 1993.[26]

---

26 Gerard Stricker, 'Religionsfreiheit in Gefahr? Zur Neuffassung des russisches Religionsgesetzes', *Evangelische Zentralstelle fur Weltanschauungsfragen* 2, 1994, pp. 33-46.

However, the political battle over this regulation was not over: it was again proposed in 1997, and again provoked a wave of protests inside and outside Russia.

Amendments to these regulations have been attempted in other countries as well, although they are not usually so drastic. In Poland, the number of members required for official registration of a movement has been changed from 15 to 100, despite some proposals to require as many as 100,000. Radical departures from internationally accepted standards of religious freedom are not expected in the countries intending to join the European Union in the future.

But the controversy surrounding the NRMs is far from over. Actively proselytizing non-traditional religions in Eastern Europe often enter into conflict with a number of groups and institutions. The succesful resolution of various controversies connected with the opening of the 'religious market', without imposing restrictions on religious freedom but by creating a system of negotiations among different interests groups, is one of the most serious tasks awaiting emerging democracy.

8 Alternative creeds among Russian youth
MIKHAIL F. CHERNYSH

Introduction

In the twentieth century few countries in the world can surpass Russia in the number and scale of social revolutions. Three of them – two at the beginning of the century, one at the end of it – attracted public attention throughout the world. However, there have been other revolutions in Russia, some of which came earlier and some later than the great social cataclysms. These were cultural revolutions, more obscure and less noticeable, but potentially more influential and prolonged in their effects than any of the political events mentioned. The first of these revolutions led to the demise of the pre-revolutionary Russian Orthodoxy that had largely governed the lives of the majority of the Russian population for at least one thousand years.

Its demise came abruptly with the enthronement of the atheistic communist regime, which consistently pursued a policy of repression against the Church and its adherents. The Russians were targeted by relentless anti-religious propaganda bolstered by repression and purges. Even as late as the 1970s and 1980s, when the Communists allegedly softened their attitude towards the Church, the open proclamation of religious feelings was punished by total exclusion from any political participation, or by forceful action to terminate the believer's professional career. Those who openly declared their religious feelings could expect to be rejected by college or university and denied entry to the political or scientific establishment. It was no coincidence that the Bible, essential to any Christian inventory, was not available to Russians, nor for that matter to the other ethnic groups living under the repressive regime. The Bible was printed by the Russian Orthodox Church in small quantities and distributed only among confirmed believers.

There is no doubt that this deliberate and consistent policy of eradicating all vestiges of religion, whatever the denomination or creed, had an indelible impact upon the consciousness of the Russians and the other ethnic groups living in Russia. There were, of course, strong-minded individuals who chose to withstand the pressure and resist secular temptations. However, they were not a mass phenomenon: at odds with the mainstream of society, they were frequently exiled or sent to prison for their stubborn allegiance to the creed. The secret police mounted operations to break into what they called closed sects – the Baptists, the Pentecostalists or the Old Believers.[1] Like the early Christians, the believers in the Russian provinces were forced to sacrifice their comforts for their right to practise their religion.

Apart from a restricted number of individuals who chose to 'render unto God what is God's', the majority of the population drifted away from religious education or ritual. The 'Way of Life' social survey conducted in the early 1980s[2] registered few church-goers: only 3 percent of respondents stated that they had occasionally attended church. An even smaller number (about 1 percent) claimed that they attended church service on a regular basis. The regular church-goers consisted for the most part of older people aged over 60 who did not have to sacrifice their careers or their children's futures by openly accepting religion. However, these figures should not be taken to imply that the society ruled over by the Communists felt no interest in religion. In the early 1990s the Institute of Sociology carried out a survey of school children aged between 7 and 14, and over 62 percent of them admitted that they regularly prayed to God, especially in times of personal crisis. The phenomenon of non-denominational belief thus revealed was no less impressive in other age groups. In contemporary Russia, seven out of ten adults claim that they believe in God. However, this belief is more instinctive than denominational: only 5 percent of Russian citizens regularly attend church services. There are still only a few Christians who possess a Bible (3 percent), and even fewer read it on a regular basis.

Meanwhile, since the beginning of the reform process, the consciousness of Russian citizens has been constantly under pressure from various alternative cults. A study conducted in the city of Moscow in 1994 showed that close to 60 percent of Muscovites believed in astrology and astrological forecasts, despite open disapproval of the practice by the Russian Orthodox Church. Almost half of all Moscow citizens had astrological literature at home, by which they meant astrological calendars, books or other similar material. Moreover, 30 percent of those who confessed to believing in astrology, UFOs or extra-sensory perception claimed that they were Christians. In other words, the belief in astrology or other similar phenomena

---

1   A former official provided the information on these operations in the Russian city of Vyatka. He was remorseful at what he had done and willing to go public in telling the story of repression against Christians.

2   The Way of Life Survey was repeated three times between the early and late 1980s. The survey discussed here was carried out in 1982. It was based on a random sample of 14,000 subjects representing all the regions of the former USSR.

was regarded by a large proportion of respondents as compatible with Christianity and its principles. Indeed, they had no difficulty in embracing these contradictory dogmas, paying fealty to all of them in equal proportions. This 'mosaic' consciousness was obviously indicative of a crisis of monotheism, and of a shift towards the alternative cult organizations which systematically attempted to recruit new adherents in an uncertain situation of consciousness.

1. The evolution of the young

The deliberate communist policy of eliminating religion from the lives of citizens affected the whole of the Russian population, but its main targets and victims were the young, who had little experience in dealing with spiritual issues and little knowledge of religion or religious ritual. Yet they had greater spiritual needs than older people established in life and adhering to certain maxims out of of sheer tradition. In the post-Stalinist Soviet Union, young people grew more and more disenchanted with the communist dogma. It became increasingly clear that none of the great communist projects was going to be implemented, that none of the lofty goals was to be achieved. A survey carried out in 1989 found that over 70 per cent of Russian young people claimed no belief in communist tenets.[3] This does not mean that they rejected the great ideals of the unity of humankind and of equality, since a substantial number of subjects (64 per cent) approved of them. However, this approval was expressed for the ideals, not for the manner in which the communist regime was attempting to bring them into being.

Disenchantment with communist dogma led young people in other directions. It was this state of affairs that created the preconditions for the rise of alternative creeds, a phenomenon explained by the situation of the Russian Orthodox Church – by tradition the stronghold of religion and therefore a natural retreat for young people in search of religious experience. However, in the post-Stalinist period, many young Russians held an ambivalent attitude towards the Church. On the one hand, the Church did little to discredit itself in the eyes of the population: in view of its function in society it was always in latent disagreement with communist dogma. On the other hand, during the

---

3   Henceforth the figures refer to the data gathered by the 1989 Social Development of Youth Study conducted in the Russian Federation by the youth research sector of the Institute of Sociology of the Russian Academy of Sciences. The survey was based on a random sample of young Russians aged from 14 to 30.

post-Stalinist period the Church never openly protested against any of the repressive actions undertaken by the authorities, silently assenting to the many policies known to be detrimental to the lives of ordinary Russian citizens. It could be argued that without such detachment the Church could not have survived. However, a detached and often cooperative attitude towards the regime was not what many Russian young people were looking for. It should be pointed out that the Orthodox Church was not the only institution in this situation. There were other churches and creeds that were forced to choose between muted cooperation with the state and an open and often hopeless fight against its powerful machinery of repression.

The alternative creeds came to Russia in the early 1960s, echoing the new youth culture and its emphasis on new values. The youth subculture of those years also included a religious component, which often took the form of oriental cults like Krishnaism or Buddhism, although a mass survey based on an All-Russia sample would not have registered their followers on a large scale. Nevertheless, the hippies were noticeable and vociferous in the Russian big cities, providing visible proof that an alternative lifestyle was possible. In the days of *perestroika* other youth religious movements arose, although these were often less innocuous than the Krishnaites or Buddhists. In the atmosphere of openness and freedom of the time, new youth leaders came to the fore, often originating from obscure and dangerous sects. Examples follow.

The White Brotherhood was founded by two former officials in the communist youth league. The head of the movement claimed to be the reincarnation of Christ and predicted an imminent apocalypse, with the possibility of salvation only for the movement's members. The White Brotherhood received substantial funding from anonymous sources, and according to the Ministry of Internal Affairs managed to recruit up to 100,000 young people in various parts of Russia and the other countries of the CIS. The second example was the Bogorodichnaya Church, often described as a totalitarian sect which practised intensive brainwashing of its members. Little is known about its number of adherents, given that it was a tightly closed community, but it is certain that the majority of its members were young people aged around 20 years old. There is evidence that the Japanese Aum sect managed to create a following in Russia. There is no information on the how it functioned in the country, but investigation of the sect's activities revealed that it had made useful connections among the Russian leadership, and had formed groups of followers in practically all Russia's large cities.

The Russian parliament, the State Duma, responded to the danger of totalitarian sects by enacting a new law on the 'freedom of consciousness'. The law stipulated that all new non-traditional religious communities must pass a test period proving their good intentions. The law stated that only four major religious communities have the indisputable right to operate in Russia: the Russian Orthodox Church, Islam, Judaism and Buddhism. After vociferous protests by the Catholic communities in the West, an amendment was passed which allowed Catholics to worship without being required to register. The law also provoked protests from other Western religious communities, since the Protestant, Krishnaite and other communities had been omitted from the list. The law does not require 'non-traditional' communities to disband, but simply states that they must report most of their activities to state organizations.

The law will hardly stop the growth of alternative or even dangerous cults: the stressful situation in Russia will continue to push young people towards sects, often to the detriment of their mental health. What life circumstances induce the young to choose alternative cults? Examination of the issue reveals a set of factors determining such behaviour.

2. Qualitative analysis

A statistical approach to the problem of 'non-traditional' cults (a conditional term) is rather difficult to implement, since their members are unwilling to participate in large-scale surveys, often viewing them as stratagems to learn more about their cults in order to damage their practices or to aid the authorities in repressing them. Therefore, in exploring the reasons for the drift by young people towards alternative creeds, informal in-depth interviewing was used in the survey described here. Interviews were conducted with five young men and five young women belonging to two cults – half of them to the Krishnaites and half to the Scientologists. The questions asked dealt mostly with the reasons for the subjects' religious choices, and they revealed several major factors.

2.1 Family problems

The expression 'family problems' is used in the broad sense to refer not only to tension in relations among family members, but also to problems facing the family as a whole. A number of respondents were from single-parent families. However, it would be wrong to link membership of alternative cults solely to the problems of the family and its disintegration. A number of respondents came from families which, they claimed, had harmonious relationships, although even these families had problems which caused hardship for their members. A member of the Krishnaite brotherhood commune said:

> I had good parents. They did not quarrel much, no more than other families. Even when they quarrelled they never went beyond a certain limit. There was no wife battering in our family, no vile words thrown at each other. In fact we were a quiet family.

Nevertheless, his quiet family life encountered the problems resulting from a stressful social environment:

> When the reform started, we had problems. I remember that in 1992, when prices went up dramatically, our family budget was on the verge of collapse. Soon they stopped paying my father's salary. He was an engineer in a research and development institute. His job had been important, and he was used to respect from his colleagues and from us, his family. However, the reforms changed all this. His job was no longer important. After a while they threw him out. He was in a state of shock. He did not know what other job he could find. He kept looking for sources of additional income. For about a year we lived only on my mother's salary.

In the eyes of this young man the episode demonstrated how fragile the family's world had been, and how wrong they had been to expect life to move along the well-trodden path:

> My parents started to care only about money. They only thought about how to feed the family, me and my little brother. This is a dead-end life. I would not like to live like this, not to waste my life as my parents did.

A similar life of stress and poverty was described by another respondent, also a member of the Krishnaite community:

> My father took to the bottle. It ended sadly - in divorce. My father did not help us at all. We were alone in the world, needed by nobody. At times we could hardly make ends meet. My mother took on several jobs, thinking only of how to feed us all.

Most respondents complained about a lack of spiritual life in families plagued by problems of survival:

> There was little time for my father or my mother to talk about spiritual life. In fact they trudged through life, without no proper thought about another world, a

world beyond their understanding. The material world crushed them and took away all of their creative being.

There was apparently one feature shared by all respondents: whatever the quality of their parents' life, they found it unsatisfactory. Their quest for a new religion was also an attempt to distance themselves from the stifling atmosphere of their parents' home, from perennial problems and daily toil, without hope of a better future. It may also be said that the search for life-alternatives would not have been so intense, had the social situation evolved in a positive direction, promising good jobs and good salaries. Economic conditions could only provide a replica of a discredited life made up of drudgery, acute problems, and personal conflict.

2.2 Blind alley situation

The interviews showed that in the majority of cases the respondent's decision to join a cult was closely bound up with a desire to escape from a 'blind alley'. One female respondent, a Scientologist, declared:

> I came into the office and realized that I would have to stay there for years with no hope, with no change. I would have to come there and work all the time, and nothing good would ever happen to me. I would have to talk to my colleagues, and the conversation would be empty. So I decided that I would not work there after all. I decided to find a job with flexible working hours so that I could have more time to develop my faculties, to study books, to improve my skills. At some point I may resume my career, but only in possession of more knowledge and a better understanding of how to get on, how to make life interesting.

Like family problems, a blind alley situation is often the result of worsening economic conditions crisis and less social mobility among the young:

> I graduated from the Moscow Physics and Technology Institute. Now they do not need specialties. The country is treading a different path where science is not needed. Personally this might be the right thing to do. Science is only one source of knowledge. It is wrong and immoral to ignore other sources when the light of knowledge is more powerful. There have always been men and women who knew more than others and could work wonders. They had no need of a formal education. Knowledge came to them from other sources.

Today, many young people have little hope of a career. A situation characterized by the breakdown of the social institutions is often conducive to the deformalization and deritualization of life. Higher education credentials now hold little guarantee of a better future. Educational establishments differ sharply in their provision for the life-chances of graduates. Trapped in unemployment, young intellectuals are often inclined to review their attitudes to the world dramatically. There is always a distinct group of educated young people who reject the world as an inadequate civilization to be replaced by a better one. Dahrendorf discusses this attitude in his *Modern Social Conflict*[4] with reference to a group of young people who encountered the perennial problem of employment on graduating from university. They founded the Green movement, but also the terrorist group that jeopardized social peace. In Russia, a social movement is less likely to arise, because of scant public experience of a civil society. A spiritual movement or a new cult is more likely to succeed.

2.3 Conflict of values

The respondents frequently mentioned a conflict of values between themselves and the rest of society. They viewed society as following the wrong course, creating unnecessary comforts at the expense of more vital values – human brotherhood, human understanding, the environment. The latter seemed to be one of the greatest preoccupations of alternative cults:

> Look what they have done to our world. Everything is polluted. To find a place without pollution you have to travel a long way from big cities. The air, the water and food is harmful to humans because of omnipresent pollution. If the same policy prevails, the world will destroy itself. The only hope is to reform human values, to make humans more aware of a new way, a world without greed and with more emphasis on the ideals of human understanding. We went to the Rainbow Festival in the Pskov region. We never harmed anyone, we enjoyed meeting our brothers and sisters. Nevertheless, they sent the police, who bullied us into moving out of our camp and accused us of drug-taking. The police know perfectly well that we do not need drugs. But they threaten us and persecute us. They feel that the ideology of life and nature conservation threatens their way of life dedicated to the accumulation of more and more wealth.

This young Krishnaite felt that his movement was in conflict with the outside world on crucial life-issues. He regarded the course chosen for civilization to be wrong and dangerous to life, finding proof and justification for his cause in the environmental problems resulting from the greed and avarice dominant in contemporary society. He felt that this attitude must be replaced by a new set of ideals, among which the environment would assume

---

4 Ralf Dahrendorf, *Modern Social Conflict*, reprinted edition (Berkeley: University of California Press, 1990).

primacy. These new ideals were expressed non-violently, but society's response to them was violence. For the members of alternative movements, violence is further proof which (i) emphasises truly important issues and (ii) provides an authentic alternative to the basic set of values.

The above-mentioned conflict of values frequently results from the passive position taken up by the mainstream creeds on the pressing problems of the contemporary world. Environmental concerns rank third after falling living standards and crime in modern Russia.[5] Of all other concerns, the environmental issue is the most life-threatening, and requires a more consistent stance from religious organizations. However, the mainstream creeds make no statement on the issue, thereby giving alternative creeds a chance to assert themselves.

2.4 The generation gap

Another frequent theme developed by the interviews was the generation gap. As a rule, alternative religious movements consist of young people. The latter often regard their actions as innovative when compared with the actions of previous generations. Particularly so in Russia, where the generation gap is being widened by the transition from totalitarian socialism to a market-based society. This is not to imply that alternative creeds are pro-market. Socially, they quite often opt for a humanized version of socialism characterized by the freedom to propagate new life-styles and at the same time restrictions on the activities of 'greedy capitalists':

> I believe that we are blundering once again. In the past there was repression and a lack of freedom. We are now faced with the same strategy in new form. The problem is that in both periods the bankrupt ideas of material prosperity were put forward as the only true goal in life. Hence derives the dissatisfaction with life obvious even among the wealthy. When they get a lot of money, they see that nothing changes. It does not matter how many television sets or cars you have. They cannot make you happy.

Conclusion

The limited survey just described does not pretend to answer the many questions that arise in connection with the problem of alternative cults in

---

5 Ekonomicheskie i socialnie peremeni: monitoring obshestvennogo mnenia, *The Russian Center for Public Opinion Research*, July-August 1998, p. 43.

Russia. The project was only the pilot stage of broader, long-term research. However, I believe that the results obtained provide a clear indication of the strategy that the study must adopt. It is obvious that the desire to involve oneself in an alternative creed arises from a feeling of social and spiritual alienation. There are two possibilities in any social crisis. One is a situation when the social or/and economic crisis is countered by a stable set of values shared by the majority of the population. A possible example of this is provided by Poland, a country in which society has maintained its spiritual integrity during transition, with an active social stance assumed by the Catholic Church. The other possibility is all-embracing crisis in both the social and spiritual spheres of life. Such is the situation in contemporary Russia where, since the collapse of the communist dogma, no adequate replacement for it has arisen. This is obviously fertile ground for the growth of alternative cults which feed on anomie and despair.

9 *Pagus et urbanus* in Iceland: conjunctions and disjunctions in neo-pagan religion

WILLIAM H. SWATOS, Jr. and LOFTUR REIMAR GISSURARSON

Introduction

Twenty-five years ago, four men – two young, two older – sat in a Reykjavík café and shared the discovery of a common inspiration: to found a group that would revive pre-Christian Norse religion in Iceland: 'the religion of the gods', *Ásatrú* (god: s. *Ás*; pl. *Æsir*). At the same time the Jesus Movement arrived in Iceland. Pétur Pétursson[1] makes the case that the media had a significant role to play in the growth of *Ásatrú* into a 'religion', and with this we whole-heartedly concur. Indeed, one might want to say that it is the beginning of our thesis, namely that *the neo-pagan 'revival' in Iceland is very much the product of urban civilization, much in the same way as fundamentalism is the product of modernism*. We will return to this theme later, after brief exposition of the unique potential contribution of the Icelandic case to theory building in the social scientific study of religion.

1. The Icelandic case

The Icelandic case is particularly valuable for comparative sociology, especially in regard to cultural systems, because Iceland has undergone rapid and thorough modernization, but it does not have racial-ethnic diversity, regionalism, or rigid status hierarchies, any of which features complicates analyses of these kinds. In addition, the absence of a pre-European native population means that there is not a double layer of cultural traditions that have intertwined and now must be carefully dissected, as is often the case in other modernizing colonial societies. Iceland has undergone, as has the rest of the modern world, a rural-urban transition. Unlike the rest of the West, however, this has not been a transition from village to city, but from

---

1 Pétur Pétursson, *'Asasamfundet på Island och massmedia'* (Stockholm: Religionssociologiska Institutet Forskningsrapport, 1985), p. 185.

individual farmsteads to cities and towns. Iceland has also undergone the important transition from colony to nation.

The concepts of *social deprivation* and *cultural wealth* encapsulate the Icelandic condition for most of the millennium of its existence. *Social deprivation* results from both colonial exploitation by the Danes and the natural environment of Iceland. At the turn of the twentieth century, for example, Iceland was barely eking its way out of one of the most catastrophic periods of its history. Earthquakes, volcanoes, and climatic changes had wreaked havoc on its population, fully a quarter of which had emigrated to the Western Hemisphere. People still largely lived with their livestock in houses of mud and grass; a leper colony persisted well into this century. *Cultural wealth* recognizes, on the other hand, that the Icelanders were the people of Edda and Saga, stars in the crown of Western medieval literature. The poet-priest Matthías Jochumsson, for example, author of Iceland's national hymn (an anthem based on a Psalm text), would write, reflecting Iceland's unique pragmatic Christianity, that the Icelandic classics and the Bible were both inspired literatures.[2] These tendencies resulted in a society that was far more culturally than economically advanced, whose past was romanticized as a God-sent golden era. It was also a culture relatively untouched by the Renaissance recovery of Greco-Roman classics as a 'European' heritage. In its subsequent religious history, furthermore, Iceland is one of the few thoroughly Protestant socio-cultural systems not to have been exposed in any significant way to either Calvinism or post-Puritan piety (e.g., Wesleyanism or specifically Scandinavian Haugeanism).

In a study of Icelandic spiritualism,[3] we have explored at length how it was that a unique interaction between a modern quasi-religious movement and the (Lutheran) Icelandic state church came to occur at the turn of the twentieth century. We argued that Iceland's tradition of spiritual phenomena – what we term 'saga consciousness' – provided a cultural substructure for distinctly modern innovations of 'new men' at the helm of Icelandic society in the church, journalism, and politics.

Through a historically unique configuration of circumstances, these innovations were given expression in the form of a semi-religious, semi-scientific spiritualism. But spiritualism was not the only 'new religion' that

---

2   Emil V. Gudmundson, *The Icelandic Unitarian Connection: Beginnings of Icelandic Unitarianism in North America, 1885-1900* (Winnipeg: Wheatfield Press., 1984); Gunnar Kristjánsson, *Churches of Iceland: Religious Art and Architecture* (Reykjavík: Iceland Review, 1988).
3   William H. Swatos, Jr. and Loftur Reimar Gissurarson, *Icelandic Spiritualism: Mediumship and Modernity in Iceland* (New Brunswick: Transaction, 1996).

appeared in Iceland at this time. We mentioned briefly *Nýall*, a unique Icelandic religion, founded by Dr. Helgi Pjeturss in c.1919, which combined elements of spiritualism, theosophy, Icelandic nationalism, eddic poetry and the sagas, and the latest scientific research of the period. It antedated both Scientology and flying saucer cults, but included elements that would appear in each.

Also Theosophy had a wide following in Iceland: indeed, it had the highest per capita membership in the population of any nation in the world in 1947.[4]

Similarly the birth of institutionalized 'religious freedom' in Iceland was occasioned by Mormonism in the late nineteenth century, as a saga recounted in the form of a historical novel, *Independent People*, by Iceland's Nobel laureate Halldór Laxness. Thus, 'new religions' did not emerge suddenly on the Icelandic horizon in the 1970s, nor is Icelandic neo-paganism as distinctly countercultural as some theories of new religious movements would suggest.

The story of Iceland's conversion to Christianity is unique in the annals of the faith. It is also a paradigm for the study of Icelandic religious consciousness. A conflict had been brewing between the independent pagan Icelanders and Ólafur Tryggvason, the king of Norway, who had accepted the Christian faith and subsequently took upon himself the obligation to bring the Icelanders under the sway of the new teaching. The stage was set for a potential confrontation at Alþingi (the Icelandic parliament) as Christian and pagan parties each began to gather strength, and as each declared that it would not live under the law of the other. The Christians then chose Hallur Þorsteinsson (Síðu-Hallur) to proclaim their law. However, apparently unwilling to be responsible for dividing the people, he instead brought the question before the Lawspeaker, Þorgeir Ljósvetningagoði, himself a pagan, whom the pagan party had already authorized to speak on its behalf. Þorgeir took the case and then, as Jón Hnefill Aðalsteinsson notes,[5] went *under the cloak*: that is, Þorgeir lay down for a day and a night, pulled his cloak over him, and spoke to nobody and nobody spoke to him, probably in an attempt to attain hidden knowledge in some ancient pagan tradition. When he finally mounted Law Rock to deliver his decision, it was for conversion, but with a series of limitations, one of which was that the worship of the old gods could *continue in private*.

---

4   Pétur Pétursson, *Spiritism och mystik på Island under 1900-talet* (Stockholm: Religionssociologiska Institutet Forskningsrapport, 1978), pp. 155-6.
5   Aðalsteinsson, Jón Hnefill, *Under the Cloak* (Stockholm: Almquist & Wiksell, 1978).

Iceland accepted Christianity by a freely-taken decision that weighed the options in light of international political and economic considerations but also in terms of domestic tranquillity. Þorgeir recognized that the country could not live under two sets of laws, but he made provision for individual differences through the caveat which permitted private devotion to the old gods: a licence that was dropped as an older generation went to their graves, and many of the *goði* who formerly ran the pagan temples sought ordination for themselves or their sons and became Christian priests, then operating proprietary churches from which they derived income as they had previously done from the pagan temples. Icelandic Christianity never lost this farmstead pragmatism, although in subsequent centuries it was threatened at times by Danish colonialism. It is this characteristic of Icelandic religious life that lies behind the observation of the present priest of the shrine church parish of Þingvellir, the site of Iceland's ancient parliaments, that 'Christianity has always been [...] *different* here [...] From the beginning there was no internal questioning of faith and little moralizing'.[6]

Using a typology derived from the psychological anthropology of Ruth Benedict, Sigurdur Magnússon[7] has observed that 'the difference between the Icelanders and most peoples in Western Europe' is that Icelandic culture is not a 'guilt culture', as is most of the Christian world (and particularly that influenced by Calvinism), but a 'shame culture', with 'a kind of "innocence" regarding the world'. Individuals in shame cultures do not relate to the supernatural in a confessional way, but do so by holding 'ceremonies for good luck'. The shame culture type thus 'seems tailor-made for Icelandic culture as it is expressed in Edda and Saga and in the basic outlook of modern Icelanders [who] despite all their cultural achievements, are children of nature [...] immature in the way youth is immature'.

Religion in Iceland has historically been a matter of the hearth. The home was the principal place of worship and teaching, with the church building serving primarily as the focal point for central life-events. In this sense, every trip to church was a pilgrimage.[8] Since Iceland was not a village but a *farm society*, the church was not the quasi-political centre of village life (as in England), but the pilgrimage centre of family life. Still today, for example, when a funeral is held on a Saturday in a country parish church – often with a congregation coming by bus from an urban centre – no 'regular' church

---

6   Louise E. Levathes, 'Iceland: Life under the Glaciers', *National Geographic*, 171(2), 1987, pp. 184-215.
7   Sigurdur A. Magnússon, *Northern Sphinx* (Montréal: McGill: Queens University Press, 1977), pp. 171-2.
8   Kristjánsson, *Churches of Iceland: Religious Art and Architecture*.

service will be held on the subsequent Sunday. Particularly important for the development of a distinct Icelandic spirituality was the institution known as *kvöldvaka*, or the 'evening wake', born out of a combination between Iceland's literary cultural heritage and cosmological circumstance: the winter noonday moon that is the concomitant of the summer tour brochures that tout 'the land of the midnight sun'. The *kvöldvaka* was at once church, school, and theatre for each farmstead. It also provided the vital link between saga consciousness and modernity, mediated by Christian literature.

While the precise origins of *kvöldvaka* are unclear, there is little doubt of its ubiquity in Icelandic society or of its persistence into the early years of the twentieth century in some parts of the country. Icelandic sod houses usually consisted of little more than a single common room plus a kitchen; farm animals lived in an adjacent room or underneath; occasionally there was also a bedroom. In the evening, which at some times of the year would have been quite early in the afternoon, the entire family, including such adjuncts as nannies or 'hands', would gather in the common room for story telling, poetry contests, reading, discussion, and so on. These evenings would include saga narratives as well as devotions from Christian books written for this purpose (*postillur*). Hymnody might also be said or sung, as the family's gifts for music would allow. The Bible was not widely owned, however, and therefore rarely formed a specific part of *kvöldvaka* devotional exercises.

Kvöldvaka is important because it placed the sagas and Christian literature in a single cultural context. This is not to imply that people did not know the difference between, for example, *Egils Saga* and Jón Vídalín's sermons (which were the most popular *postilla*). Their combination in the same evening's reading and discussion, however, created a synthetic rather than antithetic environment for the ideas expressed by each to encounter the other. Equally significant, perhaps, the 'recovery of classical learning' – that is, Greek philosophy – never took place to any significant extent in Iceland. *The sagas formed the basis for interpreting all subsequent intellectual developments independent of categories imported from either Hellenic or scholastic thought.* Iceland was not subject to the constraints of the dominant Western philosophical tradition that Matthías Sæmundsson terms 'Mediterranean dialectics':[9] the search for essences, hence inherent oppositions, characteristic of both scholasticism and Renaissance humanism. As time passed and more postillur became available, they too could be used in this way; that is to say, the old sagas and the new religious ideas continued a

---

9 Matthías Viðar Sæmundsson, 'Introduction' to *Hávamál: The Sayings of the Vikings*, (Reykjavík: Guðrún, 1992), p. 14.

process of *mutual encounter*. To these were added other publications – magazines, journals, newspapers – as they entered the cultural repertoire. Saga consciousness remained a dynamic interpretive framework for encountering the outside world, as important perhaps in 1850 as in 1350.

2. Iceland and the modern project

The *Zeitgeist* at the end of the nineteenth century in Iceland was replete with confusion, what Durkheim would legitimately call *anomie*. New techno-scientific discoveries were amazing the population, and hitherto widely accepted epistemological assumptions of how the world worked were being challenged by new experiences. In the newspapers Icelanders read that they were the descendants of apes; that they had a subconscious; that they could be hypnotized; that there were things like the telephone, telegraph, electric lights, automobiles, and flying machines. But there were also years of severe winters, great poverty and hunger, combined with such maladies as tuberculosis, tapeworm, and leprosy. The quest for political freedom figured as a major item on the Icelandic agenda, and the Western hemisphere beckoned with promises of plenty. Icelandic church administration was influenced by Danish rationalism at the end of the eighteenth century. In ironic combination with biblical pietism, this rationalism made a major contribution to Icelandic life by promoting and sustaining literacy through the work of the clergy, but it also created a spirituality among a clergy pulled between the pillar of rigid, literalistic orthodoxy and the post of rationalistic positivism.

The political struggle for independence led to home rule in 1904, with an Icelandic prime minister residing in the country.[10] In 1918 Iceland achieved technical independence and sovereignty, although the country continued to be headed by the Danish monarchy. Genuine independence and full sovereignty, with an elected president, came in 1944, when Iceland became a republic in the maelstrom of World War II. The cultural controversies of the late nineteenth century were centred on debates between two important status groups: the *bændur-literati* (farmer sages), who had dominated Iceland since its founding, and the new men of the 'cities'. An important economic shift in Icelandic economic life also took place, as fishing became its primary industry, rather than a secondary pursuit after farming. The new coastal villages were a demographic by-product of this economic shift. Proto-

---

10 Gunnar M. Magnúss, *Það Voraði Vel 1904* (Hafnarfjörður: Skuggsjá, 1970).

urbanization in turn created contestation of no little significance as it rapidly became clear that Reykjavík, not an official 'town' until 1786, was becoming the centre of power. The conflict between the *bændur* and the new men was a contest for socio-economic and socio-cultural power in the broadest terms. A new Iceland was being created. As a whole the new men were 'world open' as Icelanders had not been for hundreds of years. They were breaking out of the isolation imposed upon them by their colonial status and poverty, and they were bringing the world home with them. More and more of them were studying for advanced degrees at European institutions, principally at Copenhagen, but also at Halle and Cambridge and as they travelled to 'Western Iceland' in the Canadian province of Manitoba.

Although 'no major critique had been launched [in Iceland] against the church and its pastors before the social transformation began in the last decade of the nineteenth century',[11] religion nevertheless quickly became a mode of discourse through which socio-cultural conflicts were articulated as political freedom increased. In this setting, a unique movement emerged beginning in 1905. This was the *Icelandic spiritualism* centred on the physical mediumship of Indriði Indriðason (1883-1912), as interpreted by two of the leading 'new men' of the period, editor Einar H. Kvaran and priest-professor Haraldur Níelsson (nephew of the Bishop of Iceland, Hallgrímur Sveinsson, whose office in Reykjavík was sometimes the site of their experiments), with the additional patronage of two more well-established, if controversial figures, the poet-priest Matthías Jochumsson and Björn Jónsson, publisher, politician, and prime minister of Iceland. What makes this movement unique in the annals of spiritualism is that it arose *within* the established church, perhaps at one point including almost half the priests among its sympathisers. Within the context of the present discussion, we point out the youth of both Indriði and, comparatively speaking, of his principal protagonists, but also their connection to specific elders.

Haraldur Níelsson provided enormous legitimation to the movement. He not only attended the early séances and participated in the later organization of the Icelandic Society for Psychical Research (S.R.F.Í.), he also believed, preached, and taught spiritualism as 'the truth of Easter' with passion. His credibility could not be gainsaid in any way. His scholarship, preaching, chaplaincy to lepers, teaching, family background, and personal piety placed him beyond reproach. Hundreds, possibly thousands, went to hear him preach on Sunday nights. Furthermore, because of his position on the Faculty of

---

11   Sigurdur Arni Thordarson, *Liminality in Icelandic Religious Tradition Ph.D. dissertation* (Nashville: Vanderbilt University, 1989), p. 177.

Theology of the University of Iceland and its prerequisite status for ordination in the Icelandic church, Haraldur was able to influence the *future* of the Icelandic church and the formation of its clergy. Haraldur managed to develop a sophisticated theology that incorporated spiritualism as a part of a much larger whole, while at the same time his oratorical skills made his work accessible to the general population. Haraldur and Einar saw themselves on the brink of a breakthrough to a new religious horizon and couched some of their work in biblical terms. These connections seem to have served the function of interpreting spirit manifestations in a manner consistent with New Testament texts so these innovators acted as a bridge back to traditional, if not orthodox, religious themes.

Björn Jónsson's involvement raised the political stakes for the movement and made it a matter of immediate concern for some elements in the society. His adversaries would accuse him of playing on the superstitions of the people for political gains; he would defend himself as a seeker after truth. Neither way could spiritualism be marginalized. Haraldur's theology and preaching notwithstanding, it may well have been the *politicization* of spiritualism by organs of Björn's political party that made spiritualism a cause that could not be relegated to the esoteric and hence shunted off to 'the margin of the visible'.[12] Because of Iceland's socio-economic history, Marxism, for example, never constituted a viable alternative ethic; yet in the social dislocation that characterized the shift to a coastal urban society and a fishing-dominated economy in the dismal conditions of the late nineteenth century, Icelanders welcomed a worldview that offered consistency with both their past and future. *Scientific spiritualism* became such a programme.

In this respect, it is important to note that from the first the S.R.F.Í. remained separate from, but intimately related to, the state church. The society constantly reaffirmed that it was a *research* organization, but its leadership, with Haraldur Níelsson in the vanguard, had a significant component from the clergy, along with others principally from the professional classes. Pétur Pétursson observes, for example, that there came to be a status advantage deriving to the 'new men' from membership in the S.R.F.Í. *vis-à-vis* more pietistic groups. This may or may not have caused people to 'believe in' spiritualism, but it did give spiritualism a higher socio-structural profile than it achieved for the most part in Anglo-America. By being at the same time religiously infrastructured, the S.R.F.Í. had an implicitly religious character, even as it purported to pursue an explicitly

---

12 Edward A. Tiryakian, (ed.), *On the Margin of the Visible: Sociology, the Esoteric, and the Occult* (New York: Wiley, 1974).

scientific purpose. It was thus able to overcame the stifling effect of the realist materialism of the influential Dane Georg Brandes, which, in discounting the possibility of either personal immortality or social change, gave no foundation for personal or social morality (as, for example, Marxism did elsewhere, at least to some degree).

Although Indriði's séances were conducted with attempts to introduce scientific rigour – particularly at the hands of Guðmundur Hannesson, a professor on the University of Iceland medical faculty, who represented scientific legitimacy in its fullest flower – we would emphasise a number of religious details that characterized the séances. There was often hymnody and prayer on the part of the controls. The room in which the séances were held was arranged to resemble a church hall, with a lectern and harmonium. Einar Kvaran was the son of a priest. In addition to the relationship between Haraldur Níelsson and his uncle, theological students were generally used as assistants in the conduct of the experiments. Indriði apparently developed a friendship with the daughters of a priest in the Westman Islands. From the opposition to the spiritualist movement, too, one of the most frequent charges brought by newspaper critics was that Einar Kvaran was forming a *new religion*. Would such a charge have been made if Einar had not been the son of a priest, well-educated in theological matters, and closely in league with Haraldur Níelsson and his students? Although Kvaran insisted that he was *not* setting up an alternative church, his very protests may have as often as not been interpreted otherwise. Nevertheless, spiritualism allowed Iceland to enter into a dialogue with the modern project which enabled new religious concepts into the culture to be integrated into an environment of mutual intergenerational responsibility and interdependence. Young ideas and old concepts were creatively synthesised by Níelsson's theology and they circulated through Kvaran's editorial activities.

Spiritualism was the midwife to the birthpangs of modernity because in its approach to life here *and* on 'the other side', it facilitated the transition from the extended family farmstead with its all-encompassing life-world that transcended generations from this world to the next through the pilgrimage centres of parish church and cemetery, to the nucleated social relations of the coastal villages and urban centres. The 'scientific' ability to talk with the departed on the other side showed that change *and* continuity could be accommodated in a single socio-cultural worldview precisely because this worldview did *not* posit a closed paradigm for knowledge. The sacred acquired meaning not through 'things set apart and forbidden', as Durkheim would put it, but through penetration – as it pervades the everyday life-world in constant dialogue with the mundane demands of day-to-day existence.

3. Nýall

Because *Nýall* is not widely known outside Iceland, brief discussion of this movement, as part of the cultural context out of which *Ásatrú* would eventually emerge, is perhaps worthwhile. The movement also surprisingly anticipated many conceptual innovations that occurred in more well-known 'new religions' which did not develop until after World War II. The word '*Nýall*' originating in a book with the same title written by an Icelandic geologist, Dr. Helgi Pjeturss (b. 1872). Pjeturss had been an outstanding student at Copenhagen, where he carried out research on Iceland's geological history and completed his doctoral dissertation in 1905. *Nýall* means 'the one who brings the new'.[13] Pjeturss's book is a collection of articles published in Reykjavík from 1918 onwards and which constitute a remarkable syncretism of different elements, introducing, for example, what he refers to as astrobiology. In *Nýall* Pjeturss suggested that his research in different areas could cause a revolution for the whole of human civilization, stating, among other things, that it was not remarkable that this knowledge should come from Iceland, because the Icelandic people, during their long period of suffering and privation, had passed a unique and exceptional test of talent and gifts that would take form in his teachings.

In his research on psychic phenomena manifest through mediums and séances – some of which he organized himself for the purpose – Pjeturss achieved results that conflicted with spiritualism on important points. His main argument was that spirits were not non-material beings, but instead material beings now living on other stars and planets. Through beaming or channelling from one or more mind or brain to another, these beings could come forth at séances as materializations[14] and in people's dreams.[15] These beings were people who had at one time lived, or else who would come to live, on earth, but had left their earthly bodies to live further material lives as material beings on other planets.[16] Pjeturss writes: 'The force that is released when a person dies here on earth glides forth to another star and makes for itself, through the support of related entities and on the basis of what his whole bioradiation has created, another body from the substance of that particular planet'.[17] It was possible to talk with these beings through mediums at

---

13   Helgi Pjeturss, *Nýall: Nokkur Íslensk Drög til Heimsfræði og Líffræði* (Reykjavík: Félagsprentsmiðjan, 1919), p. 242.
14   Ibid., p. 19.
15   Ibid., p. 51.
16   Ibid., p. 312 ff.
17   Ibid., p. 268.

séances: the medium in trance obtained the consciousness of the other being.

Pjeturss also claimed that dreams were caused by other waking intelligences which materialized in the mind while a person was asleep: these intelligences also emanated from other planets. Every person had an undying quality of self through his or her inherent 'bioradiation' (*lífgeislan*) as he called it – or life-beaming – which represented a person's innermost being and personality, and which was able to travel around the universe independently of time and space. Every person, while still alive, had his or her own dreaming agent on another planet. In dreams the person experienced what another existing person on a different planet was doing. A sleeping person obtains the consciousness of another being.[18] Sleep is a form of trance, and the trance of a medium is of the same kind as sleep. Our dream-world is the same as the spirit world of the medium.[19]

Pjeturss wrote, 'Man is an associational being, like a cell community'.[20] The cells are interconnected and coordinated; if disconnected, they may die. His theory was that all life on earth as well as on other planets belonged, and would eternally belong, to the 'larger order' or 'harmony'. In this process of development, Pjeturss declared, there would be occasional backsliding. It is for this reason that there are dark planets where life is not happy and discord prevails. People on these planets – and he included earth among the dark planets – are nevertheless able to improve themselves and move to the lighter planets.[21] Dreams are the most important means to acquire knowledge about life on distant planets. The effects of theosophical teachings are evident in Pjeturss's approach, even if they are articulated in a different form. The following quotations from *Nýall* evidence this clearly:

> Human history on earth is a recounting of ever-growing suffering. What is missing is the right contact, the harmony with life on the stars, where life is truly lived. Association, harmony is the nature of life.[22]
> The more developed humanity becomes, the closer it comes to this magnificent goal, to become a single organic unity (hyperzone), because that is what it is more than anything else, a common field of force.[23]

Helgi Pjeturss wrote five other books to explicate his theories further. His teachings received some attention from prominent Icelanders, several of

---

18 Ibid., p. 227.
19 Ibid., p. 229.
20 Ibid., p. 107.
21 Pétursson, *Spiritism och mystik på Island under 1900-talet*, 1980, pp. 19-20.
22 Pjeturss, *Nýall:*, p. 270.
23 Ibid., p. 311.

whom thought that this was the original Icelandic philosophy. Copies of his volumes are still frequently to be seen on family bookshelves in Icelandic homes.

Although there was widespread interest in these teachings, no society was organized to propagate them until 1950. Some efforts had been made earlier, but they failed to achieve any concrete results. Helgi Pjeturss died in 1949, and his death prompted his followers to set up a formal society in 1950. This organization is still in operation and is called the Nýalists (*Nýalssinnar*). According to its constitution, 'The purpose of the society is to gather support for the theories of Dr. Helgi Pjeturss among Icelanders and other nations and seek, according to them, to obtain increasing and as good as possible a life and intellectual association with more developed inhabitants of other stars'. During the mediumistic sessions of the Nýalists, Pjeturss always appears as the chief control, regardless of the person doing the mediating.

More than a dozen people were present at the society's organizational meeting, most of whom had been meeting informally for two years prior to this occasion. In 1951 the Nýalists founded their own journal *Íslensk stefna* (*The Icelandic Line*), which was published for several years and then ceased. Another periodical was begun in 1975, called *Lífgeslar* (*Lifebeams*), and is still being published. In 1975 a separate society was created in Iceland's 'Northern Capital' of Akureyri, but it has since closed, while in recent years two more societies, in addition to the original one, have been founded in the Reykjavík area. The affinities between Nýalism and Swedenborgianism are significant, as are the career trajectories of Pjeturss and the spiritualist Oliver Lodge.

4. Ásatrú

Nýalism never made a claim to public status as a religion in Iceland. This was also true of theosophy, spiritualism, and freemasonry, all of which have a quasi-religious character. The great majority of their members, which included parish clergy, remained at least nominally within the state church, some actually being leaders within that body. It is of particular interest in the comparative development of *Ásatrú* that whereas the leaders of the spiritualist movement were accused by their opponents in the press of trying to start a 'new religion', they vigorously protested otherwise and worked diligently to legitimate their views within the framework of the established church. In the case of *Ásatrú*, by contrast, the media became a vehicle whereby it was able to pursue official recognition.

Of the original four men who met in the spring of 1972, it was the eldest, Sveinbjörn Beinteinsson, who was about fifty at the time, who became the first *allsherjargodi* (High Priest) of the new religion. He lived until 1993, and was succeeded in 1994 by Jörmundur Ingi Hansen, whom Pétur Pétursson[24] describes at the founding as:

> a younger man, a bohemian type, interested in esoteric teaching and Eastern religions. He was one of the foremost figures of the Hippie movement and the flower power ideology of that time in Reykjavík. His artistic talents have been useful to the group. He made the statue of Thor which stands in the centre of the cult place and reconstructed, together with the Chief Godi, the rituals and the liturgy and even the dress of the ancient believers.

Hansen is also of interest because he was not strictly speaking Icelandic, but Danish in origin, and changed his first name from Jörgen to Jörmundur early on to affect a more Icelandic style. The other two men were a student radical at the university – who never officially joined the movement when it became a religion, though he worked hard to see it established (a behaviour which was not unique to him) – and a journalist about 40 years of age, who was active in the Reykjavík Theosophical Society and interested in the history of religions.

Like the S.R.F.Í, the *Ásatrúarmenn* initially formed as a 'secret society until the leaders had the opportunity to develop its religious doctrines, the cult ceremonies and the form and constitution of the group. But the press knew about it before it was established'.[25] This prompted a series of newspaper accounts both in Iceland and abroad, mostly superficial, some sensationalist though not unsympathetic, which resulted in a demand that the leaders provide a religious system of both doctrine and rituals practically on the spot. Whereas the leaders were initially wary of the press, they soon found that the media gave them an outstanding opportunity to 'invent' their religion on a world stage. 'It was in fact a journalist who first contacted the Minister of Justice and Ecclesiastical Affairs with the question' of whether it might be possible for the group to obtain official recognition as a registered religious body, which would give the Chief *Godi* equal legal status with the pastors of the Christian bodies in Iceland. The issue having been forced in this way, legal status was applied for in the autumn of 1972, and the process was closely followed in the press. Apparently the 'minister seemed to think in the beginning that this was all a joke and took his time in answering'. Eventually,

---

24 Pétursson, *Asasamfundet på Island och massmedia*, p. 21.
25 Ibid., p. 22.

however, he followed protocol and asked the bishop of the state church for his opinion, which was to reject the application. Nevertheless, the matter was then politicized as a freedom of religion issue, and as simultaneously raising a challenge against the 'Christian Establishment' in Iceland.[26] Hence, in the spring of 1973, official recognition was granted, and *Ásatrú* became a 'religion' in Iceland. The Chief *Godi* was now a legitimate 'minister of religion' in the state's eyes, and the *Ásatrúarmenn* received tax support in ratio to their numbers. This aroused even further international interest, partly due to the formal character of the recognition, partly from a growing neo-pagan, New Age spirituality that saw the possibility for 'licit' pagan practice.

The media attention did not seem to have a direct impact on the Icelandic group itself. From its founding until the mid-1980s, its adherents remained at around 70; thereafter a period of growth began, so that by the mid-1990s its numbers had increased to over 200. The group has not been without controversies since its founding. Especially important in the first decade was the issue of Nordic purity, which finally achieved some sort of resolution with the founding of a separate association for the preservation of the Nordic race (*Norrænt mannkyn*) in 1983, inasmuch as the majority of *Ásatrúarmenn* rejected Nordic racism for a more liberal, humanistic paganism. In Pétursson's opinion,[27] the principal agent for holding the movement together was Sveinbjörn himself:

> The Chief Godi is [...] an integrative link between the different factions [...] The Chief Godi is one of the oldest members of the group, but he has the gift of getting along with the young generation [...] Together with young rock music bands he has performed on stage in concerts and restaurants the poems of the Edda and old folk verses. He also visits schools and lectures on the old religion and the old world view.

Sveinbjörn also became 'one of the best-known Icelanders internationally', since from the outset the *Ásatrúarmenn* have pursued as one of their aims the introduction of 'paganism and other ancient Icelandic cultural rites to the world'.[28]

The neo-paganism now in Jörmundur's hands is an attempt to continue reinventing a tradition that began around the café table, but at a much more sophisticated level, and still with some desire to confront established Christianity as well. For example, Jörmundur has announced plans to create a

---

26 Ibid., p. 22-3.
27 Ibid., p. 24.
28 Thórdís Bachmann, 'Pagan Congress in the Year 2000', *News from Iceland* (Nov.), 8, 1994.

world Pagan Congress in Iceland in the year 2000, which will be precisely the thousand-year anniversary of the conversion of Iceland to Christianity. The goal of the Congress would be to both to create a Pagan Charter and to establish a 'common-interest association, which could provide moral and financial support in countries where there are no pagan societies'.[29]

From a sociological standpoint, this movement displays several striking features. On the one hand, strictly speaking, the Icelandic pagan movement is a contradiction in terms, since its intention is to herald the spread of a new world religion. Whereas in classical usage, the pagan was rural, tied to local deities rather than those of the empire, Icelandic neo-paganism is now seeking to be in the vanguard of a new religious movement on a global scale – witness the Pagan Charter. Significantly, however, the movement has also sought to combine aspects of pagan belief with contemporary trends, particularly in regard to nature. Jörmundur states:

> [P]agans face the fact that man and nature are one. When you treat others, or nature, badly, it comes back to you as a negative effect. Today we see that man has polluted and ravaged nature, which is very dangerous. On the other hand overprotection is also dangerous; it solves nothing to ban all fishing and the hunting of wild animals. Balance is the key [...] Man's role, according to paganism, is to ally himself with the gods in the endless battle against the forces of destruction [...] Paganism is connected to your own reality, the place on earth where you are situated, and that which is there. It is not a written rule which says: 'Do this in this way and at this time', when that dogma may not be practically applicable. People find paganism inside themselves. It becomes a religion because it evolves among a group which lives in a common society, speaks the same language, experiences the same things, and lives in the same climate zone.[30]

Thus localism and cosmopolitanism are combined in the neo-pagan worldview. The absence of dogma allows considerable flexibility; oral tradition continues to be invented as circumstances require.

Nevertheless, Iceland offers unique cultural resources for the development of neo-paganism. Despite the avoidance of 'writing things down', it is the case that in the Icelandic Sagas and Eddas and the *Hávamál* (*Words of the High One*), Iceland has a living pagan tradition preserved through the work of Christian scholars of the early period and then passed down through *kvöldvaka* into the twentieth century. Thus there is, in fact, a set of sacred texts to which Icelanders can appeal directly. Few other Western societies are so rich in this respect. Furthermore, the central pagan act of

---

29   Ibid.
30   Ibid.

worship, the quarterly *blót* (feast), already had a precedent in late-nineteenth-century Christian Iceland, as part of admiration for the past in the annual celebration of *Þorrablót*, which was observed in the late winter. *Þorrablót* is still celebrated both in Iceland and among expatriate Icelandic societies in the United States and Europe. In the contemporary pagan *blót* people still 'drink to their ancestors and other natural forces, such as guardian spirits and fairies', something that might well take place in any *Þorrablót*, along with much feasting: 'A good feast often ends in a big celebration and there is nothing that forbids people pairing off and going home together. That is part of life', Jörmundur observes.[31] These cultural resources link the character of the implementation of Christianity in Iceland from the time of the Conversion Alþingi onwards, as recognized also in the relatively common Icelandic pattern, that 'goes far back in time', of marrying after the birth of the first child, sometimes as late as his or her confirmation: hence the Icelandic cultural historian Sigurður Nordal's comment, 'We have been bad pagans for a century and bad Christians for ten'.[32]

Not to be ignored, finally, is the way in which the neo-pagan movement inflates the importance of Iceland and its people within Icelandic consciousness. As with Helgi Pjeturss's Nýalism, there is a clear assertion that Icelandic experience can provide resources of world-shaking significance. From Ingólfur Arnarson's casting off his high seat pillars to found Reykjavík in 874 to Matthías Jochumsson's poetry, Iceland has created a religious founding myth of *specialness*. Iceland's people are not a rag-tag band in some forgotten corner of the world but special people in the centre of the world: just ask Reagan and Gorbachev. The unique claim of Icelandic neo-paganism to a historic cultural repository and living tradition now poises the *Ásatrúarmenn*, at least in their own eyes, at a critical juncture of world-historical significance: the rebirth of paganism. Jörmundur claims that there are now sixty pagan societies in the United States, and several hundred thousand pagans in all the Scandinavian countries and many European nations. (In Great Britain both the Odinshof and one of the Odinic rites have been granted trust status by the Charity Commission, which in effect grants paganism official status as a 'religion', at least in the eyes of those who wish it to be a religion.) A high point in Jörmundur's career came in June 1994 when he was asked to lead a *blót* at London's Trafalgar Square (and hence in front of the church of St. Martin in the Fields). Interestingly, however, he states, 'I

---

31 Ibid.
32 Richard Tomasson, *Iceland: The First New Society* (Minneapolis: University of Minnesota Press, 1980).

used the same basic frame as in a regular *blót* but the strong religious aspects were played down'.[33] He also claims that the greatest number of pagans per capita are to be found in the former Soviet Union, with many pagan associations, even though paganism was proscribed along with other religions during the Soviet era.

Conclusion

Icelandic neo-paganism differs from many neo-pagan groups throughout the Western world because of its living cultural heritage. Although it shares with these groups something of the 'made up' character of the religion, it is far less improvised; that is, there is a set of 'scriptures' already considered to be at least quasi-sacred by Icelanders, which are world-renowned and provide a context for the construction of present experience. In addition, ongoing custom in such activities as the *Þorrablót* makes pagan rites appear less disjunctive than elsewhere. By the same token, irony abounds in the 'civilized' context from which Icelandic neo-paganism emerged and through which it has been sustained: urban café society, higher education, liberal democracy, and above all an international mass media. Thus, Icelandic neo-paganism has become the putative centre of a world religious movement which appeals especially to young adults and their values.

---

33 Bachmann, 'Pagan congress in the Year 2000', *News from Iceland,* (Nov.), 8, 1994.

Index

Aðalsteinsson 159
Adorno 39n
Agadjanian 140n
Allport 99n
Alma 58n, 73n
Artmaier 122n
Augustinus Aurelius 77n

Baal van 81n
Bachmann 170n, 173n
Baecker 102n
Baerveldt 69, 70, 61n, 69n, 76n, 77n, 81n
Bainbridge 4, 126, 135, 136, 138, 139, 140, 5n, 126n, 140n
Baltanova 136n
Baltes 100n
Banton 96n
Barker 27, 27n, 82n, 141n
Barz 73n
Beck 100n
Becker 57n, 58n, 68n, 122n
Beckford 10n, 27n, 141n
Beinteinsson 169
Bell 2, 6, 6n
Bellah 4, 14, 17, 19, 20, 4n, 14n, 16n, 19n, 17n, 27n
Benedict 160
Berger 2, 21, 45, 2n, 21n, 45n
Bernts 58n, 65n
Beth 99n
Beyer 24n
Biemans 58n
Bjorkwist 132n
Blavatsky 137
Blumer 92n

Bochinger 45n, 54n, 55n
Bonhoeffer 19
Borchert 82, 79n, 82n
Bourdieu 15, 93, 95n
Boutinet 73n
Bovay 82n
Brake 93n
Brandes 165
Brim 100n
Bullock 84n
Bultman 19
Byzow 131n

Campbell 6, 82, 6n
Campiche 82, 23n, 57n, 58n, 59n, 61n, 73n, 77n, 79n, 80n, 82n
Capras 55n
Cassirer 53n
Cavalli 33n, 42n
Certeau 10
Cesareo 33, 33n
Champion 21, 23, 21n, 23n, 27n
Chernysh 13, 147, 182
Cipriani 33n
Claesson 134
Clark 84, 85, 85n
Clarke 96, 93n, 96n
Clévenot 38n
Clinton 144
Cobain 86
Cohen 96, 94n, 96n
Cole 103n
Coleman 3n
Corb 106n
Corsten 13, 91, 182
Cousin 73n

175

Cox 2, 2n
Craft 90

Da Matta 103n
Dahrendorf 154n
Dante 79, 80
Davidson 107n
Dawson 6n
de Certeau 10n
de Hart 57n, 58n, 60n, 62n, 63n, 68n, 75n, 76n, 77n, 78n, 79n, 81n
Dekker 58n, 60n, 62n
De Lillo 33n
De Moor 127n
De Saussure 106n
Deth 25n, 41n
Dethlefson 52, 52n
Dick 3n
Dieleman 57n, 60n
Dievturiba 137
Dillon 100n
Dobbelaere 9, 9n, 25n
Doktór 13, 125, 182, 132n, 140n
Domenach 10n
Draak 75n, 76n
Dreitzel 45, 45n
Druidry 86
Dubach 82n
Durkheim 5, 47, 75, 165, 47n, 75n, 96n, 102n, 120n
Dyer 102n

Eberhard 99n
Eco 65, 66n, 106n
Einar 164, 165
Eistenstadt 3n
Elizabeth 94n
Emert van 65n

Erikson 100n
Ester 127n

Featherman 100n
Felling 62n, 65n, 81n
Fenn 2, 2n
Fichter 5n
Filatov 130n, 131n
Fillmore 103
Fonarow 122, 94n
Forner 99n
Foucault 115, 121, 104n, 107n, 116n
Fox 87
Fraas 50n
Francis 37, 37n
Frazer 47, 47n
Fröhlich 93n
Fuchs 73, 73n, 102n
Fulton 36n, 37n, 81n
Furman 131n
Furnham 73n

Galland 42n
Gamsahurdia 137
Gandhi 19
Garde 89n
Gardnerian 90
Garelli 33n
Gebhardt 122n
Geertz 93n, 96n, 103n
Gelder 122n
Gennep 100n
Gerardts 77n, 78n, 79n, 81n
Giddens 16, 16n
Gissurarson 13, 157, 183, 158n
Glock 4, 4n, 27n, 28n
Goffman 102, 121, 92n, 101n, 102n, 107n, 109n

Gorbachev 172
Gordon 17, 14n, 17n, 133n
Gorsuch Jr. 60n, 76n
Gramsci 93
Greeley 2, 2n, 65n
Greer 37, 37n
Grossberg 95n
Gubert 34n
Gudmundson 158n
Gumbrecht 96n
Gunter 73n

Haack 46n
Habermas 6, 6n
Haerpfer 129
Hajime 20n
Hall 93n, 96n
Halman 127n
Hanegraaff 68n
Hannesson 165
Hansen 169
Haraldsson 183
Haraldur 164
Hebdige 93n
Heelas 100n
Heitink 73n
Hemert van 58n
Hemminger 46n, 51n
Henry 79n
Hervieu-Léger 21, 28, 21n, 46n
Hinnells 14n, 17n
Hitzler 93, 93n, 95n
Hnefill 159n
Höllinger 12, 45, 181
Holm 132n
Hood 60n, 76n
Horkheimer 39n
Huber 122n
Humphreys 104n

Hutsebaut 78, 73n, 78n

Iannaccone 135n
Indriðason 163
Indriði 163, 165
Inglehart 40, 41, 82, 39n, 41n, 82n

Jagodzinski 25n
Janssen 12, 13, 57, 182, 57n, 59n, 60n, 61n, 63n, 75n, 76n, 77n, 78n, 79n, 80n, 81n
Jaspers 15, 16, 18, 19, 20, 22, 15n, 16n, 18n
Jefferson 20, 93n, 96n
Jochumsson 158, 163, 172
John Paul II 138, 142, 142n
Jónsson 163, 164
Jörmundur 170

Kahn 99n
Kapica 131
Kapranov 137n
Kathleen 99n
Kaufmann 9, 9n
Kay 37, 37n
Keenan 103n
Ket 100n
Kitagawa 18, 19, 20, 19n
Klosinski 46n
Knoblauch 54n
Kohl 144
Kohli 99n
Kramer 88
Kristjánsson 158n, 160n
Krüggeler 82n
Kulikov 142n
Kundera 101
Kurtz 21, 21n
Kvaran 163, 165

Lambert 12, 15, 181, 23n, 73n
Langer 53n
Lanzetti 33, 33n
Laxness 159
Le Corre 38n
Le Pore 107n
Lerner 84, 84n
Levathes 160n
Levinson 103n
Lévi-Strauss 50, 80, 51n, 80n
Levitt 37, 37n
Lindbeck 77n
Lodge 168
Lorenzer 50n, 53n
Luckmann 2, 5, 10, 10n
Luhmann 7, 8, 106n
Lyons 103n
Lyotard 84

Macciotti 73n
Magnúss 162n
Magnússon 160, 160n
Mannheim 117, 122, 101n, 122n
Manning 103n, 106n
Marcia 100n
Marini 99n
Martin 23, 23n
Marx 55
Mauss 50, 50n
McGuire 46n
McKay 90n
Mens 58n, 68n
Metz 9n
Meyer 99n
Michelat 38, 73n
Mischke 78n
Mitterauer 100n
Moerland 69n, 81n
Mongardini 50n

Moon 89n
Moore 14n
Morfin 73n
Morrison 78
Mörth 93n
Mulgan 37n
Müller-Doohm 104n

Nakamura 20
Nearing 88
Negus 102n
Nembach 132n, 136n
Newman 99n
Níelsson 163, 164, 165
Nisarg 88, 88n
Nordal 172

Oevermann 104n, 106n
Olbrich 99n

Paine 19
Parsons 2, 92n, 100n, 101n
Pearson 68, 75, 63n
Perrijn 57n, 60n
Peters 58n, 60n, 62n, 65n, 81n
Peterson 100n
Pettersson 40n
Pétursson 157, 164, 169, 170, 157n, 159n, 167n, 169n
Pfadenhauer 122n
Pfeiffer 96n
Pinder 101n
Pjeturss 159, 166, 167, 168, 172, 166n, 167n
Platt 100n
Þorgeir 159, 160
Þorsteinsson 159
Potel 38
Pratt 75, 79, 75n, 79n

Presley 88
Prins 61n, 76n, 77n, 80n
Pruyser 63n

Rajneesh 88
Ralf 122n
Reagan 172
Rensen 99n
Reynaldo 60
Ricoeur 104n, 107n
Riffault 181
Riis 40n
Riley 99n
Robbins 3n, 27n
Robertson 3, 3n
Roerich 137
Roes 59n
Rorty 107n
Rose 129, 129n
Rovati 33n
Runggaldier 50n, 52n, 53n
Ruppert 51n, 53n, 55n
Ryder 99n
Ryff 100n

Sæmundsson 161, 161n
Saliba 27n
Scarbrough 25n, 41n
Schäffer 122n
Schlegel 80n
Schreuder 62n, 65n, 81n
Schulze 93, 92n, 94n, 95n
Schutz 92n, 106n, 107n
Searle 96n, 107n
Sellars 96n
Shakespeare 60
Shapiro 100n
Shepherd 102n
Shils 181, 92n

Shinrikyo 136
Skachov 137n
Soeffner 96, 96n, 104n
Solodnikov 142n
Spilka 60n, 76n
Spruit 58n, 65n
Stallybrass 84n
Stark 4, 126, 135, 136, 138, 139, 140, 5n, 126n, 135n
Stenger 68n
Stiksrud 99n, 101n
Strauss 106n
Straw 93, 92n
Stricker 144n
Sutter 38, 38n
Sveinsson 163
Swatos 13, 157, 183, 7n, 46n, 158n

Tacitus 79, 80
Tamayo 78
Therborn 40n
Thordarson 163n
Thornton 93n, 122n
Tillich 19
Tipton 4, 4n
Tiryakian 4, 4n, 164n
Tomasi 1, 12, 31, 181, 7n, 34n, 36n, 38n, 40n
Tomasson 172n
Tomka 132n
Troeltsch 6, 6n
Trombley 84n
Tryggvason 159
Turner 100n, 101n

van Baal 81
van der Lans 61n, 76n, 77n
van der Linden 73, 57n, 58n, 60n,

73n
van der Ven 58n, 77n, 79n
Vergote 78
Verhoeven 78, 73n, 78n
Vídalín 161
Vink 57n
Vivelo 47n
Voll 82n
Vorontsova 131n
Voyé 77, 23n, 73n

Wallis 25, 25n
Weber 6, 12, 39, 47, 48, 63, 47n, 48n, 50n, 97n, 109n, 120n
Westley 5n

Whyte 94, 121, 94n, 121n
Wicca 86, 90
Wicke 102n
Widdicombe 80n
Wilkinson 37n
Willaime 21, 21n
Willis 93n, 96n, 104n
Wilson 1, 2, 4, 1n, 2n, 39n
Wittenberg 78n
Wooffitt 80n

York 13, 83, 182, 137n

Zingerle 50n
Zulehner 128

Contributors

Luigi Tomasi is currently Visiting Professor at the Royal University of Phnom Penh (Cambodia). He received his Ph.D. in Philosophy from the Catholic University of Milan and in Sociology from the University of Trento (Italy), where he now works. He has been closely associated with the Committee on Social Thought at the University of Chicago and studied under Edward S. Shils, one of the most oustanding social scientists of the twentieth century. The editor and author of numerous articles and several well-known monographs on Youth and Religion, he is the Secretary of the Research Committee on 'Sociology of Religion' of the International Sociological Association (ISA) and the Secretary of the Section on 'Sociology of Religion' of the Italian Sociological Association (AIS).

Yves Lambert is member of the 'Groupe de sociologie des religions et de la laicité' (CNRS-EPHE), Paris, France. His chief area of research is the sociology of religion. Among his recent publications are: 'Age, generations et christianisme en France et en Europe', *Revue Français de Sociologie*, 1993, and 'Un paysage religieux en plein évolution' in H. Riffault (ed.), *Le valeurs des Français*, 1994.

Franz Höllinger is Professor of Sociology at the University of Graz (Austria). His main areas of research are: family, social networks, religion and political attitudes in cross-cultural comparison; new religious and esoteric movements. Among his published works are: *Volksreligion und Herrschaftskirche, Die Wurzeln der Religiositaet in westlichen Gesellschaften*, 1996. He is currentlyVisiting Professor at the University of

Brasilia, Brazil, where he is carrying out a cross-nationally comparative survey on 'Religion, Esotericism and Political Attitudes of Students'.

Jacques Janssen is Associate Professor of Psychology of Culture and Religion at the Catholic University of Njimegen, the Netherlands. He has published works on student movements and youth culture. He is one of the authors of *Les croyances de jeunes Européens,* edited by Roland Campiche, 1997. In his research he combines closed and open-ended techniques that he has based on a computerized technique developed for content analysis.

Michael York is Research Fellow with the Bath Spa University College in the United Kingdom. He coordinates the Bath Archive for Contemporary Religious Affairs housed in Corsham Court, serves as Director of the Amsterdam Center for Eurindic Studies in Holland and as Co-Director of the Academy for Cultural and Educational Studies in London. He teaches sociology of religion, contemporary spirituality, new religious movements and offers online course work for BSUC's New Age and Pagan Studies Programme.

Michael Corsten belongs to the Max-Plank Institute for Human Development, Berlin. He studied sociology, social history and philosophy at the universities of Bielefeld and Marburg and obtained his habilitation at the Free University of Berlin. His chief areas of research are sociology of culture, sociology of economy, research on generations.

Tadeusz Doktór graduated in 1975 at the Catholic University of Lublin and received a doctorate in 1988 from Warsaw University. Currently, he is an adjunct at the Institute of Applied Social Sciences, Warsaw University, and his main field of research is new forms of religiosity. He is the co-editor and editor of the series *Movements on the Border of Religion and Science as th*e *Sociopsychological Phenomenon*, 5 volumes, 1984-1996.

Mikhail F. Chernysh graduated from Moscow Linguistic University with a degree in languages and social sciences. He completed a graduate course at the Institute of Sociology of the Russian Academy of Sciences and has engaged in post-graduate training in a number of institutions in the West. Currently, he is Leading Researcher at the Institute of Sociology of the Russian Academy, running a project entitled *Social Mobility in the Transition Period and its Consequences.*

William H. Swatos, Jr. is Executive Officer of the Association for the Sociology of Religion and of the Religious Research Association, and Editor in Chief of the *Encyclopedia of Religion and Society*. He is also author, co-author, editor, or co-editor of almost 20 books and several dozen scholarly articles. Swatos was Fulbright lecturer in theology at the University of Rekjavík in 1982 and with Loftur Reimar Gissurarson he published *Icelandic Spiritualism: Mediumship and Modernity* in 1996. He is a Fellow of the Society for the Scientific Study of Religion and has received numerous scholarly awards and grants.

Loftur Reimar Gissurarson completed his doctorate in experimental psychology at the University of Edinburgh, having received highest honours in his preliminary studies at the University of Iceland. With Erlendur Haraldsson he has written a monograph entitled *The Icelandic Physical Medium Indridi Indridason*, published by the Society for Psychical Research in 1989, and with William H. Swatos, Jr. he has published *Icelandic Spiritualism: Mediumship and Modernity* in 1996. Loftur is also the author or co-author of 45 scholarly articles. He currently holds an executive position with the city of Reykjavík.

For Product Safety Concerns and Information please contact our EU representative GPSR@taylorandfrancis.com
Taylor & Francis Verlag GmbH, Kaufingerstraße 24, 80331 München, Germany

www.ingramcontent.com/pod-product-compliance
Lightning Source LLC
Chambersburg PA
CBHW070735230426

43667CB00030B/2384